WHY ROME FELL

Books by

EDWARD LUCAS WHITE

NARRATIVE LYRICS, *1908*

EL SUPREMO, *1916*

THE UNWILLING VESTAL, *1918*

THE SONG OF THE SIRENS
and Other Stories, 1919

ANDIVIUS HEDULIO, *1921*

HELEN, *1925*

LUKUNDOO *and Other Stories, 1927*

WHY ROME FELL

BY

EDWARD LUCAS WHITE

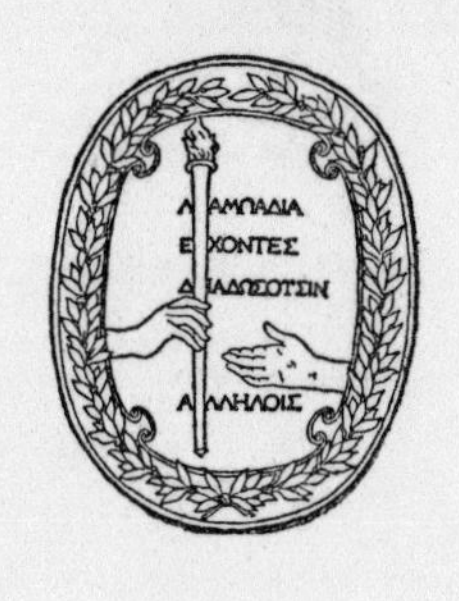

HARPER & BROTHERS PUBLISHERS
NEW YORK AND LONDON
MCMXXVII

WHY ROME FELL

First Edition

H-B

TO THE MEMORY OF

Edward Gibbon
1737–1794

THE GREATEST MODERN HISTORIAN, WHO KNEW MOST OF WHAT IS HEREIN SET FORTH IN CHAPTERS XVI–XXIX, AND WHO MIGHT HAVE SET MOST OF IT FORTH COGENTLY IN PLAIN WORDS, BUT WHO DARED NOT RISK THE PROBABLE CONSEQUENCES TO HIMSELF IN HIS DAYS, AND SO, IN HIS FAMOUS FIFTEENTH AND SIXTEENTH CHAPTERS, HAD TO WRAP UP HIS MEANING IN VAGUE VERBIAGE, OR DEAL IN GENERALITIES, OR SHELTER HIMSELF BEHIND MERE SUGGESTIONS, HINTS OR INNUENDOES, THIS BOOK IS

ADMIRINGLY DEDICATED

CONTENTS

CONTENTS

MAPS

INTRODUCTION

This book is an attempt to answer the question:

"Why did the Roman Empire, the worship of the Olympian Pantheon and the Greco-Roman civilization and culture, perish together?"

Its thesis is that, while there were many and potent negative, passive, minor, and contributory causes totally unconnected with Christianity, Christianity, throughout its rise, growth, diffusion, and success, as it was manifestly the cause of the extinction of the worship of the Olympian Pantheon, just as truly was the positive, active, major, and paramount cause of the ruin of the Roman Empire and of the annihilation of the Greco-Roman culture and civilization.

It has been found unavoidable to include in this book a concise and cursory outline of the salient incidents in the Rise of Rome.

Most, if not all, recent histories of Rome are encumbered with detailed accounts of the recurrent squabbles at Rome between the patricians and the plebeians, the aristocracy and the commonalty, the nobles and the populace, the rich and the poor; of the endless discussions and wrangles about proposed legislation.

Buried beneath and among such obscuring accumulations no average reader can descry, let alone discern, the momentous occurrences which mark the progressive extension and consolidation of Rome's external power; therefore few readers of such histories can derive from them any genuine comprehension of the causes of the majestic march of the growth of Rome's Empire.

Equally indispensable is a brief summary of Rome's achievement.

Again, most, if not all, recent histories of Rome are so absorbed in descanting on the merit of democratic government by citizen suffrage, and so engrossed in disquisitions on what the Romans did not do but might have done or could have done or should have done, that they neglect to recount and explain what, in fact, the Romans did do, and to evaluate it lucidly and fairly.

WHY ROME FELL

CHAPTER I

GENERAL CONDITIONS ON THE GREAT CONTINENT OF EUROPE AND ASIA

TO attain any approximation to an understanding of what the world lost by the Fall of Rome and of what brought about that greatest of all mankind's disasters recorded by either history or tradition, it is absolutely necessary to achieve some sort of comprehension of the conditions amid which, out of which, and either in spite of which or because of which the Roman Empire germinated, developed, and prospered. These conditions may be conveniently classified as general and local.

As a preliminary to an understanding of the general conditions it is needful to keep firmly in mind, that "Europe" and "Asia," while terms long established and universally accepted, are purely arbitrary designations of two portions of the world's greatest continent, that the division is imaginary and not real, that there are no natural features delimiting the boundary line between the two, and that, in fact, the two form but one land-mass, continuous and coherent, definitely marked off from the world's other land-masses, but itself integral and single. From the Arctic Ocean to the southernmost extensions of the Malay Peninsula, from Spain and Scandinavia to Korea and Kamchatka, it is all one continent and must be regarded as such.

On this great continent, as long as eight thousand years ago, four different ways of life had become well established and the portion of mankind habituated to each of the four had become positively differentiated, in temperament and capacities, from those habituated to any of the others.

First, along the Arctic Ocean and in the dense coniferous forests south of it, various tribes who sustained life amid cold and snow, as their descendants do today, by hunting, by fishing, and by herding reindeer, were of no account whatever in relation to the rise and fall of Rome and need only be mentioned.

Secondly, south of them, from the Dniester to the Amur, almost, in fact, from the Baltic to the Sea of Okhotsk, countless hardy nomadic tribes, very numerous in the aggregate, dwelling in tents or yourts of hides or felt, herded cattle, horses, sheep, goats, or camels, and lived on their flesh and milk.

Thirdly, not in a continuous belt, but in densely forested, swampy or mountainous regions along the southern edge of the lands ranged over by the nomads, were less nomadic and more settled peoples dwelling in log huts in villages or stockaded towns, practicing agriculture only in a rudimentary fashion and sporadically, depending much on hunting and fishing, but living chiefly on their flocks and herds. Such in Roman times were the Scandinavians, the Kelts of Great Britain and Ireland, the Germans, the races on and about the Alps, Carpathians, and Caucasus, many other stocks farther east, and the inhabitants of some isolated mountain districts farther south.

Fourthly, south of them from the regions now known as Korea and southern Manchuria, through and across China, Siam, Burma, Hindustan, Afghanistan, Persia, the basin of the Tigris-Euphrates, Arabia (then far less arid than now), and from Syria both north and south of the Mediterranean to the Atlantic in Morocco and Spain, while the degree and form of civilization varied greatly, all the inhabitants had this in common—that they lived in towns fortified by walls of stone, of brick, or of adobe or earth faced with stone; cultivated the fields close to their towns; grazed their flocks and herds on pasture lands beyond the limits of their farmlands, claimed woodlands yet farther away; and waged ceaseless war with most of their neighbors.

Disparities of latitude, altitude, climate, soil, and slope, working on differences of racial characteristics, brought about dissimilarities of development and progress among the town-dwelling population.

In many regions, though local changes were varied and frequent, there was little alteration as to general conditions. In the incessant warfare the weaker towns were stormed, sacked, and burned, and their inhabitants massacred. On lands so left unpeopled new cities were founded by colonies from prosperous towns over-populated and glad to be relieved of the resultant difficulties, or by disgruntled factions from cities cleft by dissensions. Any town strong enough to alarm those near it soon found itself fighting a league and, if it survived the onset, was left shorn of its power and no longer a menace to its neighbors. In such regions conditions incessantly fluctuated but did not alter progressively.

Wherever a region achieved some degree of orderliness and internal peace, and thereafter, by prowess, intelligence, or luck, enjoyed any considerable period of freedom from warfare, its inhabitants rapidly lost their capacity for victory and were consequently overcome by hardier neighbors and exterminated. Amid conditions such as these, improvement was impossible.

The ability of archæological experts to interpret such relics of our predecessors as have lain hidden in the earth and may be dug up and scrutinized has not yet enabled us, and may never suffice to enable us, to determine at what period men began to spare and enslave their prisoners instead of eating them or massacring them. It is an entirely reasonable conjecture that in some parts of the great continent slavery was a well-established feature of human life long before, perhaps even thousands of years before, town-walls were thought of. It is equally probable that in other districts town-walls had been not merely invented but perfected for centuries, yet the townsmen, even if they had long lost any recollection of cannibalism, were far too ferocious ever to spare the life of any captive.

Wherever and however slavery originated, whether some one individual genius first conceived the idea of saving captives alive and utilizing them as drudges, and his example gradually overspread the world, or, as is more probable, mere whim or accident, in many localities, brought about the sparing of captives and led to their utilization as laborers, certainly the inception of slavery marked a great stride in human progress.

In our day human slavery has almost vanished. It exists now only in the unexplored wilds of South America, in the least known forests and fastnesses of Africa, and in some mountainous or sandy regions of Asia. Its abolition in all civilized countries has been hailed as one of the greatest upward and forward steps in human advancement. Yet, to a certainty, the appearance of slavery on earth, as compared with its abolition, was many times as great a stride forward and upward.

Once enslavement of beaten and helpless foes had become a habit, instead of leaving behind them a devastated and depopulated waste, victors not only returned home with slaves to do their heavy work, setting themselves free to acquire greater prowess as warriors and greater skill in warfare, but they spared not merely human beings but their homes, possessions, and farms, left them the means of continuing their productive labors, and took from the vanquished the rewards of victory in the form of yearly tithes or of some other bearable tribute. Victorious towns extended their sway and acquired conquered towns and their lands as additional territory.

Not only did the custom of slavery bring about such ameliorations of the results of local warfare between neighboring towns whose inhabitants were of related stocks and spoke languages of the same type, but they even more positively mitigated the ruin caused by overwhelming invasions by totally alien races.

We can get some faint inkling of what such irresistible inroads meant to the helpless victims along about 10,000 to 6000 B.C. from reflecting on the recorded fact that the Tatar invaders of Russia about A.D. 1200 had been in the habit of sending to their paramount chief, as testimonials of their prowess, the skulls of the slain; but, as they were so far from home and the butchery was incalculable, they then compromised on sending back dried ears only, and in the course of their Russian campaigns dispatched eastward three hundred two-ox wagons heaped with human ears.

Once enslavement had taken the place of massacre and invaders had acquired a sense of the value of subjugated populations, conquerors held their hands after killing enough warriors to feel secure of the fruits of conquest. Thereafter the new overlords, however brutish, usually, whether gradually or rapidly, absorbed much of the culture of their subjects. So that promising local civilizations were no longer annihilated as the result of that waning of military capacity concomitant upon peace, prosperity, and ease; but were not only continued under alien control, but often fostered and stimulated by the infusion of immigrant energy and vigor.

In some regions the reverse process occurred, and a compact, unified race, occupying a restricted territory, steadily improved in all the arts of peace and war, steadily increased in numbers, continued to win victories and to expand, and, being adjacent to fertile areas less thickly populated by stocks on a lower cultural plane, gradually overspread them and brought pastoral life, agriculture, and civilization where the primitive inhabitants had lived by hunting and fishing.

This appears to have been what happened in China.

The great flood plain of eastern China, watered by the Hun-ho, Hwang-ho, Hwai-ho and Yang-tze-kiang and their tributaries and consisting of their present and former deltas, which rims the Gulf of Liaotung from Shanhaikwan to Laichow and abuts on the Yellow Sea and East China Sea from Kan-yu to Ningpo, was, apparently as late as 10,000 B.C. a dense, mucky, or swampy forest, comparable, although in much more northerly latitudes, to the existing tropical forest of the Amazon Valley in South America. It was of vast extent and certainly swarmed with elephants, rhinoceroses, water buffaloes, lions, tigers, and crocodiles, and probably with hippopotami and some distant congener of the crocodile, a saurian now long extinct, the attempt to depict which, copied for thousands of years since the original had vanished, has resulted in the fantastic outlines of the Chinese dragon. Chinese culture as it exists today certainly originated among nomadic herdsmen. This is proved by the national architecture, which manifestly developed from tents, as is shown by the droop of the roofs and by the usage of setting up pillars, constructing a roof supported by them, and filling in walls and partitions, if any, afterward. It is also proved even more cogently by many of the Chinese written characters; that for "justice," for instance, consisting of two signs meaning "own sheep." Apparently it was near, or perhaps even in, the Tarim Basin in eastern Turkestan, north of Tibet, now one of the driest regions on earth, but ten thousand years ago less arid and with many fertile oases, that the Chinese culture germinated. It seems to have spread eastward across what is now the sandy Desert of Gobi, then fine grazing land, to the upland regions now known as the provinces of Kansu, Shansi, Shensi, and Szechwan. There the race ousted or subjugated the aborigines and took to agriculture. Thereafter, as the highlands became overpopulated, they spread gradually eastward into the great forest, very slowly overcoming it, clearing it, exterminating its larger and fiercer denizens, and making of it some of the most densely settled farmland in all the world.

From about 2200 B.C. a considerable portion of the area later ruled by the great dynasties of the Chinese Empire had come under the sway of one paramount overlord as emperor. The dynasty of Hia (2205-1766 B.C.) was approximately contemporary with the ascendancy of the invading Semitic Hyksos kings in Egypt and with the early Minoan culture in Crete. The dynasty of Shang (1766-1123 B.C.) nearly synchronized with the period of the Egyptian Empire, with its wide foreign conquests and capital at Thebes. The Chow Dynasty (1123-255 B.C.) ruled throughout the period when Greco-Roman civilization was developing around the Mediterranean and endured until the time of the First Punic War. The overlordship of the emperors, during these two thousand years, became more and more a genuine and efficient centralized government and maintained peace much of the time, but there were many intervals of unrest, insurrections, and confusion under weak emperors, and much of that civil strife with battles, sieges, and captures, sackings and burnings of towns, which, wherever and whenever it has occurred, has so greatly hampered and retarded human progress. The comparatively brief dynasty of Tsin (255-206 B.C.) is famous for the great Emperor Wang, first autocrat of all China (245-210 B.C.), who built, along a line accurately chosen as delimiting lands to northward, fit only for the support of nomadic herdsmen, from lands to the southward capable of supporting a settled agricultural population, the great Wall of China, 1,400 miles long, 15 to 30 feet high, and 15 to 25 feet thick, which had a very definite influence on events in Europe throughout the ensuing fourteen centuries.

At a much later period something similar to what had been happening in China seems to have happened in the regions now known as Burma, Siam, and Cambodia, where alluvial plains once covered by dense tropical forests sparsely inhabited by savages living by hunting and fishing have gradually been transformed into thickly settled farmlands supporting a peaceful and civilized agricultural population, which transformation was brought about by a series of invasions and migrations from the north, northeast, and northwest, the victorious invaders bringing with them a superior culture and polity.

The aborigines of India seem to have been savages of negroid stock and to have been very early, perhaps as early as 25,000 B.C., and very gradually, displaced by a seepage from northward of the stock known as Dravidian. This dark-skinned and comparatively barbarous race had pretty well overspread the peninsula by 10,000 B.C. or thereabouts. The ancestors of the Hindus indubitably migrated from somewhere to the northwestward, probably from the valleys of the Oxus and Jaxartes, possibly from almost anywhere between the Volga and the Ob, certainly from some region where their forefathers had lived a nomadic pastoral life, and presumably entered India by the Khyber Pass about 5000 B.C. By 1500 B.C. they were well established over most of the lowlands of the Indus and Ganges valleys.

As the prehistoric inhabitants of China, Farther India, and India wrote on such impermanent materials as strips of bamboo or sections of palm leaves, their early records have perished and we know nothing of the ages of warfare between each town and its neighbors which, in the Chinese uplands and in the valleys of the Hwang-ho, Yang-tze-kiang, Mekong, Salwein, Irawadi, Ganges, and Indus, preceded the development of kingdoms and empires and intercalated between periods of efficient centralized government.

It is otherwise with the catch-basin of the Tigris and Euphrates. There mud was the most abundant and convenient writing material, and by 5000 B.C. or earlier, the inhabitants of the lower flood-plain of the Tigris and Euphrates had progressed far in the art of writing, and had developed, from primitive pictographs, useful syllabaries written with cuttings of reeds on little slabs of clay; the characters being made up of groups of wedge-shaped impressions of the triangular butt of the cut reed. By 4000 B.C. they had learnt to bake their clay slabs into almost indestructible tablets, like rough tiles. These, entire or in bits which can be pieced together and read almost as well as if unbroken, are found in great numbers in the rubbish heaps now marking the sites of their devastated towns and cities. The various forms of cuneiform script can now be read with accuracy and their meaning is generally clear. From them we have learned of long series of events in that region.

The notable occurrences were all invasions or the results of invasions.

In the valley of the two rivers civilization and culture seem to have been indigenous products and not importations. The sequence of events appears to have been somewhat as follows.

The flat land formed by the deltas and flood plain of the two rivers was in the beginning, like the great plain of China, a dense mucky or swampy forest, swarming with elephants, rhinoceroses, hippopotami, water-buffaloes, crocodiles, lions, tigers, and other beasts. Tribes along the margins of half-open glades between the forest and the fens of the delta, originally hunters and fishermen, either from innate capacity or the effects of outside influences, developed into agricultural communities. After thousands of years they cleared the forest and made of it settled crop-land. As the silt of the rivers filled in the head of the Persian Gulf, what had been sea became the new fens of the advancing delta and what had been delta became the lower part of the flood plain, the Plain of Shinar.

It is manifest that this part of the world had much more abundant and frequent rains ten thousand years ago than it has now. The primitive inhabitants cannot have realized the progressive but very slow desiccation of their homeland, but they did meet the conditions by inventing or devising irrigation and by irrigating their fields with water drawn from the Tigris or Euphrates. Many small towns arose, each incessantly at war with its neighbors. Many such cities were captured and sacked, but others were founded and, on the whole, the district flourished and became more and more populous, prosperous, wealthy, civilized, and alluring to the dwellers in less fortunate adjacent districts.

Sometime between 3600 B.C. and 3100 B.C. it was invaded and conquered by mountaineers from the northeast, who subjugated or enslaved the inhabitants and acquired much of their culture. These intruders are known to us as the Sumerians. We have not been able to make out their racial affinities, but we have succeeded in deciphering their clay tablets and so have learned their language and know much of their habits, customs, laws, history, and rulers. They also originated, developed, or imported the art of sculpture and their stone monuments tell us much about them. They never achieved any unified polity or created any kingdom or centralized government. During their overlordship or occupancy the towns on the Plain of Shinar existed as before in a condition of incessant mutual hostility and habitual warfare with their neighbors. After about three centuries of prosperity and progress the fighting qualities of the Sumerians waned and the Plain of Shinar was again invaded, this time from the west, by a Semitic race known as the Akkadians. They had been originally nomads of the Arabian desert, then had occupied Akkad, the district on the Euphrates where, many centuries later, Babylon arose, and from Akkad they overran Sumer, the lower part of the Plain of Shinar. The Akkadians, about 2750 B.C. achieved, under their King Sargon the Great, the overlordship of the entire basin of the Tigris and Euphrates and even of some lands outside it to the westward.

By 2400 B.C. the Empire of Sargon had fallen to pieces and the cities of the Plain of Shinar were again each independent of the others and each at war with all its neighbors. Later the whole land was under the government of a dynasty styling themselves "Kings of Sumer and Akkad." Some time about 2200 B.C. the Semitic Amorites of Syria overran most of the upper valleys of the Tigris and Euphrates and founded Babylon, where, about 2100 B.C. Hammurapi was king and had established his rule over the entire flood plain of the two rivers which was thenceforth known as Babylonia.

Within two hundred years Babylonia was overwhelmed from the northeast by the Kassites, barbarous highlanders who had horses, animals never before known of in that region.

Still prospering in spite of internal wars and invasions from without, occasionally from the Arabian deserts to the southwest, mostly from the mountains northeast, once at least from Asia Minor, for the Hittites subjugated all the region and ruled it for centuries, the civilization of Babylonia endured until the district was conquered by the Assyrians, a valiant and ferocious race of mountaineers who, since as early as 1900 B.C., had been steadily developing a polity, acquiring a civilization and extending their sway from along the upper reaches of the Tigris. From 750 to 600 B.C. they were irresistible, as theirs was the first army equipped with iron weapons. They subdued all Babylonia, destroyed Babylon, built for themselves a great capital at Nineveh on the Tigris, and created an empire more extensive than any earlier than theirs. Their sway extended over the entire catch-basin of the Tigris and Euphrates, far into the uplands, highlands, and mountains to the northeast, and over all Cilicia, Syria, and Palestine, part of the island of Cyprus and most of Egypt.

As a result of their innate ferocity and love of impalements and flayings-alive, and their preference for carnage as compared with enslavement, they largely depopulated the lands they subdued, and their power was not so sturdy as it might have been. It was further weakened about 632 B.C. by a terrific irruption of tribes called "Scythian," which may have been Slavs, Turks, or Mongols, who inundated southwestern Asia as far as the frontiers of Egypt, defeating every army which opposed them.

Enfeebled by such internal and external causes, the Assyrian Empire crumbled about 600 B.C., and for more than half a century Babylonia was dominated by the Chaldeans, a Semitic people, coming from the east around the upper curve of the Persian Gulf. They rebuilt Babylon and united under their control not only all the populations of the Tigris-Euphrates catch-basin, but also those of Assyria, Syria, and Palestine.

To the Chaldeans we owe our seven-day week, the names of its days, the twelve signs of the zodiac, the division of the circle into 360 degrees, and much of the science of astronomy, for they were great stargazers, greatly improved on the methods of their predecessors, and were able to foretell with fair accuracy eclipses of the moon and sun. Their importance lasted from 625 B.C. till 538, only eighty-seven years.

CHAPTER II

GENERAL CONDITIONS ON THE GREAT CONTINENT OF EUROPE AND ASIA

(*Concluded*)

EGYPT lies outside the Great Continent. But in any general survey of the development of human institutions on the Great Continent, Egypt cannot be ignored. Its situation at the northeast corner of Africa and its connection with Asia by the Isthmus of Suez made interchange of influence between Egypt and the Great Continent inevitable; and it is not too much to say that few parts of the Great Continent have influenced the rest more positively than Egypt has influenced much of it, while it is even not absurd to hazard the conjecture that no part of the Great Continent has influenced most of it more notably than Egypt has influenced all of it.

Few accredited Egyptologists or archæologists have ever claimed that civilization was imported into Egypt. Most competent archæologists and Egyptologists hold that Egyptian civilization originated and germinated in Egypt. And there is a by no means inconsiderable minority school of archæologists maintaining that all civilization originated in Egypt; that the knowledge of discoveries, inventions, and ideas first conceived of in Egypt, somehow crossed the intervening deserts and wilds and sowed the seeds of thought and action from which germinated the culture of the Tigris-Euphrates basin and the gropings toward civilization in the Oxus-Jaxartes basin and the Tarim basin; that the cultures later flourishing in India and China derived ultimately, at no matter how many removes, from beginnings in Egypt, and that even the Occidental civilizations of the Aztecs, the Mayas, the Chibchas, and the Incas originated from fortunate landfalls on the western coasts of the Americas of far-blown hulks which had sailed from India, Indo-China, or China, and so those cultures had their primordial sources in the autochthonous genius of the primitive Egyptians.

Egypt, of all districts on earth, is the most conspicuous instance of what is known as a natural nest of culture. Surrounded on all sides by waterless tracts of rocky, gravelly, or sandy desert, it is safe from any but the most well-prepared, well-led, and resolute invasion. Immigrations of tribes or casual raids or inroads by small parties of wandering savages or barbarians were all but impossible. So that Egypt was left to itself until influences emanating from it had created powerful military organizations adjacent to it. Only a trained body of hardy warriors commanded by a general at once farsighted, ambitious, energetic, and capable could, from any direction, reach Egypt in condition to inflict a serious defeat on its defenders; so that Egypt had a long prehistoric development, achieved a great civilization, and maintained its culture for thousands of years, before it was ever successfully invaded.

Egypt is and was made up of the Delta and lower valley of the Nile. The Nile is a highly peculiar river. The equatorial catch-basin of its headwaters includes a region where the rainfall is very heavy in the half year from May to October, and has much rainfall everywhere all the year round, so that it collects an enormous amount of water. From the confluence of the White Nile (the main river) and the Blue Nile (its chief tributary) at about 15 degrees north latitude the Nile flows through one of the most rainless areas on earth. From its junction, about 18 degrees north latitude, with the Black Nile (Atbara) entering it from the east and flowing from the north edge of the loamy Abyssinian highlands, no tributary adds to the volume of the Nile all the way to its outfall into the Mediterranean north of 31 degrees north latitude. In this enormous distance of thirteen degrees of latitude, a thousand miles in a straight line and hundreds of miles more along the winding course of the river, the Nile loses much water by evaporation, yet continues a great river.

The middle reaches of the Nile from the confluence of the White Nile and Blue Nile at 15 degrees north latitude run through a very arid region, and below that, to the first cataract at 24 degrees north latitude, down a narrow chasm cut through the almost entirely desert plateau of Nubia.

The lower reaches, from the first cataract to the head of the Delta at 30 degrees north latitude, flow through a valley or gorge eroded out of the plateau of the Sahara Desert. This valley, about 550 miles long and nowhere much over 30 miles wide, is Upper Egypt, the Delta being Lower Egypt.

As late as 25,000 B.C. much of what is now the Delta was a deep bay of the Mediterranean, the Nile silt not yet having filled it up. What there was of the Delta was all fens, and between the naked sun-baked rocks, gravel, or sand of the desert on either side, whatever areas inside the long gorge were reached by the waters of the river at their highest levels were clothed by a dense forest growth, with mucky or marshy strips here and there along the river. Fens and swamps swarmed with crocodiles, hippopotami, water-buffaloes and water-birds; elephants were everywhere, and in the forests rhinoceroses, many species of antelope in uncountable herds, zebras, okapi, giraffes, and other browsing creatures bred, and, feeding on them, packs of lions, hyenas, wild dogs, and other beasts of prey.

In this forest the ancestors of the Egyptians must have lived for thousands of years by hunting and fishing. Their ultimate conquest of the forest and of its denizens must have been very, very gradual. But by 10,000 B.C. or so they had turned much of it into crop-land and cultivated it intensively. They domesticated cattle, sheep, goats, swine, ducks, geese, cats, and even hyenas. We know nothing of the thousands of years during which the territory later united as Egypt was split up among hundreds of independent towns each at war with its neighbors. No traces of primitive stone walls built to fortify any town have been identified anywhere in Egypt, and, if any such ever existed, the stones of which most of them were built have long ago been removed and used otherwise. There is no known evidence of the existence of any fortified stronghold anywhere in Egypt. And probably there never was any. United Egypt never needed frontier fortresses, as its frontiers are everywhere unsurpassably fortified by impassable deserts; and frontier fortresses were built, as far as we know, only at the limit of Egyptian control southward, to guard against raids down the Nile, and at the limits of Egyptian control eastward, mostly along the Isthmus of Suez, but during the glorious period of the Egyptian Empire, far into Asia.

The predynastic Egyptians had not yet learned how to dress stone nor how to transport blocks of stone. What is more, not anywhere along the valley of the Nile is there any elevation suitable for the situation of a fortress and possessing an independent local water supply. There is not a drop of water to be had anywhere except the water of the Nile. Therefore, the strategic points the possession of which was coveted and competed for must have been the intakes of the irrigation canals. At or near these the towns must have been situated. Such locations for towns can hardly have been fortified otherwise than by ditches, earthworks, and palisades. There is no solid foundation for stone walls on the unfathomable loamy silt.

The earliest Egyptian writings were certainly on papyrus or sections of palm leaves and have perished utterly. Therefore, we can only conjecture the sequence of events. As local conditions were not uniform, in some places one town or community might occupy and control two or more irrigation intakes with the areas irrigated from them, mostly each community would possess one irrigated area and one only, in some localities two or more related and friendly communities or towns might amicably share an unusually large area irrigated from one intake. Whatever the original conditions, in the course of time the stronger communities overcame the weaker, annexed their lands, and subjugated their inhabitants. The number of independent communities decreased from age to age and the average area held by each increased. The descendants of the victors specialized as warriors and priests and controlled their disarmed subjects as agriculturalists and artisans. Before our earliest records begin, Lower Egypt, the Delta, and Upper

Egypt, the long, narrow valley, had each achieved a unified government under a king. This had come about, most probably, because of the facility with which a chieftain controlling the river by means of a fleet could move his armies to any desired point.

For centuries the Kingdom of Lower Egypt and the Kingdom of Upper Egypt were at war, whether incessantly or intermittently we do not know. The two kingdoms were finally united into one sometime after 5800 B.C., and the rulers were henceforth styled kings of Upper and Lower Egypt and wore a headdress combining the former dissimilar crowns of the kings of the two former kingdoms.

So unified, Egypt became, as it were, one vast walled city, of seven to eight millions of inhabitants, bastioned about by forbidding defenses, rocky hills, stretches of naked gravel, and vast expanses of shifting sands. Inside these it erected no fortifications of any kind. Its 1,500 to 3,000 towns lay open, without any walls, gates, or moats about any. The Nile was its Main Street.

After its unification, Egypt, on the whole, maintained its independence and conserved its civilization and culture for a very long period, certainly over twenty-five centuries, and possibly not much under 5,300 years. The chief periods of alien rule by foreign conquerors were four. The first was that of the Hyksos, or shepherd kings, who certainly came from the eastward and were probably Semitic nomads from the Arabian deserts, but possibly Mongols from the far steppes beyond the Caspian Sea, the Sea of Aral, and Lake Balkash. They entered Egypt about 2100 B.C. and ruled or dominated it until some time after 1580 B.C.

Later two different dynasties, not consecutive, of kings of Æthiopian blood ruled Egypt. This seems to indicate at least two conquests from the south, down river, by invaders of some race allied to the modern Abyssinians. The second of these Æthiopian dynasties, the twenty-fifth Egyptian dynasty, ruled from 730 to 672 B.C.

It was expelled or annihilated by an Assyrian invasion and the Assyrians ruled Egypt, mostly through vassal Egyptian chieftains governing as local princes, until 653 B.C.

There followed the brief and troubled period of independence under the twenty-sixth dynasty until, in 525 B.C., the Persians under Cambyses conquered Egypt and made it a province of the Persian Empire.

Egypt has now been subject to foreign rule of some kind for 2,451 years. Before that she was independent for at least 2,300 out of 2,525 and probably for 5,000 out of 5,300. Her native civilization and culture endured unimpaired till her temples were closed and their cult statues demolished after A.D. 381, during the reign of the Emperor Theodosius, over 4,620 years from the devising of the Egyptian calendar in 4241 B.C., the earliest certain date in human history.

Ancient Egypt was the most unified of all nations earth ever saw. All the land and all the irrigation water was regarded as belonging to the king, and all men were rated and treated as his servants.

The ancient Aryans, Iranians, Medes, Persians, Hittites, Armenians, Phrygians, Achæans, Hellenes, Greeks, Italians, Romans, Teutons, Germans, Scandinavians, Kelts, Gauls, and Britons and the modern Hindus, Persians, Russians, Poles, Bohemians, Bulgarians, Servians, Rumanians, Greeks, Italians, French, Spanish, Portuguese, Germans, Swedes, Norwegians, Danes, Dutch, English, Irish, Welsh, and Scotch and kindred peoples are spoken of as the Indo-European races, the name being given because, from the first trustworthy and datable records of them, they occupied territories extending from India to Europe.

The Indo-European languages indubitably had a common origin and derive from one primitive parent language.

Whether the Indo-European races are blood kin and descended from one ancestral stock is uncertain. But probably, if not all, most of them are so related and are, as it were, distant cousins. Many characteristics of the vocabularies of their tongues indicate that the speakers of the original common language were pastoral nomads, and it has been generally conjectured that their ancestral home was in the catch-basin of the Oxus-Jaxartes or on the Kirghiz Steppe to the north of it.

The region known as the plateau of Iran, between the valley of the Indus to the eastward and the valley of the Tigris westward, the Indian Ocean and Persian Gulf to the southward and the Caspian Sea and valley of the Oxus northward, was peopled from the northeast as early as 1500 B.C. by the ancestors of the Medes and Persians. In long wars between the Assyrians and Medes the Medes at first had the upper hand; then, about 775 B.C., became subjects of the Assyrians, revolted before the dissolution of the Assyrian Empire, were semi-independent between 710 and 640 B.C., and from 640 to 558 extended their sway over most of the Iranian Plateau; in alliance with the Chaldeans, stormed and wasted Nineveh about 606 B.C., and held the Persians in subjection.

In 558 B.C. the Persians revolted, reduced the Medes to vassalage, and created an empire far vaster than had been even that of the Assyrians. By 518 B.C. the Persian realm included the Indus Valley west of that river, most of its headwaters, the entire Iranian Plateau, the valleys of the Oxus, Jaxartes, Tigris, and Euphrates, everything south of the Caspian Sea, Caucasus Range, and Black Sea, its west shore southward from the mouths of the Danube, with all Thrace and Macedonia, the island of Cyprus, all Arabia, all Egypt, and also Cyrene to the west of it south of the Mediterranean. Except their holdings in Europe, the Persians retained all this vast empire until 334 B.C., about 184 years.

Whether or not the Ægeans were of Indo-European stock, as is probable, they certainly had occupied the Greek mainland and islands as early as before 3000 B.C. If their ancestors came from beyond the Danube, they probably crossed it about 4000 B.C. or earlier.

The ancestors of the Greeks, who later displaced the Ægeans, were certainly of Indo-European race as well as users of an Indo-European language, and they certainly came from beyond the Danube, which they may have crossed as late as 1600 B.C., though probably before 2000 B.C.

The earliest inhabitants of Italy who have left any traces which can be interpreted were apparently of Mediterranean stock, a short, dark race, allied to the present-day Berbers of north Africa. They were savages who used tools of rough stone and flint and lived in circular huts.

Indo-Europeans, apparently, first reached Italy by land sometime between 4000 and 3000 B.C., probably across the plains of Hungary, through the low passes of the Julian Alps and round the head of the Adriatic. The earliest Indo-Europeans to inhabit the peninsula are known, from the local name for the rich earth found on the sites of their villages, as the "Terramara" people.

A later wave of immigration or a more intelligent and progressive portion of the "Terramara" folk is known as the Villanova people, from the modern name of the site of one of their cemeteries, a notable and typical example of them, near Bologna. Many such cemeteries, manifestly all of a folk of identical race, religion, and customs, have been identified in northern and central Italy.

Whether the Terramara and Villanova races were ancestral to the historic Italians, or whether the ancestors of the Umbrians, Sabellians, Samnites, Oscans, Faliscans, and Latins arrived as a second or third immigration, is as yet uncertain, but they indubitably came by land round the north end of the Adriatic.

Some east-coast Italian tribes of Illyrian ancestry, however, most probably immigrated by sea across the middle or southern part of the Adriatic; and the Veneti, at the head of the Adriatic, were certainly of Illyrian stock.

The ancestors of all these peoples seemingly reached Italy before 1500 B.C.

Probably not much after 1500 B.C. the Etruscans arrived, most likely by sea and apparently from Asia Minor. Of what race they were and to what other languages their speech was related are as yet insoluble mysteries.

The ancestors of the Kelts of Ireland, Britain, and Gaul had certainly occupied those regions before 2000 B.C. When their immigrations ceased cannot as yet be determined, still less when they began, or whence.

The ancestors of the Teutonic races, Scandinavians and Germans, certainly migrated later than the Kelts, but seem to have overspread the Scandinavian peninsula, Denmark, and Germany before 1500 B.C.

All this sounds like a meaningless welter of haphazard occurrences with no common factor. But very definite common factors run through it all.

The fringe of savages along the coasts and estuaries of the Arctic Ocean, living by fishing, hunting, and herding reindeer, played no part in the great events to southward of them. They barely managed to exist, and increased not at all from age to age; for the hardships of their life kept their birth-rate low and their death-rate high. They continued in possession of their expanses of tundra, waste, and forest chiefly because, bleak and grim as were the steppes to south of them, their home tracts were more forbidding still and invited no immigrants or invaders.

Everywhere in the regions of the town dwellers, from the Amur Valley, across China, India, Babylonia, Syria, and westward to the Atlantic, any cities weakened by pestilence, failure of crops, or other similar misfortunes were likely to perish, annihilated or subjugated, and their territory annexed by stronger neighbors. More than that, any town enjoying peace and prosperity for any length of time was likely to be weakened in a military sense by the waning of the fierceness and valor of its warriors. Three generations of peace generally so lessened the dash, intrepidity and pluck of a soldiery that they failed to defend their city.

Similarly, wherever the mollifying influences of common ancestry, common traditions and customs, common religion and common language, had mitigated local hostilities and had resulted in leagues or alliances embracing the cities of a considerable territory, all the communities of such a region were very likely to be outfought and subjugated by more doughty neighbors. In general, as far as the peoples inhabiting walled towns were concerned, such occurrences brought about only local and temporary alterations, not permanent and progressive changes, for the region victorious and dominant in one age was very likely to become effete within a few centuries and fall into servitude.

As between the dwellers in walled towns and the semi-nomadic villagers of the swamps, forests, uplands, plateaux and mountains, the sturdiest, staunchest, best-equipped, best-drilled and best-led forces of long-established cities were, wherever they encountered them, sooner or later worsted by their hardier, more venturesome, more reckless, and more persistent assailants.

Life on the open grasslands, plains, and steppes anywhere between eastern Mongolia and the Baltic, at any time after the domestication of camels, horses, cattle, sheep, and goats, must have been a merciless and incessant struggle for survival. Each family, tribe, or horde, sheltered at night or during storms in tents or yourts of hides or felt, camped where convenient, when convenient, and moved in what direction seemed best as weather, pasturage, or whim dictated. If luck was with them, the climate not too severe, and pasturage not too scanty, they prospered, and their animals and their human masters increased in number. Unkind seasons might bring loss of stock by freezing, lack of forage, or long drought; murrains might sweep away their flocks and herds, or pestilences decimate the herders. At the worst such misfortunes might leave not one animal or human being alive. Even a mild epidemic, or a partial scarcity, might reduce their numbers till they were too debilitated to recuperate. Such weakened communities could not withstand more fortunate neighbors. There was no natural obstacle to prevent such pastoral nomads from roving at will. A torrent in flood might delay a tribe in motion, but after a time shrank to a fordable stream. The deepest and widest rivers were frozen over in midwinter. There was no shelter anywhere, nowhere to hide, no natural stronghold. In any clash between horde and horde the weaker of the two was certain of massacre or enslavement.

Amid such conditions the nomad stocks, from generation to generation, became hardier and hardier. They were amazingly enduring of heat and cold, hunger and thirst, idleness or fatigue, inaction or overexertion. Even in times of plenty they were frugal and sparing drinkers and eaters. As individuals they knew how to take care of themselves in all weathers at all times of the year.

They became archers marvellous for the accuracy of their aim, for the distance at which they could hit a living mark, for the force of impact of their arrows. As quartz, flint, or other stone arrowheads displaced bone, as bronze arrowheads somehow imported from southward displaced stone, they became more formidable archers from age to age. The like improvement in spearheads made them ever mightier as spearmen. Swordsmen they never were, though each, of course, carried some sort of knife, dirk, or dagger of flint, quartz, or bronze.

The riffraff among them from early times till only a few centuries ago had no better weapon than a pitiful halfway battle-ax made of a horse jaw for head, lashed with rawhide in the cleft of a stick for haft. Not quite so wretched infantry used various sorts of maces or clubs; and a favorite weapon of the more brawny was the formidable whirlbat. But among them fighters afoot were a last resort. For centuries before 2000 B.C. their well-to-do warriors had gone to battle in two-horse chariots. By 1500 B.C. many of them already rode horseback. After 500 B.C. chariots began to go out of favor with them, and by A.D. 300 they were disused and all fought as cavalrymen. Their archery continued to improve and they made marvellously effective bows, and used them from jolting chariots at full speed or from galloping horses with terrific effect of aim, distance, and impact.

In their ceaseless conflicts with their neighbors, after slavery once became a custom, hordes, prospering for whatever cause, whether luck, hardihood, valor, intelligence, or able generalship by their leaders, grew by increment or accretions to whatever numbers could not be exceeded by a unified community of nomads herding camels, horses, cattle, and sheep and living on their flesh and milk. Just what that limit of numbers was cannot be specified with confidence, but in historic times some such hordes certainly numbered over a hundred thousand warriors, with their women, children, and some oldsters, not many, for conditions on the open steppes and plains never conduced to long life nor to a hale and green old age.

Despite their incessant mutual slaughter they early populated the steppes, plains, and grasslands, whether lowland or highland, to their full capacity for supporting nomadic herdsmen; indubitably long before they ever heard of bronze and while they still had only bone and stone weapons; probably by 7000 B.C.; and almost certainly before 5000 B.C.

Apparently it was with them as with the lemmings of northwest Europe. These small rodents, more or less resembling field-rats, gophers, prairie dogs, and other such of their congeners, are always found everywhere in the regions from northern Norway across Finland and northern Russia to the Urals or beyond. Ordinarily they are not noticeably numerous. But a series of years favorable for their breeding causes them to multiply to incredible swarms, which, to the number of millions at once, migrate westward, swimming lakes and rivers, devouring every leaf and twig of vegetation in their way, keeping on, in spite of foxes, bears, packs of wolves, and flocks of crows, ravens, kites, hawks, and eagles which prey on them, till they reach the Atlantic and swim westward until drowned.

So a series of mild winters and warm summers, with sufficient rain or some similar favorable conditions, caused the nomads of the steppes to multiply beyond any possibility of living on in those regions. The results were the successive waves of migrant hordes which have swept southward since long before our earliest records or traditions. Hence originated the southeasterly migration of the ancestors of the Chinese and the migrations southward, southwestward, and westward of the various Indo-European races.

It is not to be assumed that the nomads comprehended anything of the conditions about them, realized the overpopulation of the steppes, or even that any one horde understood why it must move. They recognized an insufficiency or the impending threat of an insufficiency of pasturage for their flocks and herds and so of food for themselves. They moved as each day's convenience guided them, without foresight or plan. The nomads along the northern margin of the steppe fought desperately to avoid being driven into the forests, wastes, and tundra where they must perish. Every independent family, encampment, clan, tribe, or horde fought every other in the bitter competition for pasturage and water. On the whole, movement northward was less attractive than movement southward and, possibly, more difficult, for it is not unlikely that the nomads farthest north were the hardiest, fiercest, and most valiant. On the whole, the movement was southward, and once the southernmost hordes were in motion there was, for them, no turning back. If they blundered into waterless deserts too wide or into pathless labyrinths of mountain gorges blocked by precipices or glaciers, they perished. If, in their blind groping and fumbling southward, luck guided them into populous regions, they were irresistible and overwhelmed every army on their way; as the Scythians about 632 B.C. worsted even the terrible Assyrians, who alone were then equipped with weapons of iron, hewed a swath of devastation across their realm, and ravaged all southeastern Asia to the Isthmus of Suez.

Something not dissimilar to what actually took place would probably have come to pass in any case, even if climatic conditions on the Great Continent had remained unaltered from mankind's first chance beginnings of experiments leading to the domestication of animals.

But nothing concerning the past of any part from earth is more certain than that, from not long after 25,000 B.C. until the present, inner Asia has had a diminishing amount of rainfall and therefore gradually shrinking seas, lakes, and rivers, and vegetation ever less abundant, less nourishing for beasts and men, and scantier.

This continuous diminution in the food supply greatly exacerbated grim struggle for survival everywhere on the open steppes, plains, and grasslands, and forced more frequent and larger migrations southward, with greater impetus.

It must be noted that the desiccation of Central Asia, while on the whole continuous, has had fluctuations. There have been periods of increasing rainfall, but, on the whole, the process, while fluctuating, has been positively a progress toward desiccation.

It must also be noted that Central Asia was never well watered, and has been, apparently for millions of years, arid. But, besides fluctuations in the progressive desiccation of the past twenty-five thousand years, there have been alternating periods of somewhat similar length during which Central Asia became alternately less arid and more arid. The centuries from before the beginnings of Rome to after her fall came within one of the periods of increasing aridity.

It is not too much to say that the diminishing moisture of the interior of the Great Continent has been the paramount influence on all its events for the past fifteen thousand years and that the progressive desiccation of Central Asia was the dominant factor in the conditions precedent to and concomitant with the rise and fall of Rome.

CHAPTER III

GENERAL CONDITIONS IN THE MEDITERRANEAN WORLD

THE Mediterranean world included Egypt and the basin of the Tigris-Euphrates river system. This is what the Romans meant by the phrase *orbis terrarum* (the ring of lands), namely, the ring of lands about the Mediterranean Sea.

In this world conditions varied greatly. The climate was nowhere humid, but wide areas had a moderate rainfall; even wider areas had a rainfall scanty but sufficient to support a large agricultural population; while not far south of the Mediterranean lies the vastest desert on earth and one of the most arid, and conditions like its conditions extend all across Arabia and even into much of the Tigris-Euphrates Valley. Surfaces and soils varied from naked rock or gravel and shifting sands through many kinds of sandy loams, clayey loams, and clays suitable for dry farming, to deep alluvial silts and thick blankets of rich virgin forest mould, these last mostly in limited areas separated by less fertile highlands or by mountains.

The region was populated by races differing widely and strikingly from each other: the docile, patient, industrious, and thrifty Egyptians and Babylonians; the Syrians, instinctive merchants; the morose and bigoted Hebrews; the Phœnicians, cruel, ruthless, dexterous, and inventive, moreover enterprising traders and unsurpassable seamen; the amazingly keen-sensed, original, strenuous, and capable Greeks; the Berber Moors along the north coast of Africa, as tenacious of their mountain valleys, ravines, and gorges as are their descendants today; the intractable and high-spirited Iberians; the Celts and Gauls, mercurially valiant, reckless, and unstable; the frugal tribes of Italy, laborious farmers, among whom, in early days, no foreigner would have noticed the Latins, dour, slow-witted, stolid, plodding, dogged, heavy-hoofed, bull-necked, and bullet-headed.

Except the peculiar and unconformable Hebrews and the intrusive Persians, all these very various races had similar conceptions as to religion and a similar attitude of mind toward religion and toward its relation to government. This phase of their life will be dealt with later.

Likewise, numerous and great as were the local variations, there was a sort of family likeness and recognizable similarity, even in the most divergent variants, in the scheme and plan of their governmental polity and in the hereditary instincts, usages, and practices which maintained it.

A just conception of this general resemblance and of the factors which made it up will best be given by proceeding from typical examples of community organization to aberrant instances.

The Greeks had two words for "city"—"*asty*" and "*polis*"—from which latter derive our words "politic," "political," "politics," "polity," and such. "*Asty*" meant, collectively, all the buildings of the city, its fortifications and the land on which they stood, or the residential portion as distinguished from the citadel, which was often called "*polis*" in contrast. "*Polis*," besides, might have either of the meanings of "*asty*" and was also used to designate the entire city with all its inhabitants and the whole territory belonging to the city, with its entire population. It also meant the state, as a governmental organization. Moreover and most frequently, it was used to mean the whole body of citizens as an organized community, much as we use the word "city" when we say: "The city voted for war"; the "city approved of the proposal"; "he was preferred by the entire city."

A Greek city has been aptly defined as a military and religious confraternity encamped round a church. "Encamped" is justified, as there are indubitable instances, authentically recorded in historic times, of an entire Greek city-community abandoning their citadel, city, and territory and migrating in one body, usually by sea, to a new location. The most ancient and best-established Greek city might have been forced by adverse circumstances to such a change of abode, and the possibility seems to have been always in mind as a far-off and unlikely contingency. But most Greek cities, and especially those, like Athens, all tradition of whose origin had been lost and which regarded themselves as autochthonous, venerated their territory, the area fortified by their city walls, and especially its citadel and within it the site of their chief temple, as holy ground, clung to it with fervent affection, defended it with reckless valor and unflinching resolution, and, as individuals, looked upon exile as a misfortune comparable to death. And like feelings soon developed in colonies, if they prospered. The definition, as a whole, is adequate, since defense against attack from without was always the most urgent and important concern of every community and since no community of the ancient Mediterranean world even conceived of government apart from religion or of religion apart from government, still less of fraternity outside of the community. Its emphasis is correct, for to each city-state its temple was its most precious possession.

Greece is cleft by arms of the sea and cut across by ranges of mountains. The typical Greek city, and there were many such, possessed a small valley, more or less wedge-shaped, though mostly resembling a wedge bent, twisted, and jagged, the two long sides defined by mountain ridges, its butt along the seashore, with limits marked by surf-thumped headlands, near its point the springs of the most important of the streams watering the valley. Some square miles of meadow and cropland near the sea, hill pastures about them, and forests of oak, ash, beech, and other such trees above the pastures, pine forest higher yet, and then the rocky chine of the mountains.

Each city had a citadel on an isolated hill in the valley, or, if none such existed, on a spur of one or the other range of hills. On the slopes of this acropolis and about it clustered the houses of the city, which always had a public market-square in the most convenient locality as the center of its daily life, and which was always girt by stone walls, at least six yards high and usually much higher, with towers at the corners and at each alteration of level, and a pair of towers flanking each gate, of which there were seldom fewer than four or more than six.

The townsfolk cultivated the fields as far as it was convenient to walk out to the day's work and walk back to sleep. About larger towns were outlying farmsteads and open villages. Beyond the crop-lands flocks and herds pastured in the care of herders or shepherds. Charcoal burners sojourned in summer or harboured all the year round in huts in the forests, and there timber was cut as needed. Beyond the ridge of the mountain-range was the enemies' country. Along the seashore were fishermen's huts, and part of the population were usually capable seamen.

War, of course, was the chief concern of the community and of every man in it. Boys, watched and admonished by superannuated elders, exercised each morning in a field adjacent to the city. Lads drilled similarly. Every robust adult served as a soldier, anyone sufficiently affluent to own a fit riding horse as a cavalryman, any ordinary citizen as a heavy-armed infantryman with spear, shield, corselet, helmet, and greaves, or, if undersized or slender, as a skirmisher, archer, or slinger. Personal capacity determined the choice of seasoned soldiers for officers and commanders. Few summers passed without a campaign of defense or an expedition beyond the community frontiers. Most cities had a squadron of warships; the larger and wealthier had fleets. All men save dullards were equally at home and of use ashore or afloat. What with herding, farming, gardening, tending vines and fruit trees, timbering, fishing and seafaring, quarrying, stone cutting, carpentering, smithing and other city trades, each community was self-sufficing and most men were capable and efficient at almost any occupation or activity and fit for every sort of public duty. Each city was a world to itself, and however associated with others in leagues or alliances or as mother city to a colony or colony of a mother-city, each felt self-governing and independent.

Less tiny valleys were often divided between two city-states, with the river-bed as their boundary; larger valleys accommodated three or more. Usually cities sharing a valley were closely related in race, spoke the same dialect, and had all but identical customs and systems of law.

It is almost impossible for us to realize on how small a scale Greek city life was lived from 800 to 300 B. C. One can get an inkling of it from meditating on the recorded fact that Platæa in southern Bœotia was less than eight miles in a straight line from Thebes, the most powerful city of Bœotia. Yet the two were at war for over five hundred years, and although Platæa was allied with Athens and usually had with her an explicit treaty of offensive and defensive alliance and the distance as the crow flies between Athens and Platæa was less than thirty-one miles, this proximity did not avail to save Platæa from being repeatedly, at least three times within 110 years, captured and razed by the Thebans or as a result of their machinations.

Again in Argolis in the Peloponnesus on the Saronic Gulf the sites of Epidaurus and Trœzene were not fourteen miles apart in a straight line; yet these two city-states, with varying fortunes, were intermittently yet recurrently at war from their founding until the Romans gained control of the region in 146 B.C., a period of over seven hundred years.

In any mountainous or hilly region, as Thessaly, Epirus, Illyria, Macedonia, Thrace, most of Asia Minor, Syria, Phœnicia, Palestine, Cyrene, Africa (the modern Tunisia), Numidia (Algeria), Mauretania (Morocco), most of Spain, and Italy southward from the southern rim of the valley of the Po, allowing for mountains more crowded or farther apart, higher or lower, steeper or less steep, for hilly or rolling country instead of mountains, for plains wider and less infrequent, conditions differed in degree, not in kind, from conditions in Greece.

Exceptional were Egypt and Babylonia. In Egypt defensible and trusted frontiers had brought about the disuse of town-walls altogether. In Babylonia, the soil of which was an alluvial silt of unknowable depth without a pebble as big as a pea, and utterly without building stone, town walls were of mud faced with unburnt brick (what we call "adobe"), larger or more prosperous towns had walls of unburnt brick faced with burnt brick and some few had walls wholly of burnt brick laid in bitumen.

Except for Egypt and Babylonia the conditions were substantially alike all round the Mediterranean south of the Pyrenees, the Po Valley, the Balkans, and also everywhere south of the Black Sea, the Caucasus, and the Caspian Sea on across the Iranian Plateau into the valley of the Indus and probably over most of India.

According to the nature of the country and the characteristics of the inhabitants there were variations of detail. Broken mountains with narrow valleys had mostly small towns, with the tract possessed by each very restricted. Such a terrain made it difficult for any town to acquire permanent control over the territory of any other. The less mountainous the region the more chance had a strong town of acquiring dominion over its neighbors. The more open the country the more likely was it to be occupied by towns independent but more or less amicable and fraternal, fighting among themselves with less ferocity than against outsiders and ready to unite for mutual defense.

From the mouth of the Ganges to the Atlantic Ocean, south of the Caspian Sea, the Caucasus, the Black Sea, the Danube, and the Rhine, in the centuries between 2000 and 200 B.C. there was great variety in the results. In some districts primitive conditions hardly altered, and on the whole no community prospered more than the rest, so that all continued independent and approximately equal. In others local leagues formed, prospered, declined, and dissolved again and again. In yet others one vigorous community became prominent, extended its dominion, and made its neighbors pliable allies, obedient associates, or subjugated vassals. Many regions came under the rule of alien invaders.

The sense of local independence varied from complete self-reliance, inevitable in a community face to face with manifest and inexorable necessity of having to fend for itself as from primitive times, to a vague and attenuated ghostly tradition and shadowy memory of long-vanished self-government.

The 1,500 to 3,000 open towns of Egypt had lost all knowledge of their former independence, and from their centuries of mutual warfare no relic survived except the local animosities which often led to riotous clashes between the rowdies of neighboring villages, shindies which even taxed the repressive powers not only of the provincial police, but of the king's militia. Egyptian villages and townsfolk were completely subservient to the kings and blindly fulfilled any orders from above. Nor was it easy to arouse them to revolt against intrusive foreign dynasties.

Outside of Egypt, everywhere in the Mediterranean world, and apparently all across the Iranian Plateau and into India, the inhabitants of each town spontaneously felt and ardently cherished an intense local civic patriotism. Whether Sumerians, Akkadians, Amorites, Kassites, Assyrians, Chaldeans, Persians, or Greeks ruled over them, each of the brick-walled towns and cities of the Tigris-Euphrates Valley appears to have felt itself a nation, to have defended its independence to the utmost, to have submitted only when submission was inevitable, then to have endured a garrison and governor which it could not expel, and paid what taxes, tribute, or imposts it could not evade. There is not only no proof, there is nowhere the faintest indication that any town or city subdued or annexed by any of these empires ever acquired or developed any sense of loyalty toward the reigning dynasty.

As to the Sumerians, Akkadians, Amorites, and Kassites we can only conjecture; as to the Assyrians, Chaldeans, Medes, and Persians we know that they were devoted body and soul to the service of their kings, that the fealty their sovereigns aroused in them was as ardent as any ever displayed by any liegemen for any monarch. But these rulers never succeeded in infusing into any subjugated, tributary, or allied population any sense of allegiance and hardly even of good will. They may have appreciated the local peace and iron-handed justice bestowed on them by their overlords, but mostly they accepted all such benefits as sullenly as they paid their taxes. Their young men served in their masters' armies rather as dreading the consequences of any attempt to evade being drafted than as willing volunteers. Against Assyrians, Chaldeans, Medes, and Persians alike every tributary town was ready to revolt at the first glimmer of any hope of success.

So likewise of the population ruled over by the various dynasties which divided the conquests of Alexander the Great.

So of the towns and cities subject to Carthage.

In all the walled-towns and cities of the Greeks, wherever situated, the flame of local patriotism burned fierce and bright. They might enter a league, or accept an alliance, might submit to paying tribute, might obey an imposed governor as long as he had at his beck a garrison strong enough to overawe them, might even, sometimes, cling to their homeland after their citadel and their city walls had been razed, but they always regarded themselves as deserving of autonomy and complete liberty in all respects. Each community felt itself a permanent entity, and if subjected looked forward to regaining its freedom, whether it was ruled by a native upstart autocrat or a deputy of some foreign conqueror.

Amid all this bewildering diversity there was a general resemblance, as in their instincts concerning religion, so also in the universal possession of one institution, common to all, and, while greatly varied from region to region and race to race, yet recognizably the same everywhere.

This prevalent institution was variously called council, council of elders, town-council, city-council, college of *decuriones, curia,* and, at Rome and in towns and cities which spoke Latin or any closely allied dialect, "*senatus,*" a word which has come over into English as "senate."

The method of selection, the composition, standing, importance, dignity, prestige, influence, authority, power, and powers of such a council, *curia,* or senate, varied greatly according to locality or nationality. But the most dissimilar variants had some common features, while, except as concerns Egypt, in the Mediterranean world proper and even to some degree across Babylonia, the Iranian Plateau, and India, from the mouth of the Ganges to Ireland, such councils either retained some characteristics of an ancestral prototype or tended toward an approximation to similarity.

Whatever was the nature of the town-council or other governing or guiding body of the towns of predynastic Egypt, centuries of absolute rule by autocratic Pharaohs obliterated every trace, even any memory, of an elective system, and the councils of elders of the villages and towns of historic Egypt were groups of selectmen chosen by the local representative of the king, usually for life, but members of the council only as long as the local governor approved.

To what extent the Assyrians, Medes, and Persians possessed local elective town councils before the development of absolute autocracy by their kings is now not known. And the matter does not concern us except in so far as Assyrian or Persian rule or Median influence may have modified the institution in regions later within the Roman Empire. Evidence of modification recognizably idiosyncratic to those districts is not conclusive.

All the Semitic peoples—Arabs, Hebrews, Israelites, Phœnicians and the rest—appear in primitive times to have been under the sway of kings not only by custom paramount, supreme, irresponsible, absolute, and autocratic, but also by heredity and temperament innately arrogant, imperious, arbitrary, despotic, peremptory, and tyrannical. Ages of such rule have left their mark on all existing Semitic races. And among those of Greco-Roman times, with such a past, the town-council had been or had tended to become or had evolved from being the council of the king chosen by the kings.

In many Semitic communities, as notably in the Phœnician coastal cities such as Tyre and Sidon, the senate gained more and more importance, prestige, and authority from age to age, and the kings of such cities consulted their advisers so habitually, and so often followed their advice, that their government resembled that of modern constitutional monarchs.

Some Phœnician colonies had kings, even in long-continuing dynasties. Most, like Carthage, had two elective chief-magistrates. In some cities these were life-magistrates; in others they held power for a definite term of years only.

Most city-states of the Greeks, Italians, Iberians, Gauls, and not a few of other races about the Mediterranean, sooner or later became restive under the rule of kings, rid themselves of them and organized themselves as republics, mostly oligarchic, but in many cases, as notably at Athens and Rome, tending more and more toward democratic government.

In some of these city-states the council, *curia,* or senate existed as if from time immemorial, chose the magistrates, judges, generals, admirals, and other civil and military officials, who after their term of office became as a matter of course, by unchallenged custom or by enacted law, life members of the *curia.* In others, a *curia* was elected from time to time, which then elected all officials and so perpetuated itself until some unusual upheaval of popular dissatisfaction brought about a general abdication of office by its members and the election of a new *curia,* by a town meeting of all citizens; whereafter, things went on as before until the populace again became intensely dissatisfied. In others the whole body of accredited citizens assembled once a year and elected for one year all necessary civil and military magistrates, who, at the end of their year of office, automatically became life members of the senate. This was the type to which all such semioligarchic, semidemocratic republics more or less tended.

In some the senate, varying much in numbers, consisted solely of ex-magistrates, ex-generals, and such. In other city-states the senate or *curia* itself, from time to time, chose as additional members men who were felt worthy of magistracies but had failed of election or had never been put forward or come forward as candidates.

At Rome the censors, besides expelling from the Senate members deemed unworthy of membership, whether on account of bad character, specific misconduct, or deficient income, also chose into it men who by good character, ancestry, general esteem, or great wealth seemed well deserving of membership.

It was not usual for the voters of any city-state to elect members of their senate or *curia*. Everywhere in the Mediterranean World the council, *curia,* or senate approximated to being a body of ex-officials, after their term of office automatically life members of the senate.

CHAPTER IV

CONDITIONS IN ITALY BEFORE THE RISE OF ROME

THE word "Italy" in its modern sense as a geographical term denotes the entire peninsula south of the main water parting along the chine of the Alps, north of which are glaciers and streams feeding the tributaries of the Danube, Rhine, and Rhone. Modern Italy, as a nation, now possesses nearly all this territory. This use of the word as a geographical expression began with the Greek historian Polybius about 150 B.C. It was not so used officially, as a governmental designation, until after the death of the Roman Emperor Augustus and the accession of his successor Tiberius in A.D. 14.

Before that, not only in executive documents, but in general usage, Italy, as at the outbreak of the civil war between Cæsar and Pompey, meant the actual peninsula south of a line running up the bed of the tiny river Macra, which flows into the Mediterranean not much north of Carrara, from its headwaters along the crest of the Apennines and on down the little river Rubicon to its outfall into the Adriatic Sea, not far north of Rimini. Everything north of this line was known to the Romans of republican times as Cisalpine Gaul (Gaul south of the Alps). Later this was called also Upper Italy and the remainder Central Italy to the rivers Frento and Silarus; southward from them, Lower Italy.

The climate of Italy is nowhere extremely hot, cold, wet, or dry. The regions now parched in summer, treeless plains or rocky hills denuded of every vestige of soil, were, as recently as four thousand years ago, well wooded and moister.

The valley of the Po has yet a very fertile soil of deep alluvial silt, unexhausted. Along the western coast a strip of lowland, several hundred miles long but seldom over twenty-five miles wide, is rich farmland still. The rest of Italy now either has a thin, poor soil, long cropped out, or has been washed clean of any soil at all down to bedrock.

Four thousand years ago there was little exposed rock in Italy, only chines of mountain-ridges, summits of mountains, cliffs and isolated rock-pinnacles. The higher mountains were clothed with dense forests of pines and other evergreen conifers. Their slopes and foothills, the rolling, hilly country, and even most plains except meadows and marshes along rivers, were forested with a thick growth of mighty oaks, ashes, beeches, chestnuts, maples, and other deciduous trees. The forests swarmed with herds of deer and wild hogs; bears, lions, wolves, and foxes were common. Mankind had settled Italy, but had nowhere gained the upper hand of vegetation and wild animals.

Vesuvius is still intermittently eruptive in our days. Four thousand years ago volcanic activity in southern and middle Italy was more frequent, more intense, and more widespread than now. Much of the soil was virgin forest mould; still more of it even more fertile deposits of disintegrating volcanic ash. It was capable of supporting a large agricultural population, and its possessors multiplied until they farmed most of it.

As late as 3000 B.C. the flat lands of the valley of the Po, now known as the Plains of Lombardy, were all one vast morass. Into this, at what period we do not know even approximately, there seeped and trickled, probably very gradually, settlers from the tribes who had, since perhaps 10,000 B.C., inhabited the peculiar villages made safe from attack by being built on piles well out into the lakes of the Swiss valleys. We know that these immigrants began to arrive after 3000 B.C., because before they came they had begun to use metal, copper or bronze, unquestionably imported from the eastern Mediterranean. The remains of more than a hundred of their settlements have been found buried in the Po Valley. These villages had a very definite pattern, recognizably the same whatever its local variations, an arrangement of streets crossing at right angles, with one open square in the middle and a protecting moat encompassing the whole, indubitably the prototype of the Roman military fortified camp, in use thousands of years later, but manifestly derived from this lake-village plan.

CONDITIONS IN ITALY

By 1500 B.C. all of Central Italy and most of Lower Italy were dotted with the walled-towns of the Italic tribes, of Indo-European blood, whose ancestors had crossed the Danube sometime after 4000 B.C. and had entered Italy across the comparatively low eastward extensions of the Alps and past the upper end of the Adriatic Sea. The heel of Italy was held by tribes of Illyrian stock whose forebears, apparently, had crossed the lower part of the Adriatic in ships of some sort. But they were likewise of Indo-European blood and their towns and customs resembled more or less those of the Italic tribes.

What Italic tribes originally peopled Etruria, the south-westward slope of central Italy north of the Tiber, we do not know. But from the vestiges of them yet surviving in Roman times they appear to have been very closely related to the Latins, who possessed about seven hundred square miles of coastal country south of the Tiber, from them called Latium. East of Etruria lived the Umbrians; wedged in between them and the Etrurians and Latins, the Sabines clung to their hills; while Samnites and Oscans overspread the remainder of Italy southward.

Apparently the kindred languages used by all these Italic tribes, while divergent in many respects, had still enough likeness in their vocabularies, forms, structure, and pronunciation for a speaker of any one to be more or less generally intelligible to users of any other.

There is every indication that even while the forested areas of Italy far exceeded in extent the portions of the surface brought under the plow, competition for arable land was keen, and that every walled-town existed in a normal condition of recurrent, if intermittent, conflict with its neighbors. Even though not uninterruptedly at war with any one neighbor, any town was certain of being, at any given time, at war with some neighbor and so incessantly occupied at warfare of some kind.

The cities of the Italic tribes had a strong tendency, perhaps by hereditary instinct, toward forming leagues. Such leagues were mostly of towns using the same dialect and not merely of the same stock, but vividly aware of it. There were Latin leagues, Umbrian leagues, Sabine leagues, Samnite leagues, and Oscan leagues. But each town was fiercely independent, and although a league was likely to be unanimously harmonious while all its component communities were manifestly threatened with invasion, conquest, and subjugation or slavery by some outside foe, yet, except in times of great and imminent general danger, there were many dissensions inside each league. Any disgruntled town was likely to secede from its alliance with its kinsmen and fend for itself or join some neighboring league. So a Sabine town might be for a while a member of a Latin league or the other way about. The leagues, after the earliest dates from which reliable records have come down to us, were internally unquiet, unstable, and seldom durable. Mostly each had a tempestuous, wayward, and transitory existence.

While often, even usually, there was some one most populous, most wealthy, most powerful, and most prominent city in every league, yet, before 500 B.C. it does not appear that any league was really dominated by any one of its components.

That the Latin tribes in particular and, probably, the Italic tribes collectively, regarded war with each other as a last-resort method of settling a dispute which could not be settled through discussion, conference, or diplomacy by adjudication or compromise; that they viewed the outcome of a battle as proving which side was right and which wrong in the sight of their gods, and so regarded war and all armed conflicts among themselves as an appeal to the judgment of gods looked on as just and fair—is indicated by many recorded facts and by traditional anecdotes, details of which throw not a little light on their mentality.

Especially is it implied in the form of battle trophy called by the Romans *spolia opima* (distinguished spoils).

To win the *spolia opima* a commander-in-chief must meet in prearranged single combat, in broad daylight and in full view of both armies, the commander-in-chief of the enemy, must not only overcome and kill him, but must carry off to his home town the slain general's entire equipment of weapons and armor.

Roman legends, traditions, and records, all together, claimed no more than three instances from the foundation of Rome of the achievement of this exploit by a commander-in-chief of a Roman army.

Legend had it that Romulus, the founder of Rome and its first king, carried off and brought home the first set of such spoil taken in the name of Rome, he having killed and stripped the Latin king, Acron of Cænina. This legendary exploit was held to have occurred about 743 B.C.

The second instance was believed to have occurred about 318 B.C., when Lar Tolumnius, King of Veii in Etruria, was challenged, fought, killed, and stripped by the consul Aulus Cornelius Cossus. But there was some uncertainty about the records, and while there was no doubt that the king had been killed and his equipment dedicated at Rome to Jupiter Feretrius in his temple, there was a story that the victor in the fight had been a tribune of the soldiers named Aulus Cornelius Cossus, but not the consul, so that it was questioned whether the spoils were unimpeachably entitled to be rated as genuine *spolia opima*.

The third instance was of clear historic record. In 212 B.C. the consul Marcus Claudius Marcellus challenged, fought, killed, and stripped the king of the Insubrian Gauls, variously called Viridomarus or Britomartus, and his equipment hung in the Temple of Jupiter Feretrius by those of Acron and Tolumnius until the burning of the Capitol in A.D. 69.

Thus the Romans laid claim to only three performances of this feat in the space of 537 years.

Yet the enthusiasm with which it was acclaimed, the great honor it was held to confer on the community in whose chief temple such spoils were hung, the attitude of mind of the Romans toward it, the tone in which their historians write of it, the fact that the proofs of its accomplishment were called by a special archaic appellation, all indicate that it must have happened far more frequently during the six centuries before the foundation of Rome than during the six centuries after. Obviously, the smaller the towns at war, the more closely related in blood and the less their dialects differed, the more definitely they regarded success in war and victory in battle as proving that the gods favored the victors and disfavored the vanquished, and so as demonstrating that the vanquished were in the wrong and the victors were in the right, the more likely the adversaries were to substitute a prearranged single combat between the two leaders for a general engagement of the opposed forces, and the more likely the discomfited army was to accept resignedly what they regarded as the unquestionable and conclusive arbitrament of the gods and submissively to watch the victor despoil the corpse of their late leader.

It may reasonably be assumed that a single combat between the leaders of two armies, instead of a battle, and by prearrangement, was a very frequent occurrence and an established custom not only among the Latins, between 1000 B.C. and 500 B.C., but among all the Italic tribes for even a longer period at about the same time.

The Etruscans are the most mysterious race known to history. Dionysius of the Halicarnassus, in his *Roman Antiquities,* writing about 10 B.C., says that, as far as he could ascertain, they resembled no other people either in language or manners. And today philologists who have specialized most on the Etruscans and have assimilated all that is known of them can say no more. We have about eight thousand inscriptions in their language, mostly brief epitaphs, and know the approximate pronunciation of most of their words, for their alphabet is intelligible; but except for proper names and about two hundred words we do not know the meanings of the words, and not one word of any Etruscan inscription resembles, except accidentally, any word of any known language existing or disused, so that we have not the faintest inkling of any relationship between the language of the Etruscans and that of any other folk. And we are not close to being able to read what Etruscan writings we possess.

As to race, they certainly were not Negroid or Mongoloid. But whether they were Hamitic, Semitic, or Indo-European eludes demonstration. Such portraits of them as we have in extant statuary, reliefs, and wall-paintings mostly depict them as thick limbed, stocky, with black or dark hair and beards, often curly. On the whole they are not un-Semitic in appearance, but often their noses are not of the characteristic Semitic outline.

What is known of their religious beliefs, rites, and ceremonies proves their early intercourse with Semitic races and makes not improbable a remote common origin for the Etruscans and Mesopotamian peoples. But what we know is too vague for us to ascribe any Etruscan religious conception or manner of worship rather to inheritance than to adoption of it.

Nor is any light thrown on their origin by what we know of their form of government or methods of war.

The Etruscans certainly arrived in Italy after 1500 B.C. and before 1000 B.C. Indubitably they came by sea and probably from Asia Minor, according to the tradition that they sailed from Lydia. But their arrival was apparently earlier than the traditional date, 1044 B.C.

They soon occupied all Etruria, the region north of the Tiber to the Apennine Mountains, and their language became that of almost the entire population of that district, though the dominant Etruscans were never in the majority even there where they were most numerous. They won control of all the western watershed of the Apennines from near Genoa to the Bay of Naples and of most of the valley of the Po south of that river. They seem to have much resembled the Normans of A.D. 800 to 1500. Everywhere they became overlords of subjugated cities and regions, communities and peoples. The Latins, and even more the Sabines, had some success in keeping their racial customs and hereditary organizations despite Etruscan overlordship. But besides making all Etruria Etruscan they largely assimilated most of Campania.

In intellectual capacity and in material equipment they were vastly superior to the Italic tribes which they exterminated, subjugated, or overawed. They had better implements, better armor, better weapons, better war-chariots, and greatly surpassed the native Italians at agriculture, building, town design, drainage, and at all the arts of peace and war. They must have been, for their period, unsurpassable administrators, diplomats, and commanders. Also they were natural traders, which the Italians were not, being mostly farmers.

Whatever towns the Etruscans gained control of they fortified mightily. No city walls built in Italy before their times nor after them except by the Romans, approach in thickness, height, and massiveness the impressive Etruscan fortifications. They used large, even immense blocks of stone accurately shaped, carefully dressed, and skillfully laid.

Before Rome was founded the competition for arable land had become very fierce all over Italy proper, and what land had come under cultivation was cultivated intensively. Millet, spelt, and barley were the most usual crops for dry uplands; wheat was grown wherever it produced a good crop, as it was preferred. The productive areas of Italy, especially of Campania, Samnium, Latium, Sabinum, Etruria, and Umbria, were populated up to their limit of productivity; Sabinum and Latium were even overpopulated.

It must be kept in mind that there was practically nowhere any possibility of importing food. If the season was favorable the entire community was well fed. But each city-state produced all its own food. If the season was not favorable, many went hungry through the winter; not infrequently some starved to death, for each family was responsible only for itself. A bad year and short crops everywhere might cause a severe famine during which no inconsiderable portion of the populace would perish of starvation.

To exist, each city-state had to fend off its assailants and raise sufficient crops during the summer.

The land of the tiny fields was more often cultivated with mattocks, spades, hoes, and rakes than with plows and harrows.

The struggle for existence was more severe in Sabinum and Latium than elsewhere. There can still be seen not far from

Rome drainage channels, laboriously dug or hewn for miles through the solid tufa-rock underlying the shallow soil. These were made sometime between 1000 and 500 B.C., designed to reclaim or create or preserve crop lands by diverting flood waters from above them or near them. These works were executed with very primitive tools and it has been calculated by experts that the land reclaimed cost in human labor the equivalent of one thousand dollars per acre. One can get an inkling of how bitter was the struggle for existence when it was worth while to produce food at such an outlay of time and labor.

By 800 B.C. or not much later, while much of Italy was cultivated, much as yet forested, and not only were wild boars and deer still abundant, but there were still far too many bears and wolves for the comfort of the human inhabitants. Lions, however, were far from numerous, and, while they might be met with in any part of the peninsula, an encounter with a lion, even in unsettled regions, was no longer a frequent occurrence.

Italy, while far from safe for human beings, was less unsafe.

CHAPTER V

THE BEGINNINGS OF ROME

OUR sources of information concerning the beginnings of Rome are threefold: first, legends and traditions wherein are embedded not a few recitals of actual events usually distorted in transmission and blended with myths and inventions; secondly, the discoveries through archæological investigations in the way of skeletons, skulls, bones, graves, weapons, utensils, implements, pottery, wells, sewers, walls, foundations, and other human remains and artifacts long buried in the earth; and, thirdly, inferences made from both.

The familiar story of Numitor, Amulius, Rhea Silvia, Romulus, Remus, the she-wolf, Faustulus, and Laurentia is chiefly interesting as proving a totemistic idea or conception as part of the beliefs of the aboriginal ancestors of the Romans.

Totemism is a subject forbiddingly illimitable, unfathomable, protean, labyrinthine, and obscure. It is not rashly to be approached, and must be trespassed on, if at all, with great circumspection.

Yet it is obvious to anyone with a smattering of knowledge of totemism that the story of Romulus, in the form in which it has come down to us, had been much bowdlerized in transmission. Rough, gross, rude, and coarse as the Romans of republican times appear to us, their forebears along about 1000 B.C. or earlier must have been much rougher, grosser, ruder, and coarser.

Manifestly, in the original form of the myth, Romulus was the offspring of Mars, the war-god, and a she-wolf. The ancestors of the Romans, at some very early period, must have gloried in their ferocity, as did Ezzelino da Romano many centuries later. Presumably their token was the wolf; they likened themselves to wolves, were proud of the similitude, and exulted over their captives, more or less as follows:

"Expect no mercy from us!

"There is not a drop of human blood in our veins:

THE ENVIRONS OF EARLY ROME

"The mighty God Mavors, insatiably greedy of blood, was our father!

"And our mother was a she-wolf!"

In process of time the ancestors of the Romans or the Romans themselves grew less brutal and their natures softened. Gradually the implication of physical union between the god Mars, conceived of as of human form, and a she-wolf, came to be felt as a revolting idea, whereafter a human mother was insinuated into the story and the she-wolf reduced to the rôle of a mere wet nurse.

Yet the Romans, not only of early ages and of the period of the Punic Wars, but even of the late Empire, still derived not a little of their indomitable military morale from the belief that their ultimate ancestor had fed on wolf's milk and that the residue of it running in their veins made them the most formidable of mankind.

All other portions of the story of Romulus—the exposure of twin male infants, on whatever ground; their preservation by the kindness of a shepherd and his childless wife; their recognition by their grandfather Numitor; their expulsion of their uncle from the kingship at Alba Longa and their restoration of their grandfather to it; their love for the locality in which they had grown up and their restiveness at Alba Longa; their plan to found a city near the place of their rescue; their gathering of volunteers; their dissensions and disputes; their method of adjustment; their quarrel and the death of one at the hand of the other—are perfectly in character and in keeping with the conditions of the period and locality and may very well all be genuine traditions. The she-wolf as foster mother and the apotheosis of Romulus as Quirinus after his death are the only manifestly mythical elements of the legend.

There is nothing to discredit any detail of this narrative. All may be traditional records of actual occurrences. We may very reasonably believe that in fact, about 753 B.C., a band of youths from Alba Longa strengthened the fortifications of a wee town on the Palatine Hill, or fortified for the first time what had been a mere hilltop village, or founded a town on a hill, which, for all they knew, had never before had on it any human habitation, and so established the tiny fortress called from its outline *Roma Quadrata* (Square Rome) from which Rome grew, and that their chieftain or leader became the first King of Rome.

Indubitably, as the diggings and excavations of archæologists have demonstrated beyond question, villages existed on the Palatine, Aventine, and Cælian Hills as early as 1000 B.C., and before 800 B.C. there was a market on the site of the later Forum of Rome, and also there were burials in the Forum and on the hills of Rome as late as 600 B.C. These inferences are proved by finds of pottery and other artifacts which can be approximately, even closely, dated, with certainty.

The legends concerning Numa, Tullus Hostilius and Ancus Martius probably embody mostly traditional records of authentic happenings, but mixed with legends and inventions. The destruction of Alba Longa by a Latin king, such as the Tullus Hostilius of tradition, is not unlikely, in view of the recurrent conflicts between towns of the same race and language and the embittered nature of enmities between kinsfolk estranged.

The name Tarquinius, of which we make Tarquin, is manifestly the Latinized form of the Etruscan name *Tarkhnas* which is found on more than one Etruscan tomb.

The traditional dates of Tarquin the Elder, 616-578 B.C., coincide fairly well with the period of the beginnings of Etruscan overlordship among the Latins of Rome, as indicated by the Etruscan cemetery on the Esquiline Hill and traces of an early Etruscan settlement on the Cælian Hill.

The ascription of the mighty fortifications of Rome to Servius Tullius, according to legend the sixth king and second Etruscan king of the city, is very likely a traditional record of actual fact. According to the received account, he reigned from 578 to 534 B.C. The Servian Wall was certainly built after 600 B.C., for it is, in design and original construction, indubitably Etruscan, and when the Etruscans fortified a town they drew round it a consecrated strip of land called by the Romans *pomerium*, within which they permitted no burial or burning of any corpse. As burials in the cemetery on the site of the later Forum of Rome continued till after 600 B.C., the Etruscan fortifications must have been begun after that date. And the existing remains of the earliest portions of this enclosing wall are of building materials much used at Rome in the sixth century B.C.

Near 800 B.C. life for the Latins was hard and stern. They held about four hundred square miles of the westernmost part of Latium, south of the Tiber and inland from the sea. But their territory was populated to close upon a thousand human beings for each square mile, and the best of it even more densely, for some of it was inferior crop-land and the worst of it was not capable of bearing any crop at all and was useful only as pasture land. Also they were hemmed in on every side. The Rutulians along the seashore southward of the Tiber, with Ardea for their chief town, may have been Latins at loggerheads with the rest, but to a certainty they were seldom at peace with them. Antium, on the first seacoast headland southward from the outfall of the Tiber, was held or ruled by the Etruscans. The Volscians, a Sabellian people akin to the Umbrians and Sabines, had Velitræ, close to the southern base of the Alban Mount, and possessed the mountainous hills to the southeastward, with such strong towns as Cora, Norba, and Signia.

North of the Volscians and due east of the Latins, the Hernicians, another Sabellian tribe, held several valleys of the southwestern slope of the mountains, with such strong towns as Anagnia and Ferentinum. North of them, likewise due east of the Latins, were the Æqui, also Sabellians, mostly on the other side of the range which bounds Latium, but holding some valleys on the Latin side and even the fortress town of Bola within a mile of the eastern base of the Alban Mount.

Further eastward, behind the Hernici and Æqui, were the Marsi, a hardy tribe of Sabellian stock, usually allied with either the Æquians or Hernicians, sometimes in league with both.

In the triangle east of the confluence of the Anio with the Tiber, between these two rivers, were the Sabines.

Thus the Latins were hard pressed from every direction, by the haughty and powerful Etruscans north of the Tiber, by the Sabellian Æquians, Marsi, Hernicians and Volscians, south and east, and by the Sabines between. The Etruscans were mighty, the Sabellian tribes were fierce, but the Latins were tough, almost as tough as the Sabines. And even tougher than the Sabines were the Latin shepherds of the Alban Hills. To exist at all on those hills implied a tough constitution and a tough disposition. They had both.

Of them some youthful ne'er-do-weels and high-spirited lads, disgruntled with conditions at home, resolved to go off and set up for themselves, and constructed or strengthened a tiny fortress on the Palatine Hill, one of seven rocky eminences by the Tiber about a mile below the infall of the Anio. The hills were bare and between them wound unpleasant swamps. Only a very hardy folk could exist there at all. And, even apart from barren rocks and festering marshes, it was the least peaceful spot in Latium, close to the arrogant Etruscans and the dour Sabines.

Yet, somehow, the newcomers prospered, won mates, won battles, won territory, bred, kept alive, and within 112 years had made themselves paramount among the Latins and had razed Alba Longa, whence their founders had come.

They kept on prospering, despite many serious setbacks.

The Etruscans had made Etruria theirs in all respects, till the descendants of the previous owners had adopted their customs and language. From 800 B.C. to 400 B.C. they were supreme in Campania and greatly and permanently altered the native Oscans, making them over into half-Etruscans. But the Latins in between were more tenacious of their speech and folk ways. For two centuries or longer most Latin towns had Etruscan kings and the nobles everywhere in Latium were of Etruscan blood. But the Latins continued Latins. The Sabines and Sabellians remained unsubdued by the Etruscans; the

Latins, while subjugated, were never assimilated and finally expelled their overlords from Rome about 510 B.C.

The Etruscan kings of Rome must have been farsighted and intelligent as well as ambitious. Apparently it is not unreasonable to conjecture that they had realized that Rome, a site lending itself naturally to fortification, situated below the head of navigation on the largest and only navigable river in the peninsula proper, was the natural capital of Italy. As a matter of fact they fortified it with walls at that time impregnable and the most imposing in Italy, and to drain the marshes between the hills they constructed sewers which were the wonder of all beholders and unsurpassed in dimensions until our own times.

After the expulsion of the kings the Senate and people of Rome, organized as an independent republic with two consuls as chief magistrates, were in possession of a city with walls stronger and enclosing a larger area than any in Italy or near it. But they controlled only a comparatively small territory outside of it, and had recurrent, almost incessant, wars with the Sabines, Æquians, Hernicians and Volscians. Yet by 486 B.C., only twenty-four years after the establishment of the republic, Rome had begun to get the upper hand of these local enemies and by 396 B.C., only 114 years after the expulsion of the last Etruscan king Tarquin the Haughty, Rome had, after a siege lasting nine years, during which, for the first time, her legions kept the field all winter, captured, sacked and razed Veii, the nearest Etruscan city.

As late as 700 B.C. the Etruscans had been in full control of the Valley of the Po south of the stream bed of that river. Their capital was Felsina, later Roman Bononia, (now Bologna) and they had flourishing fortified towns on the sites now occupied by Faenza (Roman Faventia), Modena (Mutina), Parma, and Piacenza (Placentia).

Early in the seventh century B.C. some pressure from northward began to cause bands of Gauls to cross the Alps into upper Italy. Probably the Germanic tribes were pressing hard on the Gauls, very likely because they themselves were hard pressed from the northeast. What was going on beyond the Germans we can only conjecture. But it is worth noting that it is not impossible that acute distress and unusual turmoil on the steppes of Asia resulted in a general movement southward, of which two related manifestations were the irruption of the Scythians into the Assyrian Empire in 632 B.C. and this invasion of Italy by the Gauls not much later.

After 600 B.C. hordes of Gauls began to enter Italy, and they soon exterminated the aborigines north of the Po and occupied all Piedmont and much of Lombardy.

Within no long time after the expulsion from Rome of the last Etruscan king, Tarquin the Haughty, about 510 B.C. the swarms of Kelts had not only crossed the Po, but had ousted the Etruscans, driven them across the Apennines and had possession of the entire Po Valley. The Boii, the most prominent of the invading tribes and probably also outnumbering any, occupied most of the valley of the Po south of that river. The Insubrian Gauls, apparently invited or helped along or allowed to pass through by the Boii, mastered and settled all the Eastern slope of the Apennines from their crest to the Adriatic as far south as the little river Æsus, more than sixty miles southeast of the Rubicon. They pushed on across the Apennines into Etruria and about 390 B.C. laid siege to Clusium (now Chiusi), on the Clanis, a northern tributary of the Tiber. According to legend or tradition they there took umbrage at the behavior of ambassadors from Rome to Clusium and, while the Romans were not anticipating any trouble with them, unexpectedly declared war and promptly and rapidly advanced on Rome.

The Roman army, mostly sturdy spearmen afoot, with the nobles as cavalry and commanders, marched out confidently to repel the presumptuous invaders. They met them at the brook Allia, which falls into the Tiber only eleven miles north of Rome.

Now the Romans knew how to fight Latins, Volscians, Hernicians, Æquians, Sabines, and Etruscans, and how to beat them. Against any adversaries such as they were used to, however overmatched they might be and however hopeless their prospects might appear, that Roman army would have fought on doggedly to the last man.

But they had no experience of Gauls. We know hardly anything of the appearance, behavior, order, and methods of onset of the Insubrian Gauls. Manifestly, from the upshot, all or some of these were totally novel and unfamiliar to the Romans and wholly unexpected. At the crisis of any battle it is the unexpected which counts. What is unexpected is disconcerting, and when both officers and men are simultaneously disconcerted no army can hold out. The battle of the Allia resulted in a quick and overwhelming victory for the Gauls and in utter and irretrievable rout for the Romans. A defeat had not been thought of. No preparations for a defense of the city had been made. So sudden was the disaster that no messenger arrived at Rome in advance of the fleeing rabble of panic-stricken survivors of the army, intermingled with exultant pursuers. There was no time to close the gates and with the fugitives the Gauls entered the city and sacked and burned it.

The citadel on the Capitoline Hill held out against them until, satiated and out of provisions or bought off, they retraced their steps northward, leaving Rome deserted and in ashes.

It cannot be emphasized too much that up to its devastation by the Gauls about 390 B.C. Rome had been merely an Italic town differing from scores of other Italic towns only in that no other city on the peninsula had so large an area inside its walls and in that its walls outclassed all others in Italy in strength and impressiveness.

Up to the sacking by the Gauls, Rome had done much, the records of which, to anyone pondering on them, give promise of her future greatness. But practically Rome had made no progress toward greatness. She had stuck to the siege of Veii for nine years and had taken and razed it. But this had been due rather to general and progressive weakening of the power of the Etruscans than to increase in the power of Rome.

Elsewhere her all but incessant warfare had accomplished nothing.

In her wars with the Volscians, Hernicians, Æquians, and Sabines such towns as Velitræ, Cora, Norba, Signia, Præneste, Bola, and Tibur had been taken and retaken, had changed hands again and again, had been alternately Sabellian cities and Roman fortress colonies, but after more than a century of gallantry and carnage the general situation was much as just after the solid but exiguous walls of *Roma Quadrata* had been constructed on the Palatine Hill by Romulus or whoever else.

CHAPTER VI

THE EARLY ROMANS

THE Rise of Rome dates from its restoration after it had, about 390 B.C., been sacked and burned by the Gauls. Consider what sort of a populace was capable of a revival after such a disaster.

The Romans had been in the making for many centuries before the making of Rome began. To ignore all earlier influences their ancestors had had no unopposed progress from their aboriginal habitat throughout their journey to Italy.

Presumably they had fought their way across the plains of Hungary, the Danube and many of its tributaries, and the mountains east of the Alps; low by comparison with the Alps themselves, but no inconsiderable obstacle. Once in Italy, they had had to exterminate or enslave or subjugate the aborigines, and this can have been no brief or easy task, even if the invaders had spearheads, daggers and arrowheads of bronze, and the natives only of quartz or flint.

How densely primitive Italy was forested, even as late as the development of Latin as a language apart from its congeners, can be inferred from the Latin word for the sacred grove about a rural temple—*lucus* (a bright place). In the thickly populated and intensively cultivated Italy of Imperial times not only had forests vanished except on steep mountain slopes, but on the plains there were no trees whatever save those of the consecrated groves. So, amid the glare of Italian noonday, each grove was a dark place and the grammarians of those times marvelled that a dark place should be called a bright place. But, along from 1000 B.C. to 500 B.C. each sacred grove, with its hallowed and venerated trees well apart and no undergrowth, was naturally called a bright place, being such, in fact, by contrast as a partial clearing surrounded by lofty, dense and gloomy primeval forest. The prevailing forests of Italy before 1000 B.C. sheltered many wolves, bears, and even lions, and life, without regard for human enemies, was no careless ramble through a well-policed park.

Moreover, once settled in Italy on land their right to which was acknowledged by other communities related in blood and speech, even after they had fortified a town on it with good stone walls, no community had an easy time.

Farming was laborious; food was rarely overabundant and often scanty; famines were not infrequent, and warfare was all but incessant. Amid such conditions women bear many children but raise few. Any weaklings born died young and a lad must be sturdy, brave, cool, and alert to survive his campaigns and marry and raise a family. Thus, on the whole, the Italic tribes were hardy, the Latins and Sabines hardier than the general run, and the shepherds of the Alban Hills among the hardiest in the peninsula.

After the founding of Rome the selective action of all conditions was intensified for the Romans.

Whether malaria was prevalent in Italy before Hannibal's invasion is a moot point. If not, malaria was not one of the conditions which acted selectively on the Roman stock. But if exposed to malaria the early Romans certainly survived by selectively acquired immunity, which would indicate unusual vitality, for few races on earth have acquired immunity to malaria by selective survival.

The Alban shepherds may have been already by heredity immune to malaria. If not, the swamps between the seven hills of Rome, if malarious, soon brought it about that the inhabitants were, to a great extent, malaria-proof. Before many generations selective survival, if operating, had weeded out in early life all born liable to malaria and ensured that most infants were malaria-proof from birth.

Presumably the staple diet of the Romans was at first millet and spelt, a hard and hardy variety of wheat with chaff tenaciously adherent. This is indicated by the Latin word for baker—*pistor*—which means a pounder of grain in a mortar. such treatment being necessary to loosen the clinging husks from spelt. It is also implied in the tradition that, as many

Scotch crofters subsist even today on a diet of oatmeal porridge, so, for many centuries before baked bread was known among them, the ancestors of the Romans and the Romans had lived on a porridge made of spelt or a not dissimilar porridge of barley, as their usual food. Even wheat, which was preferred and grown more and more from age to age, does not plump out much with starch in the dry climate of Italy under hot sunshine and rainfall never overabundant, but its grains are hard with much gluten.

Millet, spelt, barley, hard wheat, beans, lentils, peas, cabbage, beets, turnips, and greens made up a spare and muscle-forming dietary and the early Romans did not incline to obesity.

To a certainty they evolved and bequeathed to their fortunate descendants the marvellous Roman stomach which, even when filled to satiety, was capable of digesting completely any food its owner had felt inclined to swallow, whatever its nature or variety; and which was able to extract every bit of nourishment from any substance, however indigestible and refractory, containing nutriment, and so to keep a Roman alive on the scantiest and most unappetizing rations.

Roman muscle was toughened by use.

The women were seldom idle. Wool had to be carded, spun, and woven. There was never an oversupply of clothing, and any girl or woman not occupied at something more urgently important was generally busy spinning. Weaving called for more skill than spinning and was work for women of experience, even for ladies. During over five centuries not only was all the bread for each family baked in their dwelling, but all grain was ground there. In the earliest ages it was ground in hand mills resembling querns, and so in each household the women daily spent much time at the hard labor of preparing meal or flour, as Mexican women today grind maize on a metate.

What with spinning wool and grinding grain and what else the day's work implied, the mother of each Roman transmitted to her sons no small portion of their health and strength. Each generation was, if anything, healthier than the preceding.

The men cultivated their small fields less with plows than

with spades, mattocks, hoes, and rakes. Turning clods with spades or mattocks, and powdering the glebe with hoes and rakes, hardened the Roman muscles.

There was a campaign, defensive or offensive, every summer, and every lad sufficiently full-grown to tramp all day wearing a helmet, corselet, and greaves, and carrying spear, shield, and rations, fell into line.

Weaklings, shirkers, cowards, fools, and hot-heads were regularly eliminated by the inevitable operation of circumstances. Nearsighted youths missed their aim or failed to see the hurtling arrow or spear.

There were no surgeons, doctors, nurses, nor ambulances.

"He fell" was not merely a report of an occurrence; it was generally an obituary needing no amplification or comment.

For centuries after the founding of Rome the Romans had no inkling of the rudiments of strategy and only the crudest notions of tactics. As each summer's campaign closed with the approach of bad weather, their entire army was disbanded each winter. In the spring a new levy was made, and under newly elected commanders they marched out in the general direction of the enemy. In sight of the foe their tactics seem to have been little better than some such order as:

"There they are, boys! Go get 'em."

In our days, for the rowdies of city slums, for jackies or crews of tramp-steamers or foremast hands on shore-leave, in a shindy, fracas or free-fight, the guiding maxim is always:

"Down the man in front of you; then help your side partner."

The Roman word for a fight was *pugna* (a grip), and it was often used for a battle. The Roman idea of how to win a battle was to bring it as rapidly as possible to the condition of being a great number of simultaneous single combats. Any Roman felt capable of besting any individual adversary, and his notion was to get close to him and spear him.

The Romans must have been in their day, in fact, unmatchable as individual fighters, for with new levies newly organized each spring under newly elected commanders, without strategy or tactics, they beat all their neighbors and began the conquest of the world.

One usage of the Romans was unique with them, and no other nation had ever had any similar practice. In all parts of the world in all ages camps have been fortified as seemed best when it seemed necessary. The ditch protecting the seashore camp of the Greeks before Troy is an early instance, and countless others could be cited.

But the Romans alone formulated a definite pattern for their camp, used precisely the same pattern for any one army night after night, and felt it incumbent upon them, each successive day of any campaign, to fortify their camp before dusk.

How the practice originated we can only surmise, as it was fully developed long before our earliest records of their history.

In Italy along about 1000 B.C., as all over the world, toward sunset any army on the march halted, and the men made fires, ate a meal, placed sentries, sentinels, and pickets, and lay down to sleep around their sinking fires or the fading glow of the coals where they had burned. If their outguards were successfully vigilant they all woke up alive. But, for a bold, audacious, enterprising, and venturesome enemy an open camp was always an opportunity for an exploit. A lad who knew the lay of the land in detail and was tough, intrepid, and self-confident, could strip naked, grease himself all over, take a dirk in his teeth, and, when near his enemies' camp, crawl belly flat on the earth, squirming through grass and bushes and over any surface, creeping forward inch by inch; and if sufficiently keen sensed and crafty might pass between the pickets, escape the notice of the sentinels, and even elude the sentries.

Once inside the camp, he could listen for snores and crawl among the snorers. Biding his time and making sure of his chance, he could rise, stab or slash at any near-by humpy shapes visible in the starlight, and make his escape or attempt it.

The results, next morning, would not be a heartening sight for the survivors, but rather depressing.

Now the Romans or their ancestors developed a distaste for being disemboweled or skewered or having their throats cut in their sleep. Somewhere, sometime, some one genius of a commander set his men to scratching a furrow all around their camping place, and throwing up the earth out of it on the side toward the sleepers. The idea took. A trench no more than a yard wide and half as deep was a positive obstacle in the way of any night prowler, and the slight ridge behind it was a positive advantage to the sentinels or sentries raised by it even a few inches above the level of the ground beyond the trench. In time, how short or how long we cannot surmise, accepted practice demanded a ditch a yard or more deep and wide in proportion, and the excavated earth made a worth-while embankment.

In an army so protected not only was every sleeper assured of waking unwounded, but in the unusual, unlikely, but not unheard-of event of a night rush or attack before dawn by an exceptionally strenuous enemy, the entire force could not but find it far easier to repel the assault.

Before the beginning of the Punic Wars the Romans had evolved a normal plan of a fortified camp, varied only in detail, a type to which every camp conformed. And castrametation had become an art an apprenticeship at which must be served and long experience acquired before an officer might be trusted to select the site for the night's camp, survey it, and lay off its plan.

We know nothing definite as to the plan and size of a Roman camp before the times of the third Punic War, 149-146 B.C. Polybius, the Greek historian, who was with Scipio in that war and at the taking of Carthage as a sort of honorary private secretary and aide-de-camp, describes the camp of his days in great detail, for two legions and their normal complement of allied cavalry and skirmishers, at that time a force of over 20,000 men all told, of whom over 18,000 were infantry. Such a camp was a square of 2,150 Roman feet each side, so that much fewer than 18,000 workers, for not all could be ditching, must dig over 8,600 feet of ditch in about four hours. What were the dimensions of the ditch in early times we do not know, but in Cæsar's camps in Gaul about a century later it was regularly a V-shaped trench nine feet wide and seven deep, and the rampart of earth was faced with sod or logs and was topped at its outer edge by a strong stockade of stakes. The early Romans may have been less systematic, but the soldiers probably had no easier time of it.

A camp had always four gates, one in each side. At each gate were two towers, what we should call blockhouses; there was a tower at each corner of the camp, and others as judged needful. The Latin word for camp, *castra,* is a plural word meaning "towers."

The ration served out to Roman soldiers consisted of unground wheat, some olive oil, a very little salt, and a small quantity of either wine or vinegar. The Romans never drank wine undiluted. Poor folks always mixed one measure of wine with seven of water. On campaigns the soldiers used much less wine or vinegar to much more water. The unhealthfulness of drinking water without wine or vinegar was universally known by experience. In fact, the wine or vinegar killed most of the disease-germs in polluted water. The salt flavored their porridge, or their bread, which was baked, if time permitted and fuel was sufficiently abundant. This bread must have been much like what we call "camp sinkers." The olive oil they used as we use butter. The wheat was ground to a coarse flour or fairly fine meal in hand mills, like querns. Rations were served out twice a month, thirty-two pounds of wheat for each soldier, which he had to carry, himself. What with weapons, armor, rations, and the two stakes for the camp stockade which each soldier carried, his load was never less than sixty pounds and was often much heavier. The husbanding of each man's rations was his own concern. If his discretion and self-control were normal he had about two pounds of wheat a day. Weakness or faintness from hunger for some days before the new ration was served out mostly eliminated fools and gluttons.

The normal routine of a Roman army on campaign was as follows: After the camp was adequately fortified and a minimum of pickets posted, the day's chief meal was eaten, sitting.

What sort of shelters the earliest Roman armies used we do not know. Perhaps none at all, no matter what the weather; perhaps shacks of boughs. Tents of hides were in use comparatively early. In times of which we have record a tent held ten men. Two slept all night. Presumably these unpacked the mules, put up the tent, cooked the food for the evening and morning meals (they had only two a day), took down the tent, and loaded the mules. Of the other eight two stood watch, one watch of each night, and slept three watches. Each watch was about a quarter of the length of the night, from the time when twilight was merging into dusk until the gray of dawn would make visible at a safe distance any approaching enemy. Of out pickets at night we seldom hear; everybody was normally inside the ditch and stockaded earthwork with its towers. A guard of whatever number of men judged sufficient was placed at each gate. Sentinels stood at short intervals on the earthwork within the stockade. At headquarters were, in charge of an aide-de-camp and orderlies, four baskets of little wooden paddles, each inscribed with words or characters identifying it in the series each basket contained. The paddles out of the basket for the first watch were served out to the sentinels, the same number for each man. As soon as the watch was set the captain of that watch, with at least two apparitors accompanying him, one with a bag or the basket, began his rounds. From each sentinel he took a paddle, and kept on his rounds all through his watch. When that watch was over that basket was redeposited in charge of its keepers at headquarters. So of each watch. Next morning the paddles were counted in the presence of the commander-in-chief or a properly appointed deputy and at least two accredited aides. If any paddle was missing the sentinel who should have handed it over was called up and confronted with the captain of his watch and his apparitors. Then and there it was settled before the presiding officer by statements of the four or more men concerned which man was at fault. Then and there either the sentinel or the captain of the watch was put to death. One or the other was at fault, and it was no thanks to him that the camp had not been surprised and its inmates butchered. For all of him, the army had been massacred. He was just as guilty as if it had been. The presiding officer determined who was at fault, touched him with his official bâton of command and instantly every man in sight, not on definite duty which could not be left, seized any club, cudgel, bludgeon, or anything that would serve for one, and the man condemned was beaten to death. The Romans were never encumbered by any false sentiment.

When it was barely light enough to see to walk without stubbing one's toe on stones or such inequalities, the bugles blew and the army roused. The tents came down, the mules were cinched, and the men fell into line, each with his two stakes from last night's stockade for next night's stockade. So, standing in full armor, each with his full burden of personal baggage, they ate their breakfast.

Off they marched. In times of which we have record a normal day's march was fifteen miles in six hours. Arrived at the place measured off for the night's camp and marked at every necessary point with flags or pennons of various colors on poles about as tall as a spear, they dug ditches for three or four hours.

Then the same routine was repeated.

Naturally, after they returned safe and sound, hale and hearty from a series of campaigns involving such dangers, toils, hardships, and privations, and requiring such brawn, valor, skill, alertness, resolution, self-command, self-restraint, and obedience to orders, the Romans had from their wives and children both admiration and respect.

The official designation of the Roman government was always:

"Senatus Populusque Romanus" ("The Senate and People of Rome" or "The Roman Senate and People").

The Senate was always put first.

It is worth while to remark here that the Romans never had any device analogous to a national flag. We have the Stars and Stripes as our official symbol of the nation. We put U. S. A. on a great number of buildings and other pieces of national property. The Romans used the letters S. P. Q. R. both as we use U. S. A. and as we use the Stars and Stripes. The letters S. P. Q. R. on a banner (not a flag flying to the wind from a more or less vertical pole, but a banner depending from a crossbar suspended to the pole as the sail-yard of a ship is slung from the mast) formed their nearest approach to a national flag. The letters were usually, later, of gold on a crimson banner, but for many centuries an army used a banner of any design or colors agreeable to its commander.

Wherever Roman authority was paramount the proud letters S. P. Q. R. were seen on buildings erected or confiscated by the Romans; on the banners, helmets, corselets, shields, spears, artillery, wagons, and other appurtenances of Rome's troops; on all public documents of every kind.

Under the kings of Rome the Roman Senate was the council of the King, chosen by the King, a body of three hundred advisers made up of the best qualified and most respected elders of the community, one at least from each patrician family. After the expulsion of the kings the Senate acted as the advisory council to all the magistrates of the Commonwealth. How it was recruited in the early decades of the republic we do not know. But, according to the norm for all city-states of the Mediterranean world, it was felt that every ex-magistrate was entitled to life membership in the Senate and the Roman Senate became approximately a body of ex-magistrates and so included practically all the men of worthwhile experience and of tried and proved capacity in civil and military activities who could be found in the community.

So constituted, it was respected more and more from age to age. Any magistrate confronted with any administrative problem as to the solution of which he had any doubt or with any uncertainty as to policy, felt bound to consult the Senate. Also almost always he felt bound to defer to their *senatus consultum* (advice of the Senate), and the *senatus consulta* came to have the force of laws.

From the establishment of the Roman Republic a law was an ordinance which had been approved by an affirmative majority vote of the Roman people, that is by the citizens in good standing assembled in the voting field on any one voting day. Any magistrate might propose a law, but in practice it was most unusual for any magistrate to submit a law to be voted on without first consulting the Senate. After such consultation he came before the assembly with proposals which had been fully discussed by the nation's most competent advisers and had their expressed commendation. Only very exceptionally did any magistrate put before the assembly a proposal of which the Senate was known to disapprove. Some very famous Roman laws were put to vote and became statutes in defiance of the Senate's declared disapprobation. Such laws were generally as conspicuously detrimental and failures as were the laws approved by the Senate conspicuously beneficial and successful. Thus the prestige of the Senate waxed from age to age and its formally debated and formally voted *senatus consulta* gradually acquired the validity of voted laws, even without being affirmed by the assembly.

It cannot be too much insisted on that, contrary to the false impression conveyed by most histories of Rome, the Romans, Senate and people alike, were at all times and in all ages instinctively averse to engaging in war and were only after much reluctance led or forced into hostilities.

The vigor with which the Romans pressed a war, once entered upon; the dogged resolution with which they kept up a losing, even an apparently hopeless, contest; the stern harshness with which they punished treacherous allies or insolent foes; the grim ruthlessness with which they extirpated any conquered race deemed rancorous and potentially a menace; were such salient features of the Roman character that they have distracted attention from their innate disinclination to enter into warfare.

Wherever Livy or any other of our extant original sources recounts the debates and discussions at Rome preceding a declaration of war it is manifest that both the Senate and people were anything but eager for hostilities. And the people always voted on a proposal to go to war.

The most important Roman magistrates were the consuls, tribunes, censors, prætors, ædiles, and quæstors.

The idea of having two consuls appears to have originated in the general distaste for one-man power acquired under the kings, and in the feeling that anything on which the two agreed was likely to be advisable, and that nothing on which they disagreed would be done. In practice that is just about what came to pass. When both consuls heartily approved any course of action it was vigorously pushed, and any measure they similarly commended met with general acquiescence. If one consul was bent on something which the other did not positively disapprove, he mostly had his way. Only in extreme cases did one obstinately oppose the other.

With us accused persons are protected from injustice at the hands of any one court or magistrate by the law of *habeas corpus,* under which some other magistrate can always be found to insure to the accused the assistance of his friends and legal counsel and their access to him. To accomplish analogous results the Romans, within twenty years of the establishment of the Republic, devised a new magistracy or gave a new form and new powers to a customary magistracy and instituted the tribunate. The tribunes of the people were magistrates elected by the people to protect all and sundry of the populace from any sort of injustice or oppression at the hands of the nobles or of any of their magistrates. In the course of time they gradually arrogated to themselves, with the approbation of the citizens and the more or less reluctant assent of the patricians and Senate, the right to forbid anything proposed or set on foot by any other magistrate, and this right grew until any one tribune could blockade any sort of action not only by any or all other magistrates, but even by all the other tribunes in unanimous agreement. While the tribunes might and sometimes—as notably Tiberius and Gaius Gracchus—did propose and carry legislative enactments, in practice the tribunes were officials who could initiate nothing, promote nothing, and do nothing, but could hamper, delay, block, prevent, and forbid anything and everything.

In 494 B.C. the Romans instituted the peculiar office of Censor. Two Censors, generally veteran experts who had held the most important administrative magistracies in succession, were chosen every five years to superintend the taking of the general census. Their powers naturally entitled them to make out and certify a list of Roman citizens and also one of Knights and one of Senators. This gave them the authority to deal with persons falsely claiming to be Roman citizens or to be entitled to equestrian rank. They soon acquired authority to deprive of citizenship persons deemed unworthy of it because of doings or behavior generally reprehended but not legally made punishable, and, concomitantly, to degrade from equestrian rank or expel from the Senate any man deemed unworthy of rank. Moreover, they also acquired authority to enroll as Knights, or even among the Senators, men regarded as worthy of such eminence but who, by adverse circumstances, had not attained it by the usual processes.

The Latin word *prætor* (he who goes before) originally meant a commander-in-chief of any military force. When, during the restoration of Rome after its devastation by the Gauls, in 387 B.C or so, it was realized that the consuls were overworked, a new office was devised and its incumbent dubbed "prætor." As time went on a second was added, then two more, and the number was repeatedly increased until there were eight.

In and about Rome a prætor had the duties of a sheriff and of a justice of the peace. He made arrests and tried cases. In the provinces a prætor was also the governor of his province. The jurisdiction of a city prætor was as high as that of our Supreme-court judges of criminal appeals.

The office of ædile was created at the same time as the office of prætor. The ædiles had charge of the construction and repair of public buildings and streets, of public health, of the inspection of weights, measures, and markets, and of everything concerning feeding the city.

A *quæstor* was in Rome manager of the treasury, and there were always two. With an army a quæstor was paymaster. Both in the city and on a campaign the quæstor (asker) was the man who asked, "Where is the money to come from?" and, "Where did the money go?"

In time it came to be the custom that the elective offices of quæstor, ædile, prætor and consul were held in that order by anyone passing through the normal course of promotion by popular recognition of successful administration.

After Rome began to acquire provinces and the consuls and prætors were overworked, it became customary to extend the powers of a consul for one year, as far as concerned the province assigned to him, and to which he went under the style of *proconsul* (instead of a consul), a man acting as consul.

Later men who had never been elected consuls were sometimes put in charge of provinces as proconsuls.

Similarly prætors had their powers extended for a year and were sent as proprætors to take charge of provinces.

Later it became the custom, later still the law, that all prætors spent their prætorship in Rome and each went out to his province as proprætor.

Later still men who had never been elected to the prætorship were nominated or appointed proprætors and sent out to take charge of provinces.

A dictator was not a regular magistrate of the Roman Commonwealth. When the general situation of external and internal affairs was in a snarl so hopeless that normal methods could not unravel it, the Romans reverted to a temporary nominated King and called him "dictator," (the man who has the say).

A dictator was customarily nominated by one of the consuls then in office, normally for a specified purpose only and usually only for a definitely limited time.

Imperator, from which is derived our word "Emperor," was not the designation of an official, magistrate, or commander elected or appointed. It was a complimentary title always conferred by acclamation.

The Latin word for war—*bellum*—was a contraction of an older form, *duellum,* practically the same as our word "duel," the syllable "du" being identical with our word "two" and with the first syllable of the Latin word for "two." *Duellum* originally meant a contest between *two* men, armies, or nations.

The original form of *imperator* was *induperator* ("the man who can make good in a contest between two," "the man who can make good in war," "the man who knows how to take care of an army and lead it to victory," "the man who can go it alone in a war," "the man fit to command").

From time immemorial, by ancestral custom, probably according to innate racial folk ways, most likely far antedating the foundation of Rome, when a Roman commander-in-chief ended up an adroitly managed campaign with a single hard-fought battle which turned out an overwhelming victory, his delighted soldiers, by spontaneous universal impulse, greeted him with shouts of "*Induperator,*" later, "*Imperator,*" signifying that they regarded him as fully fit by himself to lead an army through any difficulties to certain victory, as fit to command and give commands, as a competent autocrat.

Salutation as Imperator voiced the conviction of his men that the man so acclaimed had a peculiar personal right to the *imperium,* possessed by every commander of a Roman army. The imperium was the equivalent of the absolute authority of the former kings. Every dictator had it fully, everywhere, as did every general in the field; and every Roman governor, whether pro-prætor, pro-consul, prætor or consul, within his province. In peace the imperium, in Italy, was limited in various ways, more so within the pomœrium of Rome, and the imperium of a prætor ranked below that of a consul.

CHAPTER VII

THE RISE OF ROME

AFTER their deliverance from the Gallic raiders the Romans discussed whether to rebuild Rome or move to Veii. The latter minority proposal was overwhelmingly outvoted. Whether the walls of Rome had been mostly or partially thrown down by the exultant and malicious Gauls or had merely come to need repair through lapse of time and neglect, we cannot know. Certainly, within thirty years after her sack by the Gauls, Rome was girt by walls not merely unrivaled in circuit; but in thickness, construction, height, and strength stupendous. The far-seeing Etruscan kings had included within their *pomerium* an area capable of housing comfortably a population of 400,000 persons and affording them room for all necessary civic activities. Their clever engineers had taken advantage of every feature of Rome's topography which lent itself to their purposes. The Servian Wall was mostly built on the scarps of the Cælian, Aventine, Capitoline and Quirinal Hills. Where, east of the Quirinal, Viminal, and Esquiline, there were no steep scarps, but a space of almost level ground, they had dug for 1,400 yards a prodigious ditch a hundred feet wide and thirty feet deep, the earth out of which they had heaped up on the inner side in a long embankment known as the *Agger* (earthwork) of Servius Tullius. To retain this they had constructed along its front a massive wall nine feet thick and thirty feet high, of large blocks of accurately dressed stone. On the agger they erected walls even thicker and higher than those on the scarps of the hills, and towers even closer together and more lofty. No army ever dared to assault these defenses.

Perfecting these mighty fortifications and reorganizing the governmental administration seem to have absorbed most of the energies of the community for about a quarter of a century. By that time the vigor of Rome was not merely restored, but enhanced beyond any previous maximum.

ITALY IN THE TIMES OF THE ROMAN REPUBLIC

Horde after horde of Gauls raided almost to the walls of Rome, but each inroad ended in discomfiture for the invaders and victory for the Romans. One after another ancient and opulent Etruscan city found its massive walls insufficient to withstand assaults by Roman armies. By 357 B.C. the Romans were supreme in southern Etruria. Within six years more they had effectually crushed their inveterate foes the Volscians, Æquians, and Hernicians, after over four centuries of recurrent, almost incessant, warfare. In 343 B.C., for the first time since her foundation 410 years agone, the help of Rome was asked by aliens, the Etruscanized Oscans of Campania, the Capuans and the Sidicini of Teanum, who were hard pressed by the Samnites of the mountains, also Sabellians, but hostile and given to forays. The first Samnite War lasted only two years and was ended in 341 B.C. by a treaty favorable to the victorious Romans.

It came just in time. For the ensuing spring most of the Latins revolted against the overshadowing leadership of Rome, long steadily aggrandized. The Latin War lasted four years and ended in a complete general victory for the Romans. The Latin League was finally and forever dissolved in 338 B.C., in which year the greatness of Rome began. Each Latin city-state was compelled to ratify an individual treaty with Rome. These were all of a like tenure. Romans and Latins might intermarry, trade, make contracts, acquire landed property in each other's territory, bequeath and inherit legacies from one city to the other and all on a footing of mutual equality. But all such intercourse and all such dealings between the Latin towns was forbidden.

These treaties marked the inception of the broad-minded, farsighted, judicious, just, and beneficial policy which made Rome great.

The Romans, from the foundation of the Republic to the dissolution of the Empire, were instinctively averse to exerting their power or asserting their mastery more than was absolutely necessary. If vanquished adversaries, whether inveterate foes or discomfited insurgents, promised to be faithful allies in future, appeared to have both the intention and disposition to keep their word, and were judged reliable both as individuals and as a community, Rome treated them almost as well as if they had been steadfast confederates from the first. So that, except a few allies on practically equal terms, cities which of their own accord had come to Rome's aid in time of need, communities which had asked help of Rome, and been assisted, towns which had submitted after a brief resistance, stubborn foes and recalcitrant vassals, while the treaties with them varied almost infinitely in detail, were all made *municipia.* The word *municipium* has, in Latin, two meanings inseparably blended. *Munus* meant both a right or privilege and also a duty or obligation, and *capere* (softened to *cipere* when part of a compound word) meant "to take" both in the sense of "to win" and "to assume." *Municipia* were city-states which had both won rights and privileges from the Romans and assumed duties toward them. They kept full rights of autonomy, and local self-government, with uninterrupted continuance of their ancestral customs as to election of magistrates, constitution of their *curia,* and administration of justice. They won the privileges of intermarriage, of trade, of mutual contracts, of buying and selling real estate, of making bequests and enjoying inheritances. They assumed the duties and obligations of keeping the peace with all allies of Rome, of going to war with all enemies of Rome, and of maintaining contingents in all Roman armies.

Communities judged untrustworthy, whether as not genuinely loyal to Rome but making a pretense of loyalty; or as unreliable because of instability of temperament, even if well intentioned; or as having a minority nursing a smouldering animosity toward their conquerors; or towns considered incapable of self-government because of local feuds or a tendency to petty wrangling, were accorded all other privileges of *municipia* and assumed all their duties, but their curias were abolished, and they were not allowed to elect their magistrates any longer, but were controlled by governors appointed by the Roman Senate. Such a governor was called a *præfectus* (man put in charge), and such allied communities were therefore called *præfecturæ.* Most præfectures after a probation long enough for the irreconcilables to die off and be forgotten and for local feuds to evaporate under the influence of a series of competent and tactful prefects, finally became full municipia.

Such allied towns paid no tribute to Rome. Of course their obligation to maintain a contingent in the Roman army was a costly burden; but while expensive, it was not humiliating, as a tribute paid in kind or coin would have been. With the touchy and high-spirited Italian city-states that made a great difference.

Some conquered peoples were manifestly sullen in their submission and likely to revolt at the first opportunity. From the time when her power began to increase, the policy of Rome was to plant colonies in such districts. A colony was usually a body of three hundred Roman citizens and a greater number of citizens of allied Latin towns, seasoned men in the early prime of life, accompanied by their families. They became a sort of local garrison and constabulary, with an eye rather to keeping their district peaceable than to suppressing insurrections in their neighborhood.

The colonists were always put in full and exclusive control of the citadel of the town and were usually assigned one-third of its residential area, with the existing houses to live in; also one-third of the town's territory for farms, pasture land and forest allotments. Such colonists elected their own magistrates and so gradually constituted a local senate or town *curia.* They served in the army not as legionaries, but as allies.

Sometimes a colony took the entire territory of a town which had been practically depopulated in the course of its resistance, or which had been stormed and the survivors of its inhabitants sold as slaves.

Colonies made up wholly of Roman citizens, usually with complete possession of their town and its territory, were planted as thought best along the seacoasts of Italy. The inhabitants of these colonies were exempt from all other military service except what was needed to protect themselves and keep their neighborhood in subjection, being regarded as local garrisons. No colony paid any taxes.

Within a very few years after the expansion of Rome's power began, the Romans realized that founding colonies in conquered territory, sending colonies to important cities brought under Rome's control, and concluding treaties by which allied states became municipia was not enough to assure her sway wherever it extended. To move armies promptly and easily to threatened points, to insure quick communications with her colonies and allies, to encourage traffic between Rome and towns forbidden some of the essentials of commercial intercourse with each other, Rome must create roads. Thereupon, in 312 B.C. the great censor Appius Claudius let out the contracts for the construction of the superb highway from Rome to Capua, called after him the *Via Appia* (the Appian Way), Rome's Great South Road. As Capua was, at all periods, next to Rome the most populous and prosperous city in Italy proper, this always remained Rome's most important and most used highway.

Ultimately, twelve such highways radiated from Rome in all directions, surveyed everywhere as nearly straight as possible. Each was about fourteen and a half feet wide and paved with hard stone. As horseshoeing was not yet invented the size of the paving blocks did not matter. The Roman phrase for constructing a road was *iter munire* ("to fortify a road"), as the work resembled that customary in fortifying a camp. In later practice a broad trench was dug and its flat bottom rammed hard. On this was laid a layer of carefully fitted flat stones, above that two feet of coarse rubble, then eight inches of stones set in lime, then a fourth layer, three inches thick, of fine-grained rubble, then the pavement which was always cambered enough to shed rain water.

From these magnificent highways adequate side-roads branched to the colonies, *municipia,* and allied cities near each.

In dealing with any beaten state whose citizens they regarded as incapable of laying aside their animosity and becoming loyal allies, the Romans were absolutely ruthless. Such cities were totally destroyed, as Alba Longa, Veii, Carthage, and Numantia. If a city had been insulting or treacherous, especially if it had pretended to submit and then rebelled, most of all if it had massacred the Roman governor and garrison, the victorious Romans invariably razed the city and sold as slaves any survivors of its storming. So they dealt with Corinth and Palmyra.

This policy of habitual mercy, mildness, and fairness, punctuated with the most extreme severity where manifestly deserved, made the Romans not only universally feared, but won the allegiance and respect, even sometimes the affection, of their vassals.

The aggrandizement of Rome all along the west coast of Italy as far south as the bay of Naples, and far inland on the coastal plain, irritated and alarmed the Samnites, and the resulting second Samnite War lasted from 326 B.C. to 304 B.C., twenty-two years. Fortune fluctuated; many little states changed sides, not a few more than once. Rome suffered a notable disaster in the defile called the Caudine Forks in the Samnite mountains. In 312 the forty years' peace with the Etruscans expired. All their independent cities entered the war, so that Rome had to fight on two fronts. Within four years Rome's enemies had had enough. The first Roman war fleet was created, and convoyed round the southern headlands of the peninsula an army which invaded Samnium from the coast of the Adriatic. The upshot of the war was a positive though not overwhelming victory for the Romans, and they finally and forever obliterated as separate peoples the Volscians, Æquians, and Hernicians who had revolted and joined the Samnites. Rome founded many new colonies and increased the number of cities allied to her.

The third and last war with the Samnites lasted only eight years, but was desperately contested. The Samnites had help from Lucanians, Umbrians, Etruscans, and Gauls. The war ended with a bare victory for the Romans, but they gained more allies and founded more colonies.

Within five years the Romans had to cope with a general coalition including Lucanians and Bruttians in the toe of Italy, and Umbrians, Etruscans, and Gauls north of Rome. The upshot was a complete Roman victory. The surviving Senones were driven north of the Rubicon and the coastal plain of the Adriatic between the Æsus and Rubicon, as the first land held by Gauls to be annexed, was, to the end of the Empire, even after all Gaul was Romanized, known as the *ager Gallicus* (the Gallic piece of land). Thereafter, for over 250 years, the Rubicon, the Apennines, and the Macra formed the northern boundary of what was then called Italy.

No sooner was Rome safeguarded to northward than fresh and worse trouble broke out in Lower Italy. A Roman war fleet on the way to the Adriatic anchored in the harbor of Tarentum. By former treaties, long obsolete, Rome had agreed that no warship of hers should sail that far east. Some hotheads in Tarentum stirred up a riot, attacked the ships, and captured five, whose crews were either butchered by the mob or sold into slavery by the city government. The Tarentine populace insulted the Roman embassy which came to request amends. Rome thereupon declared war and Tarentum secured the help of King Pyrrhus of Epirus, a capable ruler and a paragon general. He brought with him war-elephants, novel and appalling to the Romans, and he beat them twice in successive years; but he won the battles by so narrow a margin and his losses were so severe in each, that a Pyrrhic victory has been proverbial ever since. The third battle was a decisive defeat for the foreigners. After ten years of war (282-272 B.C.) Tarentum surrendered and its walls were razed, but the inhabitants were spared and accorded self-government. By 266 B.C. Roman command, Roman authority, Roman control, Roman influence, in varying degrees in various districts, were supreme throughout all Central and Lower Italy south of the Macra, Apennines, and Rubicon to the southernmost headlands.

At this time Carthage, a Phœnician colony on the north coast of Africa, near the modern Tunis, had been in existence six centuries, for it had been founded about a century earlier than Rome. Carthage had prospered greatly, almost continuously, and possessed or dominated northern Africa between the desert and the Mediterranean from Cyrenaica westward. She also had flourishing colonies and a wide strip of territory along the southern coast of Spain from the Straits eastward, and held the Balearic Islands, part of western Corsica, nearly all of Sardinia and the western half of Sicily. Carthage claimed all the Mediterranean westward from Sicily, Sardinia, and Corsica as her sea, and from the first had made a practice of sinking with all on board any ship of any other nation found sailing that sea, if any ship of hers could overtake and capture it. There had been intermittent warfare between Carthage and the Greek cities of Sicily for more than three centuries.

In 264 B.C. Rome's help was asked by some unattached Campanian mercenaries, called Mamertines, who had gotten possession of the important Greek city of Messana in Sicily at the strait dividing it from Italy, and who were hard pressed by Hiero, King of the Greek city of Syracuse on the east coast of Sicily. Others of the Mamertines asked help of Carthage and welcomed Carthaginian warships into the harbor and a Carthaginian garrison into the citadel of Messana (Messina).

Meantime the Roman Senate and People, after much debate and hesitation, had voted to help the Mamertines and had sent to their assistance a fleet of ships of their Italian allies and an advance guard of Roman legionaries. These expelled the Carthaginians and occupied Messana, which a Carthaginian fleet promptly besieged and which the Roman consul relieved.

Thereafter the First Punic war lasted for twenty-two years, with varying fortunes on both sides. The Romans won their first naval victory off the north coast of Sicily west of Messana in 260 B.C. In 256 B.C. they completely defeated the Carthaginian fleet off the south coast of Sicily in sight of Mount Ecnomus, in a battle notable because over 300,000 men were afloat in the ships of the two fleets, a number never equalled in any naval battle before or since. As a result of that victory the Romans landed successfully in Africa near Carthage an army under their consul Regulus who harried all Africa (the modern Tunisia) outside of the walled cities, and failed to negotiate an advantageous peace only because of the arrogance of the conditions he demanded. He was defeated and captured, but the remnants of his army were rescued by a Roman fleet.

After more than two decades of superhuman exertions on both sides, involving severe imposts upon all citizens and allies of the contestants, vast expense, extreme exhaustion, stubborn endurance, appalling carnage, prodigious valor and marvellous daring, the war was brought to an end by a decisive naval victory. In 241 B.C. the Romans annihilated the Carthaginian fleet off the western end of Sicily. Thereupon Carthage sued for peace, paid a huge war-indemnity, and evacuated Sicily, the western part of which was organized as the first Roman province; that is to say, it was made the sphere of authority of a Roman official who was absolute ruler of it. Not long afterward Rome got full possession, except for unsubdued aborigines in the interior, of Sardinia and Corsica, and they were organized as the second Roman province. Each of these provinces was intrusted to a proconsul, an ex-consul who, at the expiration of his year of office, had had his full powers as consul continued for a year, within the bounds of his assigned province.

In 229 B.C., within twelve years of the end of the First Punic War, Rome was compelled to send a fleet and army to Illyria to break up the piratical activities of the Illyrians, as truculent as their modern successors the Albanians. This was the first appearance of Roman forces on the mainland of Greece and the first instance of help from Rome to Greek cities proper.

In 225 B.C. a great horde of Gauls crossed the Apennines and advanced on Rome. But the Romans were able to meet them with large forces and sent both consuls, each with an army, and a third army as a reserve. At Telamon on the coast of Etruria, uncomfortably near Rome, was fought a terrific battle, in which the Romans were overwhelmingly victorious. They then vigorously invaded the valley of the Po. There the Boii submitted and were allowed to remain on their lands about Bononia (Bologna). After crossing the Po the Roman army crushed the Insubrian Gauls. In 222 B.C. their capital, Mediolanum (Milan) was captured, and Comum (Como). Roman colonies were founded at Placentia (Piacenza) Cremona, and Mutina (Modena).

The Greek historian, Polybius, in the preface to his great *History of Rome,* remarks that no one could be so indifferent or so indolent as not to wish to know how and under what system of polity the Romans in less than fifty-three years had succeeded in subjugating almost all the inhabited world to their sole government. He meant the years from 220 to 168 B.C. and reckoned from the first intimations of the impending Second Punic War.

Among the Carthaginian commanders in the First Punic War, Hamilcar, surnamed or nicknamed Barca, which means Lightning, had been preëminent for brilliant and spectacular exploits on land and sea. He had harried the coasts of Italy year after year, had eluded great fleets despatched to sweep the seas for his tiny squadron, had won battles, had taken by stratagem or surprise walled cities rated impregnable, and had held fortresses against enormous odds through sieges of amazing duration. He had proved himself a genius as an independent commander, whether general or admiral. After the close of the First Punic War he saved Carthage by annihilating a horde of her former mercenary allies who had mutinied and horribly ravaged the country. Five years after the peace with Rome he was put in charge of the Carthaginian province in southern Spain; colonies from Cadiz to Cartagena and a strip of coast. He saw the possibilities of reviving the power of Carthage by creating for her a great empire in Spain and speedily conquered all of the southeastern part of the peninsula from modern Algarve to Valencia and inland to Toledo. Spain then abounded in silver lodes, some barely worked, some newly opened, many as yet undiscovered. Spanish rivers had not yet been washed clean of placer gold. Carthage was at once and vastly enriched by Hamilcar's conquest. After nine years of success he fell in battle and was succeeded by his son-in-law Hasdrubal, who continued his policies and successes. On his death in 221 B.C., twenty years after the peace with Rome, Hamilcar's son Hannibal, then twenty-eight years old, was so manifestly the darling of their armies in Spain that the Carthaginian Senate could not but acquiesce in their choice of him for supreme command, though a majority regarded him as a young firebrand. Rome and Carthage had a treaty by which the Carthaginian conquests in Spain were to stop at the river Ebro, and Greek seacoast cities in alliance with Rome were not to be molested. The most important of these cities was Saguntum. Hannibal knew that his war-party was in a minority at Carthage and that the party in power was for keeping the peace with Rome. He was resolved on forcing a war. The story that Hamilcar had indoctrinated him from his cradle with implacable hatred for the Romans is by no means unlikely. Indubitably, Hannibal had from his versatile and experienced father a military education almost as good as that which Philip of Macedon had given Alexander the Great. Hamilcar was as absolute in Spain throughout his nine years there as if he had been a king and was practically independent of the Carthaginian Senate. Hannibal succeeded to all his powers, and had even greater genius. He felt a justifiable self-confidence. He picked a quarrel with Saguntum and in 219 B.C. took it after an eight months' siege, one of the most arduous and brilliant recorded in history. His party at home jockeyed the Carthaginian government into forcing Rome to declare war. The Roman Senate started preparations to invade Africa by sea and sent a small force to Spain by land under the consul Publius Cornelius Scipio. Hannibal had laid plans which only a great genius could have conceived, and in the spring of 218 B.C., leaving enough troops in Spain to garrison it, set out by land for Italy. He forced his way across the Pyrenees, eluded Scipio at the Rhône, and was the first general to lead a disciplined army across any pass of the Alps. He had set out from Spain with 50,000 infantry, 9,000 cavalry, and 37 elephants. Late in August or early in September he was in the rich lowlands west of Milan with 26,000 effectives, all told, and a few elephants. With this force he confidently attempted to destroy a nation which, as is proved by the extant records of the Roman census of 225 B.C., could levy from Italy men enough to have under arms at one time, ashore and afloat, forces totalling over 700,000 combatants. Hannibal's capacities, training, experience, and genius very nearly succeeded. The Romans were taken by surprise, with only small forces in the valley of the Po and with recruiting for the contemplated invasion of Africa proceeding unhurriedly. Scipio had sent on his army to Spain when he learned that Hannibal had eluded him and had returned to Italy by sea. He pushed on with a small force to meet Hannibal, who had been joined by contingents of the Insubrian Gauls, beaten and partly subjugated by Rome, but disaffected and rancorous. There was a clash, scarcely more than a cavalry skirmish, on the Ticinus, a northern tributary of the Po, west of Milan. Scipio was badly wounded and barely saved by heroism of his seventeen-year-old son, who lived to achieve, sixteen years later, the final defeat of Hannibal at Zama. This victory on the Ticinus won for Hannibal widely heralded prestige among the Gauls. Scipio retreated, crossed the Po, camped awhile near Placentia, and then entrenched a strong camp on the east bank of the Trebia, a southern tributary of the Po. There he was joined by the other consul with reinforcements. In December 218 Sempronius thought he saw a chance to crush Hannibal and allowed himself to be enticed by a clever stratagem to order his men, early of a chill morning and fasting, to wade a cold river armpit deep and attack a well-fed and cunningly arranged army. Of 40,000 Romans barely 10,000 escaped to Placentia. At once practically the whole population of the Po Valley took sides with Hannibal. Over 60,000 Gauls joined his army.

Next spring, both Roman consuls led armies against him. One marched to Ariminum (Rimini) on the Adriatic; the other, under Flaminius, the conqueror of the Gauls, into Etruria to Arretium (Arezzio). Hannibal outflanked both by crossing the Apennines far north and floundering through the bogs along the lower Arno. When Flaminius learned that Hannibal was between him and Rome he set out to find him. As consul he had annihilated a vast horde of Gauls in the monstrous battle of Telamon; he had ravaged and plundered their home-lands; out of the loot he had, as censor, erected for his fellow citizens their first stone circus where they might in comfort watch chariot races, and had built more than a hundred miles of Rome's Great North Road, called after him the Via Flaminia, ultimately completed to Ariminum. He was naturally confident of crushing Hannibal and marched toward Perusia. Hannibal was informed of his movements, divined both his objective and his intended route, and lay in wait for him by Lake Trasimene. Along the lake shore the marching was easy, but close to the lake were rugged hills then already deforested, but shaggy with a scrub of saplings, shrubs, and brush. Among these Hannibal's forces ensconced themselves, the most notable of the few instances recorded in history of an entire large army lying in ambush. The Romans advanced as had every Roman army, without plan, without reconnoitering ahead, 40,000 men, each carrying his sixty pounds or more. When their long column was precisely between the lake and the ready, lurking array, Hannibal gave the signal, his men rose, yelled, and charged the astounded Romans. After three hours of easy butchery, with few Carthaginians even wounded and not 2,000 Gauls killed, 15,000 Romans were dead along with Flaminius, and as many more prisoners. Ten thousand stragglers escaped.

Naturally there was a panic at Rome, but Hannibal did not venture to march on the city.

After his victory on the Trebia he had set free all prisoners not Roman citizens; so now again, and he proclaimed that he had come to fight Rome only and to set free all Rome's vassals. But not one town opened its gates to him. He marched into south Italy where supplies were plentiful and whence, by sea, he could communicate with Carthage.

As usual in a serious crisis, the Romans appointed a dictator. He was Quintus Fabius Maximus, whose famous policy was to postpone a battle, scout and reconnoiter cautiously, hang on Hannibal's flanks and rear, and allow the invaders to wear themselves out or die of old age. This dawdling did not please the populace and for the next year, along with a veteran nobleman, they selected the lowborn Gaius Terentius Varro, who declared that he believed a Roman army could beat a Carthaginian army and that, if elected, he would march on Hannibal and fight him. He did, at Cannæ in Apulia near the heel of Italy, in 216 B.C. Within three hours 70,000 Romans had been killed and many captured; the 20,000 who escaped were in detachments and unorganized. Varro had only about 400 men with him. This was the worst defeat Republican Rome ever suffered.

As a result of this disaster the Lucanians and the Samnites, many other tribes of southern Italy, most of its towns and even Capua in Campania joined Hannibal. About the same time the only Roman force in the valley of the Po was massacred by the Gauls.

But the Roman Senate kept up heart. Every man capable of serving was drafted into the army; every volunteer slave was promised freedom at the end of the war. Hannibal's offer of exchange of prisoners, or of release of his Roman prisoners on ransom, met with a refusal even to admit into Rome his envoys.

The next summer, 215 B.C., the consul of the previous year, Marcus Claudius Marcellus, acting as proconsul, came off best in a minor battle with Hannibal at Nola. This lost Hannibal much of his prestige. He was no longer invincible. Also, he could no longer continue offensive warfare. The initiative passed to the Romans.

Otherwise this year was discouraging. Philip V of Macedon made an alliance with Carthage. Also Syracuse in Sicily, after a local revolution, took the Carthaginian side. Yet within three years, after a two years' siege, Marcellus had stormed Syracuse. And the same year, 212 B.C., a league of Greek states joined Rome in her war with Macedon. But on the other hand, that same year, in Spain, Hannibal's brother Hasdrubal won a great victory, killed both the Scipios, who had been fighting him since Hannibal entered Italy, and chased the remnants of Rome's armies north of the Ebro. In Italy, Hannibal, by treachery, got possession of the citadel of Tarentum, in south Italy. He also defeated a Roman army in Apulia and another in Lucania, marched into Campania, and compelled the Romans to desist from the siege of Capua. But he soon had to retire to Tarentum, whereupon Capua was promptly reinvested.

Next year Hannibal had to try to relieve Capua. He tried and failed. In the hope of drawing off the besieging army he marched on Rome and camped within sight of the walls. While there he learned from a prisoner that one of the fields inside his camp had been offered for sale in Rome and promptly found a purchaser at its full normal value. Also, what was less insolent, but more important, that a considerable reinforcement for Spain had marched out of Rome to Ostia. Twice Hannibal's army and the Roman forces faced each other in full array, eager for a pitched battle; twice a violent thunderstorm with hail drove both armies to the shelter of their tents. This on two successive days was taken by all as an omen. There was no further offer of battle by either side. Hannibal conned the stupendous fortifications of Rome, in any case, as then garrisoned, impregnable to the force with him even if he had had a siege-train. He marched away, and within that year (211 B.C.) Capua surrendered. Of the citizens blamed for its defection the Romans beheaded fifty-three, sold the others into slavery, and made the city a præfecture. The rest of her former allies hastened to desert Hannibal and make what terms they could with Rome.

In 210 B.C. Publius Cornelius Scipio, then twenty-five years old, was appointed proconsul to recover Spain and avenge his uncle and father. Hannibal won a minor victory in southern Italy. The Romans captured Agrigentum on the south coast of Sicily. During the next two years, in Italy, Marcellus had the worst of one battle with Hannibal and the best of another, and later was killed in a skirmish. In Spain Scipio captured Cartagena and fought a drawn battle with Hasdrubal, but could not keep him from starting for Italy with reinforcements for Hannibal.

The Romans were not an inventive race. They originated few ideas. Nor were they quick to take a suggestion or to adopt foreign ways. But once they comprehended the worth of any method or device, they outdid their teachers. The fortifications of Rome as they completed them about 360 B.C. surpassed any dreams of Tarquin the Haughty, a century and a half earlier. The massacre at Lake Trasimene had taught the Romans the value of reconnoitering, scouting, and stratagems. Within ten years they had learnt much of the art of war.

Hasdrubal crossed the Pyrenees, Gaul, and the Alps. But the two consuls intercepted his messengers to his brother, kept Hannibal in ignorance and stationary in Apulia, and overwhelmed the invaders near the river Metaurus, in Umbria on the Adriatic side of the Apennines. Hasdrubal's head was thrown among Hannibal's pickets outside his camp near Canusium. Hannibal withdraw into Bruttium (the toe of Italy) and there held out for four years more.

Meantime the Roman generals, after nine years of the First Macedonian War, had forced Philip of Macedon to sue for peace, and Scipio had captured Cadiz, the last Carthaginian hold on Spain, had made an alliance with Masinissa, King of Numidia (modern Algeria), had landed in Africa, and had won a victory.

Carthage thereupon, in 203 B.C., recalled Hannibal from Italy. He did what he could to defend his country, but next year there was fought one of the most decisive battles in the history of the world, in which, at Zama, south of Carthage, Scipio annihilated the Carthaginian army. Hannibal escaped. Carthage was granted peace on condition that she renounce all claims to Spain and the islands of the Mediterranean, recognize Masinissa as King of Numidia, reduce her navy to ten warships, surrender all her war elephants and engage to catch and tame no more, pay 200 talents ($250,000) yearly for fifty years, and engage in no war without Rome's authorization.

All southern Italy was reorganized with decreased local autonomy and more Latin colonies.

Within two years Rome had finally subjugated the entire valley of the Po. South of the Po many colonies were founded in the territories of the exterminated Boii; north of the Po the allied towns were soon Romanized.

Not long after Zama, Rome's help was asked by Athens, Rhodes, and Pergamus against Philip of Macedon. After a three-year Second Macedonian War Philip was decisively beaten at Cynoscephalæ in Thessaly in 197 B.C., and made a treaty agreeing to keep inside Macedonia and pay a war indemnity. The Romans proclaimed all Greek city-states free and independent.

At Carthage Hannibal had convinced the populace that he had not caused the war with Rome, and that his political adversaries were to blame for the trifling assistance he had had from home and so for his failure. He was elected chief magistrate of Carthage and within five years had revived her agriculture, mining, manufactures, trade, and commerce, reformed her laws, brought prosperity to all classes, kept the peace, and so managed her currency and finances that not only were the installments of the war-indemnity paid Rome promptly, but the Carthaginian treasury had a growing surplus. Convinced that he was preparing for a war of revenge, Rome demanded his surrender; he fled to Syria.

There Antiochus III, heir of one of the successors of Alexander the Great, who asked Hannibal's advice about everything but never followed it, soon declared war on the Romans, enticed into it by the few Greeks disaffected toward the Romans and misjudging the number of these malcontents. By 189 B.C. Antiochus was thoroughly vanquished. He agreed to give up all claims to territory in Europe or in Asia Minor, pay an indemnity and surrender Hannibal. Hannibal escaped and lived a few years longer.

Perseus, King of Macedon, son of Philip V, thought he could beat the Romans and make himself supreme in Greece. After a four-year Third Macedonian War he was decisively defeated at Pydna. Twenty thousand Macedonians were killed and Æmilius Paullus found himself with 11,000 prisoners, Perseus among them. This happened in 168 B.C.; by which year Polybius, writing some forty years later, held that the Romans had made themselves supreme throughout the entire Mediterranean World.

The freedom and independence which, twenty-nine years before, Rome had proclaimed for all Greek city-states they had generally misused by recurrent petty wars among themselves, cabals and leagues against Rome, and even by aiding her enemies.

The Romans razed seventy of the guiltiest cities, mostly in Epirus, after plundering them and selling the inhabitants into slavery. All Greek states were made subject to Rome as allies, municipia, or præfectures. And the like was done with many states in Asia Minor.

Meantime Carthage was prospering and Rome grew more and more uneasy. Marcus Porcius Cato, an austere and bigoted chauvinist, had long argued that Rome could never be safe while Carthage existed. He won the Senate to his view and the destruction of Carthage was decreed. Scipio, son of Æmilius Paullus and adopted son of the victor of Zama, was detailed for this unpleasant duty. The Carthaginians at first submitted, but later the irreconcilables got control and Scipio had to beat down a hopeless but desperate resistance. In 146 B.C., after the Third Punic War had lasted three years, Carthage was taken and razed and its survivors sold into slavery.

The ruthlessness of the Romans has so horrified modern historians that few set forth how sagacious, farsighted, judicious, logical, and sensible was this grim decision. By it they ensured their descendants and heirs mastery of the Mediterranean world, general peace, and amazing prosperity for full four centuries. In the same year the four-year Fourth Macedonian War, incited by an impostor posing as a brother of Perseus, was brought to a close and Macedonia was made a Roman province.

That very year the Greek cities of the Achæan league, misled by recalcitrant irreconcilables, defied Rome and fought the hopeless, though desperately contested, Achæan War, which

Mummius ended at the Battle of Leucopetra, after which he occupied Corinth, sent its art treasures to Rome, and sold the inhabitants into slavery. The Roman Senate held even this insufficient punishment for the mobbing and insulting of Roman ambassadors, and ordered Corinth razed as an example to all and sundry.

Since Spain had been organized as two provinces in 205 B.C., more than sixty years had passed in continuous guerilla warfare, punctuated by more or less general insurrections.

In northern Spain, in the mountains between the Ebro and the Duero, was then the populous and strongly fortified city of Numantia. Of the Numantines we know even less than of the Etruscans; their origin, kinship, and language cannot even be conjectured. They were certainly magnificent warriors. From their eyry they raided in every direction. The Romans warned them to cease from forays on their allies. They replied that they had raided the lowlanders since long before any Roman, or even any Carthaginian, had set foot in Spain. The Romans never failed to protect vassals. They declared war. The Numantines stood them off for eleven years until Scipio, the subverter of Carthage, was sent against them. He, after a siege of fifteen months, took Numantia by storm, most of the inhabitants fighting until felled.

Rome now had eight provinces: 1, Sicily (241 B.C.); 2, Sardinia and Corsica (231); 3 and 4, the two provinces of Spain (197); 5, Cisalpine Gaul (Gaul south of the Alps—that is, northern Italy from the Macra, Apennines, and Rubicon) (181); 6, Illyricum (Dalmatia and Albania) (167); 7, Africa (Tunisia) (146); 8, Macedonia, which at first included all of Thessaly, Epirus, and Greece now left partly free as allied states (146).

THE ADMINISTRATIVE DIVISIONS OF ROMAN ITALY

CHAPTER VIII

THE CIVIL WARS

MARIUS AND SULLA

WHEN Numantia was razed the Roman Commonwealth had existed for 375 years and more. During those three and three-quarter centuries there had been many dissensions in Rome between patricians and plebeians, between the Senate and the people, between the nobles and the commonalty, between the rich and the poor. Some of these discords had been very bitter. But every one had been settled, (and settled, be it noted, as must always be the case in a commonwealth where measures are put to a general vote, more or less in favor of the people, the commonalty, the populace,) even after heated and long debates, by some sort of compromise, without actual violence. And no wonder. With Spain seething with sedition, as with all Greece plotting revolt, almost as much as when Hannibal was ravaging Italy at will, or when the Insubrian hordes were in Etruria, or when the Samnites and Etruscans were in arms again, or when the very Latins rebelled, or in still earlier days when the Hernicians, Æquians and the Volscians raided each summer almost up to the walls of Rome, or when, in her earliest years, young Rome saw Etruscans, Sabines, and Hernicians, Æquians and Volscians threatening her from every direction, the Romans realized that any failure of civil concord meant immediate and total annihilation for Rome. Internal conflict meant speedy destruction from without; only unanimity could keep Rome in existence. While in daily and hourly dread of menacing near-by foes, political antagonists, no matter how unmeasuredly they detested each other, could not but put aside their animosities and stand shoulder to shoulder in defense of their country. But when the frontiers of Rome's dominion had been pushed so far away that no enemy was any immediate menace to Rome, political adversaries or factional rivals began to feel a keener sensation of hate for each other than of dread of alien foemen. This greatly diminished their self-control and mutual forbearance in the heat of debate, so that argument degenerated into altercation and remonstrance into invective.

Besides the disappearance of manifest danger from abroad, another cause operated to worsen the conditions affecting city politics at Rome.

In 338 B.C., at the end of the Great Latin War, the citizens who assembled in the *comitium* to vote on the proposals concerning terms of peace were the very same men who had fought and beaten the Latin rebels. Similarly, in 326 the citizens who assembled in the comitium to vote whether or not to go to war with the Samnites were the very same men who, burdened with a load of sixty-five pounds or more apiece, hiked fifteen miles or more a day, dug ditches, and stood watch too, throughout much, most, or all the twenty-two years of that war. As from the times of Romulus, so in those days, as for all the intervening four and a half centuries, the Roman voters and the Roman soldiers were the same men, the Roman populace and the Roman army were the same.

After 338 B.C. this condition of affairs altered steadily. Every colony founded put three hundred or more Roman citizens where they could seldom or never again stand in the comitium at Rome to listen to proposals and arguments and vote on them. From year to year the voting citizens who elected the magistrates and so determined the character of the Senate, who pronounced upon projected legislation, who decided for peace or war, were a smaller and smaller fraction of the fighting men of the Commonwealth; from year to year the army had fewer and fewer of its members participating in voting and less and less voice in elections, lawmaking, and momentous decisions concerning national policy.

For Rome never devised any system of representative government. As long as the Republic lasted a town-meeting of citizens present in Rome, less and less representative of the total of the citizens, more and more irresponsible, determined, in accordance with or in defiance of the advice of the Senate, grave national and international issues of peace or war.

The period of the civil wars was the century and more during which the Romans, without any one of them ever comprehending the precise nature of the crucial difficulty, were groping for a solution of the problems presented by this continually worsening discrepancy between the voting-rights and voting-opportunities of Roman citizens.

As the citizens of the colonies totalled larger contingents in the field-armies than did the city voters, the members of the voting-assembly were less and less likely to have to bear the burdens of the policies they voted for and so less and less cautious and conscientious as to how they voted.

As the men who bore the brunt of battle and won treasure and territory for Rome had less and less participation in the decision as to how the prizes of war should be disposed of, so discontent intensified. Before long demagogues in Rome utilized and exacerbated this discontent. The first and perhaps the most notable of the long series of such demagogues were the two brothers Tiberius Gracchus and Gaius Gracchus. They were well-born, handsome, gracious, ingratiating, high-minded, well-intentioned, plausible, and eloquent doctrinaire fanatics. Dishonest and boorish demagogues are far less dangerous and pernicious.

For twelve years the two, in succession, kept Rome in turmoil and uproar. A riot is actually a sort of informal and unorganized ephemeral civil war. The proposals and popularity of these two fascinating and unpractical brothers led to more than one riot. By 120 B.C. both were safely dead.

Within ten years Rome had on hand a serious war in North Africa. Micipsa, Sultan of Numidia, had bequeathed his kingdom to two sons and a nephew. The nephew, Jugurtha, a typical Berber, but with a Greco-Roman education and speaking and reading Greek and Latin fluently, who had had much experience of war and had brilliantly distinguished himself at the siege of Numantia, set Hiempsal and Adherbal to quarrelling and soon had both dead and buried. As suzerain, Rome could not countenance such nefarious and flagrant rapacity. Moreover, their injunction that he should not molest Adherbal had been defied. Jugurtha stood off some commanders, evaded others; one he defeated; some quarrelled with each other; some he bribed.

Gaius Marius, the son of a day laborer near Arpinim in that part of Latium where once the Volscians and Hernicians had flourished, had had a minor command in the armies operating against Jugurtha. In 107 B.C. he was elected consul as champion of the populace and put in charge of dealing with Jugurtha.

Marius introduced many novelties into Roman army organization, drill, tactics, and equipment. His first and greatest innovation was to call for volunteers instead, as always before, of drafting all men capable of military service and choosing the best. Within two years Jugurtha had starved to death in the lower dungeon of the Tullianum, deep in the rock of the Capitol Hill at Rome.

Meantime there had been unusual distress or commotion in Central Asia. Pressure diffused thence pushed the Western Slavs against the Germans and forced the Germanic peoples on southwestwardly. In 113 B.C. a vast horde of Cimbri had approached the eastern Alps and among their northern foothills had beaten a Roman army headed by a consul, in a hard-fought battle in which they were severely mauled. They then turned west, crossed the Rhine, vanquished a second Roman army, and rambled about Gaul, moving on aimlessly when they had eaten up a district. The Teutons, another Germanic tribe, with some allies, took advantage of the confusion also to cross the Rhine. In the Garonne Valley they defeated a third Roman army, under a consul. In their wanderings the Cimbri annihilated a fourth Roman army and then a fifth, both large.

Naturally there was a panic at Rome. Marius was consequently again elected consul.

Meantime the Cimbri had been rambling about Spain, quickly eating up its not overabundant supplies. When Spain was mostly ravaged they recrossed the Pyrenees and again ate up Gaul. The Belgians withstood them and they turned south again and united with the Teutons and their accretions.

Meanwhile Marius had been elected consul five times consecutively. Each spring he had messages from the home government urging him to find the enemy and force a battle. Each time he replied that he was not the sort of man to risk a defeat and did not intend to enter on a battle until he saw a fair chance to win it. Each year he was further urged to make an end of the war within his year's term, as it was not customary for any man to be chosen consul two years in succession. Each time he replied that he did not hanker after his command nor any command; if they were not content with him they might send some one else. Each time he was overwhelmingly reëlected.

Marius had been playing the Fabian game with the barbarians, and of course they, as the less civilized, tired of it first. Unable to elude him or force him to a battle, they resolved to part and to try to enter Italy separately, the Teutons along the Riviera, the Cimbri by the eastern Alpine passes.

Marius had his chance at last. East of the delta of the Rhône, at Aquæ Sextiæ (Aix in Provence), he annihilated the Teutons and captured their King. Then he hurried across the Little St. Bernard pass to the help of his colleague, whom the Cimbri had defeated and driven south of the Po. With both armies united under his command Marius turned on the Cimbri, drove them into Piedmont, and annihilated them also, at Vercellæ. The hordes of prisoners from both victories were such that the price of a likely slave-lad was less then than that of an average horse.

The year after this reassuring victory, as their dread of assault and sack had evaporated, the Romans again rioted in Rome, in which riots the demagogues Saturninus and Glaucia both lost their lives.

For years discontent had been growing throughout Italy proper, south of the Macra, Apennines, and Rubicon. The descendants of the subjugated races disrelished more and more the domination of the Romans. A minority of the Etruscans and Umbrians, and the remnant of the Sabellians, Marsians, Samnites, Oscans, Campanians, and Lucanians revolted all at once and started the Social War. The Marsians in the lead, they organized a federal republic, selected for their capital Corfinium in the district of the Pælignians, and called their commonwealth "Italia." They won many victories over various Roman armies. Marius fought the Marsi and their neighbors, with some checks, but with ultimate success. In Campania, Samnium, and Lucania the insurrection was overwhelmingly successful. Warned of the impending defection of the remainder of the Umbrians and Etruscans, the Romans enacted a law conferring Roman citizenship on all the Latins and on all communities in Italy which had been loyal to Rome. Rapidly then the insurgents weakened. A second law offered citizenship to all Italians who might ask for it. At once the uprising collapsed by 88 B.C.

It was time. For before the end of that year not only was a redoubtable foe assailing the Roman power in Asia, but actual civil war had broken out in Italy.

Mithridates, Sultan of Pontus, was a very notable man, a fine horseman, a great hunter, so dosed from childhood with antidotes that he ate any food offered him without fear of poison, and, at the height of his power, able to understand and talk every one of the thirty-odd languages used by his vassals. From Pontus he had conquered all the eastern shores of the Black Sea round to and including the Crimea. He also extended his rule westward and southward into Asia Minor. At the behests of Roman governors he at first withdrew from Cappadocia and allowed them to reinstate its king. But he soon reconquered it and also invaded Bithynia, which was under Rome's protection, vanquished three Roman generals and expelled King Nicomedes. In most of the Greek cities of Asia Minor and Syria his machinations resulted in the seizing of the government by the anti-Roman party. Then he suggested a simultaneous massacre of all Roman citizens in such cities and more than 80,000 were butchered in one day.

As to the civil war, it must be repeated that by that period it had come about that the armies of the Commonwealth were manned chiefly from the colonies. The soldiers, as Roman citizens, had the right to participate in all assemblies at Rome and vote on all proposals. But few of them ever had been in Rome or would ever be there. In earlier days every Roman soldier had voted at the election of the commander he obeyed, and on the declaration of the war in which he was engaged. The war was his war and the general his general. Racial and national habits are so strong that, in the intervening periods of gradual and unperceived change, even after only a minority of any Roman army were Romans born, and actual as well as potential voters, no thought of questioning a national policy ever entered the head of any Roman soldier. All implicitly acquiesced in anything voted at Rome, whether it was an order, a prohibition, an assignment, or what else.

But for some, probably for many years before 88 B.C., the soldiers had come to feel ill-treated by the city voters; submissiveness had not only waned, but had vanished, and a tendency toward non-compliance was burgeoning even if not yet manifest.

Also many armies had been flagrantly ill-treated when it came to voting how to dispose of the lands they had conquered and of the spoils of war they had won for the Commonwealth. Many times had it happened that a general had had to plead for fair treatment for his soldiers.

Not merely had many an army seen the national treasury enriched while they got no share in the division of the spoils they had brought home, but many an army had had to wait long for mere normal stipulated pay, had known its commander to have to urge and argue before he succeeded in having them paid.

So the soldiers, in general, had come to look upon the city voters as their personal enemies and upon their general as their personal champion.

Lucius Cornelius Sulla was of a noble Roman family and of an aristocratic disposition. He had been quæstor under

Marius in Numidia and had personally captured Jugurtha, from which time he and Marius were at odds, as rivals. Yet he continued under Marius throughout most of the war with the Cimbri and Teutons. But he transferred to another commander before the victories. Thereupon he was under a cloud for some years. After his prætorship he went to Cilicia as proprætor in 92 B.C. and restored Ariobarzanes to the throne of Cappadocia, from which he had been ousted by Mithridates. He and Marius grew even more jealous of each other. But during the Social War they laid aside their mutual animosities and fought their best for Rome.

Sulla was elected consul for 88 B.C. and was appointed by the Senate to chastise Mithridates.

No man on earth, as far as records tell us, ever could levy an army; sort and sift the drafted recruits; conceive, devise, and put into use improvements in their equipment and organization; organize and equip them; put over them the very best men available for officers; drill them; care for them; feed them; keep them healthy and contented; infuse into all ranks of the entire force confidence and enthusiasm; lead them according to sound principles of grand strategy and with sure instincts; choose with unerring prescience the place and time for joining battle, or conduct a battle with masterly tactical dispositions better than Gaius Marius. As a military genius he was all but unmatchable.

But this unlettered lout of a laborer's son had no other good qualities. He was no politician, no statesman, no patriot. He was inordinately vain and not only unwilling to share any glory with anyone else, but greedy of more acclaim than even his incomparable services to the state deserved. He put Gaius Marius first, his family, kinsfolk and friends second, his party third, and Rome last. Never content out of office, he was insatiably eager for command and power. Being by nature envious and spiteful, he was determined that he and not Sulla should win the renown of abasing Mithridates. When Sulla was on the point of starting from Italy with his army, Marius made a deal with the tribune Sulpicius, a popular demagogue, by which he would throw the weight of his influence with his former soldiers to have them vote for a bill Sulpicius had proposed if Sulpicius would attach to it a rider ousting Sulla from the command of the war against Mithridates and substitute Marius.

The bill, with its rider, was passed.

Sulla, in his camp at Nola, assembled his legionaries, explained what had occurred, and appealed to their sense of justice. Then first did Roman soldiers regard a decree sanctioned by a majority vote of the assembly of Roman citizens in the *comitium* at Rome not as indubitably a hallowed mandate of Jupiter Maximus Optimus swaying from his abode on the Capitol the preferences of the voters, but as a piece of crooked political jugglery engineered by an adverse minority faction made up of their personal enemies. Be it noted that Sulla's men did not rate their loyalty to him as paramount to their loyalty to Rome. They accounted Sulla not merely their champion against the malignant mob, but the only genuinely accredited representative of Jupiter and Rome.

Yet their action initiated the substitution of force for suffrage as a method of deciding questions of government policy in Rome. From this beginning grew the pernicious Roman habit of civil war, which persisted for over four and a half centuries.

As his was the only army in Italy, Sulla occupied Rome at once. Sulpicius, with a few others, was killed, unofficially. Marius escaped to Africa. Sulla put the Roman government in good working order and at the end of the year set off as proconsul to oppose Mithridates, who meanwhile had gained control of so much territory and had grown so strong that he menaced not only Rome's Empire, but her existence.

During his absence Cinna, one of the consuls, tried to overturn Sulla's arrangements. There was a riot and he fled from Rome, but returned soon with an army of rabble and liberated slaves and besieged Rome, which capitulated, starved out when Marius captured Ostia.

Marius was then over seventy, a pursy old beast with a flabby mouth half full of straggling, tilted, yellow-brown teeth, who slobbered his gravy all down the front of his garments. He and Cinna had all their political adversaries and personal enemies butchered, and confiscated their property. They systematically had made out and posted in public lists of all such persons and of all folk of wealth who had not actively favored them. They had themselves nominated consuls for 86 B.C. Marius died within a month and Cinna was autocrat of Rome till full three years after its capitulation to him.

During these three years Sulla was fighting Mithridates, whose armies had overrun most of Thrace, Macedonia, Thessaly, Greece, and Epirus, to the Adriatic. His general, Archelaus, was competent and his forces vastly outnumbered the 30,000 legionaries with whom Sulla landed in Epirus. But against appalling odds he won by personal military genius and indomitable Roman pluck. In 87 B.C. he cleared most of the lands toward the Adriatic. In 86 he took Athens after a terrific siege of nearly half a year, and routed, at Chæronea in Bœotia, Archelaus with five times his forces. In 85 he beat him again at Orchomenus with reinforcements as numerous. In 84, Lucullus, with a hastily collected fleet, was of much assistance to Sulla, who marched through Macedonia and Thrace, crossed the Hellespont, and compelled Mithridates to sign a treaty by which he gave up all his conquests, consented to the reinstatement of Nicomedes in Bithynia and Ariobarzanes in Cappadocia, surrendered his fleet, and agreed to pay a huge indemnity. Thus ended the First Mithridatic War.

Sulla then dealt with the army which the Marian faction had despatched against Mithridates in order to discredit Sulla's right to conduct the war. As the soldiers inclined to Sulla, Fimbria, the Marian commander, committed suicide. Sulla left Fimbria's army to keep Mithridates to his agreements, put Murena in command, and assigned to Lucullus the task of dealing with the Greek cities which had sided with Mithridates. These were let off with fines of various amounts upon pledging their future loyalty.

Before Sulla landed with 40,000 legionaries at Brundisium in Italy, Cinna was dead. But the Marian faction stubbornly resisted under such leaders as a son of Marius and that brilliant military genius, Sertorius. Two years passed in ruinous and bloody warfare all up and down ravaged Italy. By the autumn of 82 B.C. so many Romans had fallen on both sides that the envenomed irreconcilables among the remnants of the Samnites and Lucanians got control of those peoples and thought they saw a chance to rush, storm, loot, burn, and raze Rome. Sulla, although hard pressed in Etruria, left a skeleton army under a subordinate to hold off vastly superior Marian forces and hurried southward to save the city. In sight of her walls before the Colline gate, in a hard-fought and closely contested battle, he barely worsted his adversaries. Very prudently he ordered the few prisoners immediately put to death. Soon afterward Italy was entirely cleared of the Marian party, but its remnants resisted a while in Sicily and Africa. And in Spain Sertorius, a paragon general and a man of admirable character, who had endeavored to dissuade Marius from butchering members of Sulla's party, held out for more than ten years of guerilla warfare.

Sulla repelled the suggestion of a general massacre of all who had taken sides with Marius. But he took energetic measures to run down and put to death every Marian who had led, supervised, participated in, abetted, or profited by the orgies of butchery and confiscation in which Marius and Cinna had revelled.

During the long years of his desperate warfare with the generals of Mithridates he had been repeatedly, almost continuously, buffeted with appeals and prayers for help from members of his party in Italy. Horrible as their situation was, and agonizing as were their pleadings, his reply was always that his duty was first to Rome and that unless he vanquished Mithridates there would be no Rome to rescue. Many of his dearest friends had perished miserably at the hands of the Marians. The women and children who survived had suffered penury and worse horrors. Now the time had come for retribution on the caitiffs.

Once unopposed in Italy, Sulla, in Rome, convened what was left of the Senate and had himself appointed, not, as had always been done in all previous cases, Dictator for a definite purpose for a limited time, but Dictator for reorganizing the Commonwealth, with no time limit set.

Lists of those who had taken part in the Marian massacres and sequestrations were made out and posted. The persons thus proscribed numbered over 4,700. Sulla's henchmen managed to have many of their personal enemies outlawed and plundered by means of surreptitiously having their names included in these lists. Sulla did all he could to keep them free from any taint of injustice, and merely grimly and sternly retributive.

Cities which had taken the Marian side he deprived of their privileges and of part or all of their land.

On lands thus confiscated he settled most of his ex-soldiers in many colonies, dotted all over Italy.

He reorganized the government and again put every department—judiciary, treasury, and the rest—in good working order.

While Sulla was clearing and reorganizing Italy, Murena had had to fight Mithridates for nearly three years, almost ever since Sulla left for Italy. This Second Mithridatic War ended with the Sultan of Pontus again penitent and promising to fulfill his treaty obligations.

In 79 B.C. after holding it for over three years, Sulla, to the amazement of all classes in Rome, abdicated his dictatorship. He did not live long to enjoy the ease of retirement, but died the next year.

No sooner was he dead than two attempts were made to overset his reforms, one by voting in the city, the other by marching an army on Rome. Both were foiled. This was in 77 B.C.

CHAPTER IX

SLAVERY AND THE SERVILE WARS

IN NOTHING did the Greco-Roman world differ more from ours than in the universality and importance of slavery. From very early times every prosperous and wealthy city had in it more slaves than free persons. After Alexander's conquest of the Persian Empire the consequent blend of Greek and Persian customs resulted in something like a systematization of the traffic in slaves, influenced most by the eminence of Alexandria in Egypt. In its character of a hallowed isle, sacred to Apollo and Artemis, open to and welcoming votaries of every race and clime, Delos became the most important free port in the Mediterranean and the great market for slaves. Prisoners of war or other aliens bought by international slave-dealers were habitually taken to the island of Cyprus to be put into the pink of salable condition by rest, care, out-of-door living, and liberal feeding, as the climate of Cyprus was then accounted salubrious, and there food was cheap and escape impossible. Later they were taken to Delos for sale.

From the time of Alexander's death the traffic became increasingly selective. Pretty girls who could learn jugglers' tricks, acrobatic feats, dancing, or singing, or who were capable of committing to memory long poems and reciting them intelligently (a very popular kind of public or private entertainment among the Greeks), were put into training for one of those arts. So likewise with girls who gave promise of becoming proficient at embroidery, fancy weaving, and such feminine crafts. Boys who showed any signs of an aptitude for singing, acting, public recitations, or for painting, sculpture, carving, vase-painting, glass-making and the like, were given every opportunity to cultivate their talents. A lad who developed a good handwriting was likely to be sold to a rich man for his private secretary, or to a publisher as a professional copyist, or to become a public letter-writer as the property of a capitalist who invested in such slaves; and slave-dealers maintained schools for such boys.

Some large publishers had schools of their own. There were even established slave-dealers' colleges of medicine and surgery where likely lads were taught by the best experts and, if they turned out well, sold to potentates, noblemen, and capitalists as household physicians. These were found all over the Alexandrian world, and, later, all over the Greco-Roman world, and were highly esteemed, implicitly trusted, and, naturally, very well treated.

All such specially trained slaves were, if successful, assured of a life of ease and luxury, pampered in every possible manner, well clad, well fed, well housed, and with other slaves assigned to wait on them; in the case of the more distinguished even troops, retinues, hosts of slaves.

If the pupils could not learn, they were taken out of training and sold for what they would fetch.

The like was done with all crafts—woodworking, metalworking, pottery-making, stone-cutting and the rest.

Every Greek city was policed by Scythian slaves owned, drilled, and equipped by the government. Such Tatars could be relied on to carry out any order, whereas no Greek would ever arrest any member of his own family, guild, or political party. Nobody could make a Scythian work, but give him a sword, spear, shield, bow and quiver of arrows, and he would keep a gang of stevedores at work or guard a gateway dependably and inexorably. They were mostly wiry, but some were stalwart, lusty brutes.

In the Roman or Romanized parts of the Mediterranean world there were yet lower classes of slaves. Those at once muscular, stupid, untrustworthy, and contumacious were penned up in strong prisons (called *ergastula*), usually in basements, always with heavily barred windows, where, mostly also chained, they were kept at work grinding grain in hand mills, under slave guards not unlike the Scythian policemen of Greek cities.

Those too brawny, burly, savage, and truculent for even an *ergastulum,* were put into training in the schools for gladiators, so that their blood might comfort the spirits of the honored dead, and their combats mark the anniversaries of distinguished heroes, and also divert and entertain, as eager spectators, the celebrants of these commemorations.

Although an insurrection in Rome itself, involving 2,500 slaves and exiles, and also a conspiracy of slaves to set fire to the city and in the resulting confusion seize the Capitol and Citadel, are chronicled long before the sack of Rome by the Gauls, yet slaves cannot have become, proportionately to free citizens, numerous in Rome or in Roman colonies or in Central Italy at large until victories over the Carthaginians, Illyrians, and Gauls began to result in hordes of prisoners purchased at once by slave-dealers accompanying Roman armies and resold by them direct into Rome and its neighborhood.

Thereafter house-slaves became usual and numerous. The Roman women did not have to toil from dawn till dark at grinding grain in hand-mills, bread-making, other cooking, spinning, and weaving. Slaves did the heavy work and slave girls the spinning, even some of the weaving. Roman noblewomen had leisure for the refinements of life, for social intercourse, for caring for their looks, for self-adornment, for cosmetics, for everything that goes to make women ladies. Romans did not have to till their own fields; spading or plowing was done by slaves. Romans had more time for setting-up exercises on the drill-ground, for target-practice with their spears, for fencing, and not only for such martial training, but for practice at oratory and other arts of peace.

As a result of this inflow of slaves for sale cheap, moneyed men soon bought farms for sale cheap and created larger and larger estates worked by slave-gangs superintended by overseers. This practice, once begun, grew popular and greatly increased the slave population of Latium, Italy, and the provinces.

The practice had many advantages, but even more disadvantages.

After the appalling disaster at Cannæ all slaves who volunteered and were found fit for service were accepted and 8,000 were bought from their masters and armed. Characteristically,

Livy remarks that this was highly agreeable to the authorities, as buying such slaves outright was cheaper than ransoming Romans made prisoners of war by the Carthaginians. The Roman point of view was that an untried slave was likely to turn out a better soldier than a Roman born who had surrendered instead of keeping on fighting until killed. These slave-recruits fought well, and some two years later the survivors, after a cheering victory, were declared free men. Such freedmen, who had won Roman citizenship by merit and prowess, were valuable members of the community. And slaves manumitted by their masters made worthy citizens. If a master stipulated in his will that a slave was to be given his freedom, that was a trustworthy testimonial as to his character. So also of skilled slaves whose masters equipped them to set up in business for themselves as cobblers, weavers, carpenters, potters, or shoemakers or what else, and allowed them to buy their freedom with their savings. They made estimable citizens.

But most slaves were too cowardly to volunteer for military service, too stupid to acquire any manual skill or learn any trade, and too doltish to make even passable drudges. These had no hope of bettering themselves and were mostly brutish and reckless.

Just after the end of the war with Hannibal many slaves, along with some Carthaginian hostages, in a sudden and formidable outbreak in Latium itself, seized three fortified towns within six miles of Rome.

And a few years later there was a widespread insurrection of slaves in Apulia, the heel of Italy.

While any slave, female or male, promising to fetch a dealer a high price or for whom a master had paid a high price, was well treated and kept both comfortable and content, the ordinary run of unskilled slaves were, from our point of view, not from the ancient point of view, horribly ill-treated.

We can see today in existing Egyptian and Assyrian reliefs that slaves were looked on as were domestic animals of any other kind. Intelligent slave-owners housed, clothed, and fed their slaves so as to have them really fit for work and moreover did not overwork them. But such owners were few among many. The run of slave-owners in the Roman world no more considered the comfort of their slaves than the run of American farmers consider the comfort of their hogs, and fed them no more judiciously or generously than the run of American farmers feed their farm animals. We never concern ourselves about the needless miseries of millions of hogs all over this continent. Most slaves went barefoot all the year round, wore patched and ragged tunics and cloaks, and were sheltered in huts or shacks, often old, tumble-down, and leaky. They kept alive on their porridge made of inferior or spoiled grain. They were habitually struck, beaten, lashed, and scourged for even such small faults as laziness, slowness, or inattention, and unmercifully for blunders, disobedience, contumacy, theft, or worse delinquencies.

Their feelings were never considered. It is improbable that any average Roman slave-owner ever thought or could have been convinced that a slave had any feelings. From a female slave an owner expected just about such compliance as an American farmer expects from a cow: occasional resistance might call for occasional compulsion, but any treatment was borne and anything enjoined was done as a matter of course. A cow often lows for days after her calf has been taken away; a slave-woman probably was in tears for days after her child had been sold; a Mediterranean slave-owner in ancient times bothered about the sobs no more than does a modern farmer about the lowing of the bereaved cow. A cow is not expected nor permitted to have a will of her own about anything; nor was the slave girl of any Mediterranean slave owner, Roman or what else. Any suggestion of willfulness or of hesitance at obeying a master's will was a heinous offense from a slave or slave-girl.

Badly as most owners treated their slaves, their overseers of gangs of slaves on large estates treated theirs far worse. As in Egypt thousands of years before, as in Babylonia and Assyria and Media and Persia, slaves were merely the most useful and valuable live-stock on an estate, considered and sold for as much or as little as the horses, mules, asses, cattle, sheep, goats, and hogs. They endured all sorts of discomforts, hardships, and miseries.

There had been created in Italy in the neighborhood of Rome, in Etruria, in Campania, and generally throughout central and southern Italy, countless extensive estates manned by large gangs of slaves. In Sicily the estates were vast and worked by slaves in droves.

The first great insurrection of slaves, known as the First Servile War, broke out in Sicily in 135 B.C., led by a Syrian slave named Eunus who called himself King Antiochus and gathered a huge rabble of runaways. He displayed no mean capacities as a leader, worsted more than one Roman army, captured Tauromenium (Taormina) and also Henna at the central point of Sicily, and held out for more than three years; the first Servile War began during the siege of Numantia in Spain and outlasted it.

Thirty years later, also in Sicily, a worse insurrection of slaves broke out in 103 B.C. Their armies numbered more than 40,000 fighters, led by two elected "kings"; Trypon in central Sicily, Athenion eastwardly. At first they overmatched and overwhelmed the Roman forces on the island. Even when routed in the field by Lucullus, they held out in Triocala, their chosen stronghold. This Second Servile War began while the Cimbri and Teutons were most threatening, and the last remnants of the insurgents were not rounded up until two years after the annihilation of the Teutons at Aquæ Sextiæ and of the Cimbri at Vercellæ.

Such droves of prisoners of war were in Marius's hands after these two victories that it was difficult to find purchasers for them. They sold so cheap that anyone could afford to buy, and soon there were few households in any Italian town without a slave from one or the other invading horde. Most farms, all over Italy, had more than one such slave. Many of these had been captured as full-grown men and were dangerous farm laborers. Even those who had been mere boys could not but remember some years of rambling about Spain and Gaul, killing farmers, burning barns and houses, carrying off fowls, pigs, lambs, and other loot, and generally doing as they pleased and as was diverting and exciting. Farm life irked them. They hated its monotony and they detested farm labor. By 73 B.C., twenty-eight years or so after their capture, the oldest prisoners made then were not over forty-five and still vigorous, and the youngest who could recall freedom and license were not much over thirty-five. Thousands of muscular, ferocious, and bitterly discontented barbarians scattered all over Italy were potentially dangerous. With such quantities of such inflammable fuel about, a spark might start a mighty conflagration.

Capua, even after its chastisement for taking sides with Hannibal, was, next to Rome, the most populous, prosperous, and wealthy city in Italy. Naturally it cultivated all the luxuries of life, gladiators among them. Capua had many large gladiatorial schools, training-barracks for fencers to the death. In these were hundreds of gigantic, robust, and bloodthirsty savages, Spaniards, Gauls, Germans, Illyrians, and Thracians. One of these, Spartacus by name, had been at home at first a shepherd, then a soldier, then a brigand. He was captured while raiding and sold as a slave into Italy. Manifestly he was fit only for a gladiator and was put into training. But he had in him the memories of leadership and the capacities of a leader. He and two Gauls headed an escape from the barracks, got weapons from a town-armory, and took refuge in the old crater of Vesuvius. That volcano had been inactive for centuries and the crater was a great bowl watered by abundant springs, rivulets, and lakes, densely forested, with grassy glades here and there and even wide meadows on its floor and swarming with such game as hares, deer, and wild boars. The escaped gladiators were joined by such runaway slaves as learned of their liberty and location. Presently Spartacus had so numerous a band that they could not live on the game in the crater nor on loot from its vicinity, and, moreover, were strong enough to sally out.

The rumor ran all over Italy and many farm-slaves who had been with the Cimbri or the Teutons at once set about escaping from their masters and joining Spartacus. Bands of them were soon in every wooded and mountainous district, all making their way to join Spartacus. There had been myriads of such war-prisoner slaves on the farms of Italy, and soon Spartacus had a rabble numbering over 100,000 men; and he knew how to organize, arm, and lead them. He worsted four armies of seasoned Roman soldiers led by experienced Roman officials. His tumultuary forces got out of his control and compelled him against his better judgment to march on Rome. Naturally there was a panic in the city. But whether the sight of the walls awed the insurgents or something else turned them, they did not attempt to assault Rome, but rambled about Italy, looting and burning. They took few towns, but it was proverbial that not a pint of wine in all Italy escaped them. They ravaged the peninsula from its southernmost capes to the foothills of the Alps. When the Po Valley was eaten bare they had to run southward again to find food, and Marcus Licinius Crassus, prætor for 71 B.C., afterward famous as an associate of Pompey and Cæsar, defeated the host in a great battle and chased them southward. In a second battle, on the river Silarus in Lucania, he annihilated the horde. Spartacus fell.

Thus ended the Third Servile War.

CHAPTER X

THE CIVIL WARS

POMPEY AND PIRACY

THE slow, steady, imperceptible drift of Rome away from a commonwealth managed by a citizen electorate toward monarchial government has not often been veraciously elucidated.

The Roman voters were not suddenly robbed of their liberty and prerogatives by ambitious upstarts; consciously or unconsciously, they gradually forewent them of their own accord.

The progressive steps were five.

First: the time-honored Roman custom of electing each commander for one year only and having him resign his command at the end of the year and turn over his army and campaign to a newly-elected successor, which, contrary to all probability, had worked well against the Volscians, Æquians, Hernicians, Etruscans, and Samnites, was found very far from satisfactory against adversaries such as Pyrrhus, Hamilcar Barca, and Hannibal; and the Romans were compelled, much against their inclination, to prolong the term of a capable general and keep him at the head of the army he had led auspiciously, until the campaign was won.

Secondly: whereas from the establishment of the Republic men elected to military commands had mostly turned out competent and successful, and on the other hand bunglers and blunderers had been very exceptional as commanders, after the capture of Numantia in 133 B. C. there was a perceptible and progressive alteration for the worse in the proportion of deadlocks, drawn battles, repulses, setbacks, and retreats to victories, advances, conquests, and annexations.

Thirdly: the Romans in general and the populace especially grew unpleasantly outspoken in their expressions of displeasure, disappointment, and even derision.

Fourthly: there was less and less eagerness and willingness and more and more disinclination to accept public office, and promising candidates were harder and harder to find and scarcer and scarcer, and shrank more and more from their prospective responsibilities.

Fifthly: when a thoroughly competent man like Marius was in evidence there was a general tendency to put more and more authority and power into his hands and to feel that it was advisable to let him do everything and keep on doing everything, as bunglers were so plentiful and experts so hard to find.

More than that of any other man, the career of Gneius Pompeius Magnus, whom we call Pompey, exemplified this ever-increasing proclivity of the Roman voters.

Before he was eighteen years old Pompey was an officer in the bitterly contested Social War in the army of his father Gneius Pompeius Strabo, who was an honorable, capable, and competent general, but a martinet so strict, harsh, and severe that he was hated by his legionaries to that degree that they broke up his funeral, dragged his corpse through the streets, and execrated his memory. The name "Strabo" was so unpopular and abhorred that Pompey dropped its use as his family name, for no one of that name could possibly have any chance of being elected to any office.

Pompey eluded the ferocity of the Marian faction while it was in power, avoided notice as much as possible, and so managed to keep alive. When, in 84 B.C., news came that Sulla was preparing to return from Greece to Italy, Pompey hurried into Picenum, where his extensive ancestral estates were farmed by thousands of tenants, and soon had enlisted over fifteen thousand volunteers. These he quickly organized into three legions, and although he had the help of many seasoned ex-sergeants, it was manifest at once that he himself was an adept at every phase of the organization, equipment, and training of an army.

The skill and craft with which he led his raw levies among and through superior forces of the Marian faction proved him a master of strategy and stratagems.

When he succeeded in joining the army of his chief, Sulla saluted him with the complimentary title of "Imperator."

By the time Sulla was in complete control of Italy his feelings toward Pompey were mixed and contradictory. On the one hand Pompey was his ablest henchman, on the other Sulla was not a little jealous of him.

Pompey made no claims to special recognition or preferment, but volunteered to undertake any duty assigned to him.

Sulla dispatched him to clear the Marians, who were strongly in full possession, out of Sicily. It looked like a hopeless task. Apparently Sulla calculated that if Pompey failed he would thereby be rid of an inconveniently brilliant and popular subordinate, and if he succeeded, so much the better, for Sicily had to be recovered and no conceivable deputy promised as well as Pompey. Like Dion before him and Garibaldi after him, Pompey overran Sicily with ease and speed really miraculous.

Sulla's mingled joy and embarrassment accentuated.

Pompey, bland and subservient, again offered to go wherever he might be sent.

Sulla suggested that he undertake to recover the province of Africa (modern Tunisia and eastern Algeria), which was held by the Marians in great force under experienced commanders. Again he seems to have calculated that whether Pompey perished or prospered he himself would be better off. Pompey's achievements were so dazzling that when he returned to Rome with his elated troops in 81 B.C. Sulla, face to face with so large an army flushed with victory and adoring their young leader, could not refuse Pompey a triumph, although a special enactment had to be made to permit, for the first time, a general under age, who had never held any public office, to lead his army in triumph through the streets of Rome, as he did that September.

It was then, as he had abandoned his hereditary family name and had none, that Sulla accorded him the surname of Magnus (Great Man, practically Mr. Greatman) which, instead of the abominated name Strabo, he used for the rest of his life.

After Sulla's death Pompey spent some years in Spain operating with much credit to himself against that invincible paragon, Sertorius. Once he was dead, Pompey made short work of his armies and their Marian leaders. He marched home through Gaul, winning not a little prestige by refusing the customary transit payments demanded by the mountain tribes and fighting his way across the Pyrenees and Alps. As he neared Rome in 71 B.C. he exterminated the remnants of the hordes which had followed Spartacus.

He and Crassus were consuls next year and passed or helped pass many popular laws. As a result Pompey was the darling of the populace as well as of the soldiery.

Piracy had been more or less rife in the Mediterranean from the earliest ages. Wherever there grew near a seashore town timber suitable for shipbuilding, tools were available, and a bevy of lusty lads found time hang heavy on their hands, nothing was more natural than for them to build a ship, rig her, man her, and sail off in search of communities wholly alien in blood and religion, well stocked and less warlike, a raid on which would enrich them with loot of slaves and goods. Such raids by Phœnicians or Greeks on the coasts of Egypt were esteemed manly warfare in the early days, for instance.

And it was a matter of course for such a vagrant freebooting ship to chase and capture any alien craft of which she caught sight, and either make a prize of her or loot and sink her.

But no matter how great the temptation, raids of Greeks on any other Greek city or seacoast, or piratical capture by Greeks of any Greek ship, were acts rated criminal and shameful. Similar feelings grew up as between Phœnicians among themselves. So of each race.

Quite early Egyptian fleets patrolled the southeastern Mediterranean, to some degree safeguarded Egyptian merchant ships, and to some extent discouraged piracy. The like was more widely effected by the warships of the Persian Empire, from 525 B.C. on; and from about the same time the Carthaginian claim to all the seas westward from Sicily, Sardinia, and Corsica and their habit of sinking without mercy any and every alien ship encountered in these waters, made piracy extremely risky in the western Mediterranean.

After the destruction of the Persian Empire by Alexander the Great, there was a gradual recrudescence of piracy in the eastern Mediterranean, as his successors were chiefly occupied, from his death in 323 B.C., with incessant wars among themselves.

After the extinction, by the Romans, in 201 B.C., of the naval power of Carthage, piracy gradually spread to the western Mediterranean, especially as, after Antiochus III had been squelched in 189 B.C. and Carthage razed in 146 B.C., the insistent demands of the Roman voters for economy wherever possible caused the Senate greatly to reduce their fleet. Moreover, as the Roman power extended, many of the irreconcilables of each seacoast district annexed or controlled took to piracy rather than submit to Roman rule.

Roman administration of Sicily, Sardinia, Corsica, the Balearic Islands, southern Gaul, Spain, and the province of Africa and also the configuration of the coasts of those regions made it difficult for the natives to engage in piracy without detection and retribution. But wherever there was much deep-sea fishing some piracy was likely to be managed, and Mauretania was not yet annexed or even controlled and from its coast not a few piratical craft sneaked away to sea. But surreptitious piracy such as this did little harm in the aggregate.

East of Sicily conditions were very different. Although nationally organized piracy by the Illyrians (the modern Albanians) had been ended forever in 228 B.C., ten years before the outbreak of the Second Punic War, when their Queen Teuta was humbled by a Roman fleet of two hundred sail, yet no patrol, although incessant and by many cruisers, could prevent some piracy from the uncountable islands off the Dalmatian coast on the northeast side of the Adriatic.

And the deeply indented coasts of Greece proper, of the entire Ægean Sea, of most of its islands, and of southern Asia Minor, from Caria eastward along the sea fronts of Lycia, Pamphylia, and Cilicia, were ideal eyries for pirates.

What with the irruptions of Mithridates' armies and fleets and the outbreak of civil war between Marius and Sulla, from about 88 B.C. confusion reigned over most of the Mediterranean and might was mostly the only right on its waters and coasts.

During this period of anarchy and license pirates prospered; not merely the one-ship local native pirates, never quite suppressed and always on the lookout for opportunities, but still more towns or communities given to collective piracy and capable of operating corsair squadrons, and most of all the obstinately irreconcilable remnants of nations and races formerly independent, whether Iberians, Gauls, Corsicans, Sardinians, Ligurians, Etruscans, Illyrians, Greeks, islanders, Lycians, Pamphilians, Cilicians or Syrians, some of whom had squadrons that were almost fleets.

All these diverse elements had in common an appetite for loot and a hatred of control and authority in general and of Rome in particular. There soon grew up a practically universal understanding among them by which they abstained from mutual conflict, left any prize or booty to whichever one of them first captured it, made common cause in all matters looking to finding purchasers for their loot, and notified each other of the approach or neighborhood of warships.

From this it was but a step to the informal organization of leagues of pirates and of their confederation into a sort of Mediterranean Pirate Republic and Commonwealth, with headquarters in Cilicia and Crete, agencies at Delos, in Cyprus and at Alexandria, and agents in all cities where the whole community or any considerable fraction of it was friendly. Many towns not one of whose inhabitants ever had or ever would participate in piratical activities were not at all disinclined to buy cheap from pirates whatever they had to sell, afford them entertainment for liberal cash payment, and sell them what they needed at remunerative prices.

The pirates even had secret agents and spies in cities inflexibly hostile to them and undeviatingly loyal to Rome; even in Rome itself.

Portable plunder, whether jewelry or what else, was taken to Delos for sale, even ships with their cargoes. So of slaves, for prisoners were their most profitable booty. They made forays in force, swept whole districts clean of inhabitants, took fortified towns by surprise and later by assault, and terrorized the whole Mediterranean.

They were so united that it was possible to make agreements with them collectively and for them to guarantee the fulfillment of their pledges. Merchants paid so much a year in advance to have their ships let alone, and such insurance was effective.

But they grew overconfident. They not only stormed wealthy towns and sold the wretched inhabitants into slavery, but they even, in more than one instance, found a Roman governor so rascally that they were able to make a deal with him by which he ordered elsewhere forces that should have protected an opulent city, on condition of sharing the profits of their sack of it.

They raided the very coasts of Campania and Latium, revenged themselves on such Roman commanders as had chastised them by burning their villas, kidnapping their children, and even, more than once, making prisoners of ex-admirals. They positively captured Ostia, Rome's port at the mouth of the Tiber, looted it, and burnt the ships in the harbor.

They even entered into a compact with a ring of grain importers at Rome by which they not only let their ships pass in and out, but captured or sunk all other ships. Whereupon the price of grain at Rome doubled and quadrupled and the members of the grain-ring made enormous profits.

The Roman stomach promptly reacted, as the pirates, if more perspicacious, might have foreseen.

Since 78 B.C., nine years before, Roman squadrons and Roman fleets had scouted for, chased, fought, and sunk pirate ships, and, more than once, had been worsted by pirate fleets. Such fleets were so powerful that Roman commanders were wary of sending troop-transports to sea, even under strong convoys, except at night and in bad weather.

The knowledge of such an humiliating state of affairs aroused Roman pride even more positively than the grain-blockade and bread-scarcity pinched the Roman stomach.

Matters had come to this pass in 67 B.C. when the tribune Aulus Gabinius proposed a law conferring on Pompey supreme command against the pirates, with unlimited authority over the entire Mediterranean and all its coasts for fifty miles inland from any point on its coast line, with full control of all arsenals, warships, and land and sea forces.

This, of course, was the logical thing to do from a military standpoint—unified conduct of the war by one commander. But it was far from advisable, even as an emergency expedient, for a nation governed by the suffrage of a citizen electorate. Hortensius, Catulus, and other sage nobles warned the voters of the pernicious tendencies and inevitable results of such a measure.

But the people's enthusiasm for Pompey, their confidence in his qualifications, probity, and trustworthiness, their mortification at the shameful conditions, and their fury at the price of bread and against the grain-cornerers, gave Gabinius an overwhelming majority in favor of his law.

Pompey organized his offensive with amazing promptitude, posted a strong squadron at the straits between Italy and Sicily and stronger squadrons between Sicily and Africa, and then, with a numerous fleet, swept the western Mediterranean.

Upon news of his appointment the corner in grain at Rome had broken, the price of wheat and the price of bread had fallen below anything ever before heard of, and the populace was jubilant.

Within forty days Pompey cleared the entire western Mediterranean. Keeping his guard squadrons on duty, he posted another at the mouth of the Adriatic and then swept the eastern Mediterranean. Within fifty days more he had sunk or captured every pirate ship afloat and had stormed every pirate stronghold which did not surrender at discretion. He at once set about punishing guilty communities and towns, reimbursing those which had suffered for loyalty to Rome, and reorganizing Cilicia.

When he intimated that his authority extended over all Crete, Metellus, who had already subdued it with much effort, vowed he would fight rather than lose the glory of having subjugated the island. Pompey, always easy-going, let him have his way. Mithridates had then for seven years and more been at war with Rome for the third time and had again overrun most of Syria and Asia Minor. Lucullus, who was a thoroughly competent official and a capable general, had beaten him completely and was on the point of ending the war gloriously when his infamous brother-in-law, Clodius, fomented among his troops a mutiny which undid all the successes of Lucullus. Mithridates yet again overran all Syria and Asia Minor, and was threatening those Greek cities along the coasts which had been loyal to Rome.

Such was the situation in the Levant when Pompey was completing his annihilation of the pirates.

Thereupon the tribune Gaius Manilius proposed a law giving Pompey, in addition to his already vast authority, supreme command of the war against Mithridates, and conferring on him any and all powers necessary to crush and make an end of this pertinacious and menacing foe, who had been at war with Rome, off and on, for twenty-two years and had even made an alliance with Sertorius in Spain and had projected concerted and simultaneous advances on Rome by his fleets under his admirals, by his army under his own command round the north of the Black Sea and across the Danube and eastern Alps, and by Sertorius from Spain.

Again Catulus and Hortensius and other experts warned the voters of the probable consequences of such legislation.

Cicero, unquestionably sincere in his opportunism, spoke ably for the bill and it passed by an enormous majority.

These two enactments, the Gabinian and Manilian Laws, taken together, constitute by far the longest single stride toward monarchy in the history of the Roman Commonwealth.

Pompey made short work of Mithridates, and not only drove him back into Pontus but through and out of it and finally into the Crimea, where he committed suicide. Unhampered by any hint of mutiny such as had undone all the work of Lucullus, he made Roman influence paramount as far as the Caucasus and the Caspian. Mithridates' son, Pharnaces, he allowed to retain the kingship of territories beyond the Caucasus. He permitted Tigranes, Mithridates' son-in-law and ally, to keep his kingdom of Armenia on payment of a large indemnity, restored Ariobarzanes to the throne of Cappadocia, and rewarded for his loyalty Deiotarus of Galatia by giving him the title of King.

Then turning south, he deposed Antiochus, King of Syria, the last descendant of Seleucus, and made Syria a Roman province. As usual there was civil war among the Jews, and one side asked Pompey's aid. Since the other side had the upper hand and would not listen to reason, Pompey had to storm Jerusalem, where he restored as King and High Priest, Hyrcanus, who had sought his help.

While Pompey was about making all these conquests and organizing the annexed territories, there occurred at Rome the famous abortive conspiracy of Catiline, who, unsuccessful as a candidate for election to office, hoped to attain power by plotting insurrection and massacre. It is notable chiefly as unique in that it was foiled not by force, but by the four speeches of Cicero, the first of which completely unnerved Catiline, who fled; the second heartened the populace; the third proclaimed that the regularly constituted authorities had legal written proofs of Catiline's treasonable plans; and the fourth brought about the prompt execution of the accomplices Catiline had left behind him in Rome. As a result of the clever detective work of Cicero's secret-service men and of his eloquent presentation of the facts, Catiline suddenly ceased to be regarded as a promising reformer and was revealed as a dangerous rascal, after which his insurrection failed and he himself was killed when his dupes were defeated in a hard-fought battle in northern Etruria.

When Pompey set out for home the Commonwealth had thirteen provinces, for, in addition to the province of Gallia Narbonensis (Gaul beyond the Alps, named from its capital, Narbonne), he had reorganized Asia (the western end of Asia Minor), and had newly organized Bithynia and Pontus (northwestern Asia Minor) as one province, Cilicia (southeastern Asia Minor) as a second, and Syria as a third.

Pompey had been absent five years. He disbanded his army at Brundisium. He had had one triumph when only twenty-five years old, a second ten years later, and now, when just forty-five, achieved a third triumph.

On the banners carried in his triumphal procession through the streets of Rome were blazoned his exploits: He had subdued fourteen nations, captured 800 ships, 900 towns, 1,000 forts; the treasure he turned in to the treasury amounted to 20,000 talents ($25,000,000), and the increase in the yearly revenues of Rome due to his annexations and reorganizations would be 35,000,000 sesterces ($1,750,000).

CHAPTER XI

THE CIVIL WARS

CÆSAR AND POMPEY

GAIUS JULIUS CÆSAR was born in 102 B.C. just before Marius annihilated the Teutons and Cimbri. He came of a patrician family which had never been of any importance. They were on the Marian side of the first civil war. Marius had married Cæsar's aunt, and he himself married Cinna's daughter Cornelia. Sulla wanted him to divorce her and marry some girl whose father was a partisan of his. Cæsar declined and had to leave Rome and hide in various out-of-the-way places in Italy until Sulla's wrath was cooled and he would listen to pleas for the lad. Later Cæsar was in Asia Minor, where as a staff officer he won distinction for capacity and valor. After Sulla's death he quickly made his mark as a precociously promising advocate. On his way to Rhodes to learn more of oratory there, he was captured by pirates. When they named twenty talents ($25,000) as his ransom, he said he was worth at least fifty ($62,500), but they had best let him go unransomed; if they did he would requite the favor; if they insisted on ransom he would certainly revenge himself by capturing and crucifying the whole band. They roared with laughter at the joke. While waiting for the ransom he wrote a tragedy which he read aloud to them. Their verdict was that his Greek was unpolished, his verse harsh, and his play poor, anyhow. He said he hadn't really meant to crucify them, but now he would; they deserved it for their bad taste. When the ransom arrived and he was liberated he landed at Miletus or Ephesus, and when his father's banker, on whom he had a credit of only ten talents, pulled a long face over having advanced fifty, he laughed and said that was nothing; he wanted two hundred more. How he persuaded the banker is not recorded, but he got the money, advertised for volunteers for a profitable venture the nature of which was not to be disclosed, had his pick of more volunteers than he could enlist, hired ships, captured the pirates with a great quantity of their booty, and sent a message to the Roman governor of that region to come and try them. Then, when someone informed him that the governor was in secret a partner of the pirates and got a share of their profits, he had the pirates crucified in a row along the cliff above the beach, and on the arrival of the governor told him derisively that he might now do as he pleased with his old friends.

Out of the pirates' booty he had captured Cæsar repaid his father's banker, distributed a handsome gratuity to his volunteers, and had enough for himself to need no remittances from home during his sojourn at Rhodes and elsewhere in the East.

When, in 74 B.C., he returned to Rome, he was twenty-eight years old. He at once, although of patrician stock, set himself to becoming what we should call a downtown-ward political boss. In an amazingly short time he had made himself the darling of the slum populace. Also he ran with what we would call the fast set in upper-class, wealthy, fashionable Roman society. Among them he splurged and became notorious as a fop, gourmand, toper, gamester, spendthrift, and gallant. Though addicted to wine, women, and song, he not only kept his health, but was capable of amazing exertions and was very quick-witted. His popularity won him early election to the quæstorship in 67 B.C., and as quæstor he did well in Spain and acquired experience. As ædile he strengthened his hold on the populace by the magnificence of his public spectacles.

There has been much discussion of his relations with Catiline. Apparently he arranged to be personally safe, whether Catiline succeeded or failed, by keeping clear of his conspiracy, but avoiding overt opposition to him. When it came to the question of what to do with Catiline's city accomplices, Cæsar behaved like what we should call a typical peanut politician. He proposed that instead of being executed they should be imprisoned for life in various allied towns in Italy, one only being assigned to a town and it being enacted that no one should ever move a repeal of the ordinance. Of course he knew that no town would consent to undertake the care of such a prisoner, that the Senate had no means of compelling or inducing any town to accede, that there was no precedent for such a proposal, that even if the enactment were made it was certain to be repealed, and he knew that everybody else knew it. But his proposal enabled him to escape any future accusation of having voted for the execution of the conspirators in duress or of having favored them; which cleared his skirts and was all he wanted.

Next year, 62 B.C., Cæsar was city prætor and conducted himself so as to please all classes and both parties and win high credit.

Next year Cæsar, as proprætor, was governor of Spain, showed himself an able general in much guerilla warfare in difficult mountain country, and was so capable an administrator that he not only enriched himself, but had all Spain praising him for the economy and efficiency of his administration, during which taxes had been low and he had begun or completed many public works, in the way of roads, bridges, town halls, temples, and such like. He returned to Rome with an enhanced reputation and cash enough to pay all his debts and have a surplus.

When he returned, in 60 B.C., everything at Rome was completely deadlocked. Few of the Roman voters had served in the armies for whose legionaries they were asked to vote pay and bonuses. So most of the voters felt no responsibility for the pledges they were invited to ratify. Likewise most of those same voters knew that it would fall to others to carry out whatever policies they might indorse. So most of them felt no concern as to how they voted, for what or for whom. It resulted that the Roman voters in 60 B.C., like Vermont farmers along about 1900 and perhaps later, declined to vote at all unless previously bribed by both sides, and then mostly voted according to the mood of the moment. The natural consequence was that the prospective minority on any question started a riot before it could be voted on. And Rome was holy ground where no armed soldier might intrude except on the rare occasions when a notably victorious army was allowed to march in triumph along the specified consecrated route to pay their respects to Jupiter Maximus Optimus in his temple on the Capitoline Hill. Also, no adequate policing of Rome had ever been instituted. Therefore, election thugs had things all their own way on the voting-field and no contentious legislation had any chance of passing.

So Pompey could not succeed in having his ex-soldiers paid, still less in having them voted a bonus from the vast spoils he had brought home from his campaigns in Asia, Syria, Palestine, Pontus, and Armenia and had turned into the treasury of the Commonwealth; and there seemed no chance whatever of his veterans getting their promised allotments of land in Italy.

Marcus Licinius Crassus, who had fought well under Sulla, had vanquished Spartacus and his rabble hordes, and who had been consul with Pompey ten years before, was now the richest man in the Roman world and the most prominent and esteemed of Roman capitalists, who in general followed his lead and looked to him for guidance. He and they had been unable to invest their large surpluses profitably or promisingly, as no important public contracts could secure ratification by the voters.

Cæsar, well off as he was after his return from Spain, needed much cash for his canvass for the consulship and, popular as he was, was unsure of election when rioting was probable if any minority chose to start rioting.

The deadlock was broken by a private, personal gentlemen's agreement among Cæsar, Pompey, and Crassus, brought about by Cæsar's astuteness and the persuasiveness with which he induced Crassus and Pompey to lay aside their mutual animosities.

This compact among the three was known afterward as the First Triumvirate (committee of three).

By the terms of this agreement Crassus paid off Pompey's veterans at once and at once advanced Cæsar whatever cash he needed; Pompey, since it was known that his veterans would follow his lead wherever he led, was able to overawe the voters and insure decent order at elections; Cæsar arranged for majority votes on all bills necessary to reimburse Crassus, give him and his associates the public contracts they desired, ratify the measures Pompey had taken to organize his Asiatic conquests, ratify the payments and bonuses which Pompey's veterans had received, allot them the lands they craved, and otherwise carry out whatever projects the three triumvirs approved. Cæsar was assured of election to the consulship.

As colleague in this office he had an old noble named Bibulus, who turned out such a nonentity that people jokingly dated their letters in the year when Julius and Cæsar were consuls, which year was 59 B.C.

Pompey married Cæsar's daughter and the two were for the time, close friends.

Cæsar received by vote of the people the governorship, with full proconsular powers, for five years, of Gallia Cisalpina (that is, all northern Italy from the Rubicon, Apennines, and Macra to the chine of the Alps) and of Illyricum (all the northeast coast of the Adriatic down to Scutari). On Pompey's motion they added Gallia Narbonensis (Provence, southern France all the way from the Alps to the Pyrenees).

Cæsar's enemies, without anyone objecting—for neither Cæsar nor any of his associates then realized its implications, but took it as meaningless and perfunctory—had the Senate pass a resolution that whoever had charge of Roman Gaul should see to it that nothing menacing the welfare of the Roman Commonwealth should be allowed to happen in wild Gaul.

To comprehend the effect of Cæsar's conquest of Gaul at Rome, it must be kept in mind that, when he entered on his term of proconsulship, in 58 B.C. the Romans had been fighting the Gauls for 332 years; that, in the course of 695 years Rome had been entered by foreign foes but once, and then by Gauls; and that in the more than three and a quarter centuries of warfare between Gauls and Romans, while the Romans had won every war, because Romans never ceased fighting until they did win a war, yet if a reckoning was made of battles won and battles lost or killed and wounded on both sides, the Gauls had inflicted on the Romans defeats as many as or more than and losses as great as or greater than they had suffered from the Romans. Since the discomfiture of Mithridates by Pompey and his death the Gauls were the only foreign foes whom the Romans genuinely dreaded, and with much more cause then they had had to fear Mithridates. For every war against Gauls had been won by great exertions, by a narrow margin, and after many reverses in its course.

To comprehend the effect on his army of Cæsar's exploits it must be kept in mind that he was a city high-liver and ward-politician, in his forty-fifth year, bald and leaden-complexioned, who had had no military experience except a brief course as a staff officer in Asia Minor and some trifling chasing of brigands and humbling mountain tribes in Spain.

Also, at the start, one of his best legions had been lent Cæsar by Pompey, adored him as the greatest of military leaders Rome had ever produced, and expected little of their new commander.

When Cæsar took charge the Swiss were just about to attempt bettering their condition by abandoning Switzerland, making an irruption into Gaul with all their women, children, and possessions, and choosing for their future home whatever part of Gaul they liked best, confident that they could subjugate the Gauls and lord it over them forever.

Likewise there was already in Gaul, on the west side of the Rhine in what is now Alsace, a large body of Germans, of several tribes, at first invited as mercenaries to help the Sequani against the Hædui, then remaining, as they liked the country and were irresistible.

Knowing that the resolution of the Senate, that whoever had charge of Roman Gaul should see to it that nothing detrimental to the Roman Commonwealth happened in wild Gaul, put Cæsar under obligation to attempt to deal with the migrating Swiss and the intruding Germans, his enemies were chuckling at the prospect of his inevitable discomfiture, and the Senatorial party, enraged at the laws he had had passed in his consulship, were confident that they would soon be rid of him forever.

Cæsar found one legion in Transalpine Gaul and more than 300,000 Swiss, with fully 90,000 fighting men, on the point of pouring out of the valleys of the Alps. He fortified the only points at which they could cross the Rhône into Roman Gaul, recrossed the Alps, then primeval mountains without any roads, levied all the troops he could raise, and hurried back to Geneva. Thereafter he combined amazing speed with great caution. As the enemy were crude barbarians, he could utilize against them the simplest stratagems, and by and by began by catching the Swiss when most of them had already crossed the Saone, and he could easily lead his troops to surprise at dawn and butcher the one-fourth of the Swiss host left on the east side of that river. This clever success made his men less inclined to look down upon him.

After completely vanquishing the Swiss in a well-led and hard-fought battle, he marched against the Germans, on his way neatly forestalling an incipient mutiny and utilizing the revulsion from it to work his men up to a high pitch of martial valor. His battle with the Germans was even better led, harder fought, and more decisively the end of the campaign than his battle with the Swiss.

From then on his men esteemed him an unsurpassable general.

Next summer the Belgians, the northernmost and most formidable of the Gauls, incensed and concerned because a Roman army had wintered in wild Gaul beyond the frontiers of the Roman province, and not so savage but that they comprehended the defensive value of a prompt offensive, prepared to march on Cæsar. Cæsar was even more prescient and prompt. He was beforehand with them.

But here it is worth noting that whereas Napoleon had had a sound military education in an excellent military college, and Alexander and Hannibal had had fathers each of whom was an unsurpassable military, diplomatic and administrative college all in himself and so each of these three had had from boyhood a thorough grounding in all the underlying principles and most important maxims of warfare, Cæsar had had no formal military education whatever. So he, the greatest of the four, was guilty of oversights and heedlessnesses and committed errors of organization and management of which any one of the other three was inveterately incapable.

Cæsar's reconnoitering was inefficient and his army began ditching their camp within striking distance of six times their number of as good fighters as ever were. The Nervii, as Cæsar puts it, *flew* at them out of the forests across the Sambre, and the Romans escaped massacre and won a great victory by mere Roman training, Roman discipline, Roman toughness, Roman pluck, Roman doggedness, and Roman valor. It had been touch and go for more than two hours.

The next summer Cæsar, who was a soundly instructed and brilliantly original engineer, won, because of devices he had had installed in his warships, a decisive naval victory off the westernmost headlands of Gaul, and mastered all the indented and sinuous coasts of Brittany and Normandy.

Next summer, 55 B.C., Cæsar had to deal with a most formidable horde of Germans, fully 400,000 Usipetes and Tenctheri already across the lower Rhine near the infall of the Meuse. When he found them they were camped near the point of the wedge-shaped region between the two confluent rivers. They asked a truce and Cæsar granted it, but next day some of their young men could not resist such a temptation to easy fun as a chance to stampede and chivy ten times their number of Cæsar's auxiliary cavalry from southern and central Gaul. They had their frolic and killed many victims.

Next morning at dawn, while the German host was yet asleep, their chiefs, full six hundred of them, came into Cæsar's camp to propitiate him. He asked them why they had come. They replied that the leaders of the horde disclaimed any responsibility for the skirmish of the day before; it was just kittenish playfulness on the part of some romping lads, and they wanted to apologize. He explained that he was asking why they had ventured into his camp unheralded, without asking permission, without any pledge from him of safe conduct. They answered him that they relied on the truce he and they had negotiated. Cæsar quickly told them that they should have known better; the truce had been broken the day before and by them; there was no truce; and he instantly gave orders to hold them under arrest and to sound the bugles. Promptly the legionaries fell into line; swiftly they marched on the German camp. The myriads of savages were brawny, skilled, and brave, but they had no pickets out; every one of their chiefs was in duress in Cæsar's camp, and they were hampered by their blankets, women, and children. The Romans were on them before they suspected any danger and, except the few who swam the Rhine, all 400,000 of them were dead within four hours.

It is characteristic of such fighters as the German chiefs that, when Cæsar, after the extermination of their horde, granted them their liberty, they one and all enlisted with him. He had massacred their wives, children, and subjects. We should have expected that they would hate him. Yet, they seem to have acknowledged that he was not only right but fair in his claim that they had broken the truce and so no truce existed. They seem to have regarded him with admiration for his quick subtlety and prompt action. They all served him faithfully throughout the Gallic War, and helped mightily to the final victory. Some survivors even fought for and with him all through the civil wars.

That same summer Cæsar displayed his originality as an engineer by designing a novel plan for a bridge needing not a tenth as much timber as any wooden bridge Romans ever had previously constructed. His bridge over the Rhine was thus a marvel of engineering skill as well as a notable exploit, for the Rhine had never before been spanned by a bridge. The achievement of leading an army across the Rhine on a bridge and getting it back safe was comparable to Hannibal's feat of being first to lead an army through a pass of the Alps.

That very same summer he achieved a third and still more marvellous exploit by being the first commander of a disciplined army to cross with his troops from Gaul to Britain. This first crossing was merely a reconnaissance in force. Next year, 54

B.C., he invaded Britain with five legions and marched inland as far as St. Albans, some twenty-five miles north of the Thames. In the four crossings of the Channel not one single soldier was lost, demonstrating the clever management of both expeditions.

Next year Cæsar lost a legion enticed from its winter quarters and massacred by the Belgians. He learnt then and there what Alexander, Hannibal, and Napoleon learned as lads, never to entrust any fortress, force, or expedition to joint command by two officers of equal rank. The following summer, 53 B.C., he again crossed the Rhine.

These four spectacular exploits, the two crossings of the Rhine by bridge and the two invasions of Britain, were undertaken, apparently, for the purpose of bringing about what they actually accomplished, the instilling into all and sundry of the lasting convictions, first, that armies of the Roman Commonwealth could go anywhere, that the Roman Commonwealth was therefore to be dreaded, respected, and generally deferred to by all races and nations however distant; secondly, that Roman commanders could succeed at ventures which would result in disaster for commanders of any other breed; thirdly, that Julius Cæsar could perform exploits beyond the capacity of any other general earth had ever produced, Roman or alien. Indubitably, these four exploits greatly enhanced the prestige of the Roman Commonwealth and the personal prestige of Cæsar with all who knew of him—foreigners, provincials, Italians, Romans, members of his political party, and the soldiers under his command.

Next year, 52 B.C., the seventh of his proconsulship, Cæsar had to cope with a general insurrection of all the Gauls except the Remi, from whom Rheims is named, who made the enduring fortunes of themselves and their descendants by their loyalty. The insurgents had as leader a veritable military genius, the young Arvernian Vercingetorix. Cæsar met his first personal military failure when he had to abandon the siege of Gergovia. But Vercingetorix and his Gauls were no match for Cæsar and his Romans in the open field. After an ambitious attack which ended in rout for his Gauls, Vercingetorix, with all of 90,000 warriors, took refuge at Alesia on a mountain deemed impregnable. Cæsar, with only some 40,000 legionaries, not only besieged him, but blockaded him with eleven miles of encircling earthworks, and then, at news of a vast enlistment to rescue him, dug fourteen miles more of ditches turned the other way against the on-coming army of relief. It came, 350,000 strong. Though outnumbered eleven to one, such was the strength of Cæsar's earthworks and such the tenacity and valor of his men, that Cæsar beat off the outsiders and forced the capitulation of Alesia with its surviving defenders, after a siege unexcelled in history for difficulty and success except by Alexander's capture of Tyre.

The two ensuing years Cæsar put down minor local insurrections and so, within ten years, had fought, conquered, subdued, and subjugated a people against whom Rome had fought with only slow success for over three centuries.

By the autumn of 50 B.C., Gaul was so thoroughly and completely subjugated that the Gauls never so much as debated revolting during the ensuing civil wars, but settled down to agriculture and handicrafts and became rapidly Romanized and prosperous.

Cæsar had been able to make a clean job of subjugating Gaul because, at a conference at Lucca in 56 B.C., he, Pompey, and Crassus had agreed to prolong his term as proconsul of Gaul five years more, and to give Pompey all Spain for five years, and Crassus Syria and the whole eastern frontier. In 53 B.C. Crassus perished at Carrhæ, with most of his army, on a mishandled expedition beyond the Euphrates against the Parthians. Cæsar's daughter Julia, Pompey's wife, had died the year before.

This left Pompey and Cæsar manifestly the two foremost Romans.

And Pompey was increasingly disquieted and uneasy. He had had his term of authority in Spain extended from five years to ten and was governing Spain through his deputies. He was in Italy struggling to diminish disorder and to establish and maintain order in Rome. But riots were ever more frequent, involving more participants and more violent.

Also Pompey could not view the general situation with complacency. His exploits in the East in promptly and neatly disposing of Mithridates after twenty-two years of his outrageousness, and in annexing such vast and valuable territories after his incredible career of youthful successes, had overshadowed all previous records of military achievement. He had felt secure of enduring fame not only as the greatest Roman ever, but as the greatest Roman forever.

And lo! within ten years an upstart of a man-about-town, a city dandy, a voluptuary, had performed exploits which outshone his and had won renown certain to outshine his for all time.

What was more, it was plain that Cæsar's legionaries regarded his competence and his miraculous achievements as proving him not merely a man stamped with the seal of Jupiter's favor, as deputized by Jupiter for supreme command for life, but positively as a superhuman being, as a man hallmarked as destined to be welcomed as a fellow god among the gods of Olympus after he left this earth, as indubitably a god on earth.

"Imperator" was not a sufficiently laudatory title for him, they thought. They called him *"Imperator unicus"* ("the only commander-in-chief"), as if there not only was no other on earth to compare with him, but never before had been on earth a real, genuine commander-in-chief worthy to be called Imperator, as if all other imperators were mere forecasts of Cæsar.

After much legislating, in which it appeared that Pompey and his faction were unwilling to be fair to Cæsar, after much negotiation, in which appeared the like and also that Cæsar was very willing to be fair to Pompey and the Senate, it became obvious that civil war was inevitable, for, while Cæsar might submit to the injustice with which the Senate plainly meant to treat him, his legionaries were certain to insist on his fighting for their due rights, as well as for his own.

The Rubicon was the southern boundary-line of Cæsar's province. North of it he was legally absolute ruler; south of it he had not only no rights with an army, but as an individual he was, as proconsul of Gaul, specifically forbidden to cross it. To cross it was a defiance of the Senate and a declaration of civil war.

Cæsar's words just before he moved to cross have been much misunderstood by readers of histories written in English. He spoke Greek, the natural language of all cultured Romans in his day, and the imperative mood of a Greek verb had implications and connotations which can hardly be translated into Latin and are still harder to render into English. He said, "*Anerriptho kubos,*" which does not mean "The die is cast," but "Let it be a die which has been thrown *up,*" the "an" in *anerriphtho* meaning "up"; the implication of the metaphor being not merely that the die, once thrown, could never be recalled, but that no one could tell how it would fall while it was in the air and it would be up in the air till the end of the war. What Cæsar meant was: "With all my skill as a leader, war is mostly chance, after all. Not even I can tell how this will turn out until the war is over. It is win or lose, but chance may disfavor me."

A modern leader might say, under similar conditions, "Oh, hell! This is just like flipping a coin!"

Cæsar crossed the Rubicon with only one legion, but his advance was so rapid and his strategy so clever that he met with little opposition. Pompey, with most of the Senate, fled to Brundisium in the heel of Italy, the port from which crossings to Greece were usually made. Cæsar, overtaken by a second legion, captured Corfinium in Sabinum, east of Rome, and, joined by a third legion, besieged Brundisium, trying to prevent Pompey's crossing to Greece. But Pompey escaped. Cæsar levied three more legions, had the construction of a fleet begun, and went to Rome.

There, instead of massacring his adversaries, he put no one to death and forgave everyone who promised support or nonresistance in future. He put all departments of the government in good working order and set out for Spain. There, as in Rome, he displayed an amazing reluctance to shed the blood of his fellow Romans. In fact, no great commander of whom we have any authentic record was as averse to killing as was Cæsar. When it seemed necessary and advisable he could have his men butcher 400,000 Usipetes and Tenctheri in four hours. The Germans across the Rhine needed a lesson and he gave it. But, not only in the Civil War, but also in his wars with the Gauls, he repeatedly made plain his conviction that there was nothing to be done with a dead man except bury him or otherwise get rid of his corpse; whereas a live man might be set to useful activity.

Pompey's deputies in Spain, Afranius and Petreius, were duffers, and Cæsar might have made short work of them. But shrinking from causing the death of any Roman citizen, Cæsar played military chess with them on a large scale and came near being vanquished. Ultimately he forced their surrender and, taking as recruits the few men who volunteered to join him, allowed the rest to go where they pleased on pledging themselves not to fight against him, which pledge most of them promptly broke and hurried eastwards to join Pompey in Greece. Meantime Valerius had won Sardinia, and Curio Sicily, for Cæsar, and the danger of Rome starving was averted. Curio went to Africa and Cæsar, on his way back to Rome, forced Marseilles, long besieged by Decimus Brutus, to surrender.

At Rome Cæsar abdicated the office of Dictator, which had been conferred on him in his absence, and had himself appointed consul for the next year, 48 B.C.

That spring he crossed to Greece with forces insufficient to attack Pompey, and wasted some time waiting until Mark Antony, eluding Pompey's fleets, which had control of the Adriatic, brought over more soldiers.

Then Cæsar attempted to blockade Pompey in Dyrrachium, although Pompey's forces greatly outnumbered his. After what he had accomplished at Alesia, Cæsar seems to have felt that he could capture any garrison, however large, with any force, however small, by dogged spade work. It came to a battle, at, on, and over the unfinished siege works, and Cæsar was so thoroughly beaten that any other man would have given up the war and surrendered. He got away by an incredibly swift and lengthy three days' march, revived his men's drooping spirits by storming Gomphi, a town in Thessaly which made the mistake of refusing to admit him, and, when Pompey followed him overconfidently, drew him on to battle at Pharsalus, where, with only 22,000 legionaries, he won a complete victory by tactical skill and vigor over more than 47,000 under Pompey, who fled to Egypt and was there murdered by a henchman of its king.

Cæsar, again showing his lack of a sound military education, rashly landed at Alexandria with only 4,000 men and very nearly lost his life for his temerity. But by early in 47 B.C. he had completely won the so-called Alexandrian War, in which Ptolemy, the young King of Egypt, was accidentally killed and his sister Cleopatra came into Cæsar's possession. Cæsar immediately fell in love with her, and by marrying her according to Egyptian law, became, also according to Egyptian law, Pharaoh and owner of Egypt.

That spring he went to Pontus and won an easy victory at Zela over Pharnaces, the son of Mithridates. Promptly Cæsar put in order all Rome's provinces in Asia, Cilicia, and Syria. Then he returned to Rome, where in his absence he had, with complete fulfillment of legal formalities, been made Tribune for life, Dictator for one year, and Consul for five.

At Rome he quelled an appalling mutiny of his best veterans by facing them and, when they quieted enough, beginning his address with the word "*quirites*" ("civilians"). He had always, of course, addressed them as "fellow soldiers" or "my lads." At that one word, which indicated their discharge from the army, precisely what they had asked for, they came to their senses and roared that they were no civilians but soldiers. Cæsar asked whose soldiers they were, and they roared that they were his. He then remarked that soldiers obeyed their commander, and they roared willingness to obey him. He ordered them to their quarters and that ended the mutiny.

Cæsar then set off for the province of Africa (modern Tunisia), again with insufficient forces. He was very nearly annihilated, along with his men, but won out by the amazing genius with which he made the most of the worst possible situation of affairs. At Thapsus, in 46 B.C., he completely vanquished greatly superior forces led by Pompey's son Sextus, by Labienus, who had been Cæsar's most capable subordinate in Gaul, by the fanatical Cato and other Roman nobles, with much help from Juba, King of Numidia.

Cæsar had given orders to spare the lives of all who surrendered, but the legionaries, after victory was assured, grimly pinioned their centurions and other officers, remarked that they had fought and beaten these same adversaries once in Spain and once again in Greece and that, now that they had fought and beaten them a third time, they did not propose to have to fight and beat them a fourth time just because Cæsar was so merciful, and butchered all the 50,000 not already killed in the battle.

When Cæsar was again in Rome he celebrated four triumphs on successive days: for Gaul, Egypt, Pharnaces of Pontus, and Juba of Numidia. He was appointed dictator for ten years and censor for three.

That winter he went to Spain a second time to deal with Pompey's sons and their followers, and in March of 45 B.C. ended all resistance by a decisive victory at Munda, in southern Spain, after a battle so furiously contested and so extremely close that he said he had for the first time fought for mere life.

At Rome he set about reforming all the departments of the government. He had the Senate appoint him consul for ten years, and then dictator and censor for life. Also he had borne, since before his departure for Egypt three years previously, the title Imperator officially conferred on him by the government, as indicating that he possessed the *imperium*—that is, the right to the fullest civil and military authority in all things. He remarked in conversation that his word was law.

in Gaul, he had been one of Cæsar's most capable, valiant, and reckless officers, and won glory at the siege of Alesia. He fought mightily for his uncle all through the wars against Pompey and his partisans, and led the left wing of Cæsar's army in the crucial victory at Pharsalus. He was consul with Dolabella at the time of Cæsar's assassination.

Also in Rome was Marcus Æmilius Lepidus, forty-six years of age, who, as prætor in 49 B.C. at the outbreak of the civil war, had had Cæsar proclaimed dictator. He had fought for Cæsar all through the war with Pompey and his faction, had been consul with Cæsar in 46 B.C., and as Cæsar was again dictator at the time of his death, was then his second in command. He had been assigned Gallia Narbonensis (Provence) and northern Spain as his province for the coming year, and had an army not far from Rome. With it he aided Antony in overawing Cæsar's murderers and their fellow-conspirators.

As Cæsar had been chief Priest of Rome and the dignity had no incumbent since his death, Lepidus, at Antony's instance, was appointed to the vacant office of Pontifex Maximus.

But the two could not prevent the Senators from voting amnesty for all the assassins and their accomplices. However, Antony induced the Senate to ratify all Cæsar's acts and accord him a public funeral. Antony's address on that occasion so roused the populace that Brutus, Cassius, and their associates thought it best to leave the city, Marcus Brutus for Macedonia, Decimus Brutus for Gallia Cisalpina (northern Italy from the Rubicon, Apennines and Macra to the chine of the Alps), and Cassius for Syria, which the Senate had assigned them as provinces.

Returned to Rome, Augustus displayed powers of self-possession, self-command, self-control, self-confidence, intelligence, tactfulness, acumen, insight, foresight, wariness, discretion, caution and wisdom downright miraculous in a mere lad.

When he found that Antony had treated all Cæsar's ready cash as the property of the State and had covered it into the treasury, which he controlled, Augustus, by sales and borrowings, turned his inheritance from his father's family and

Cæsar's real estate into cash and paid all the donatives Cæsar had willed his legionaries and officers, which act enhanced his popularity, already great; for the more valuable, though intangible, heritage he entered into as Cæsar's heir was the love of the Roman populace and the loyalty of Cæsar's legionaries, which they at once transferred to him, as the near blood relation, adopted son, and chosen successor of their idolized champion.

Antony seemed in a fair way to make himself master of Rome and Rome's Empire. He had the Senate assign him as his province Macedonia with five of the six legions Cæsar had sent there as part of his preparations for a great expedition beyond the Euphrates.

Then he had the people vote him the province of Gallia Cisalpina.

As Decimus Brutus maintained his claim to this province assigned to him by the Senate, civil war broke out between him and Antony, who besieged him in Mutina (Modena).

The Senate, alarmed at such an assumption of power and stimulated by Cicero's torrents of invective upon Antony, hoped to utilize against him the affection of the soldiery for Augustus, and there were secret negotiations between him and the Senate. They gazetted him a proconsul and this legalized his command of two legions which had already welcomed him as their chief. With them he joined the consuls of 43 B.C., Hirtius and Pansa, in an attempt to chastise and abase Antony, now, at the instance of Cicero, proclaimed by the Senate a public enemy. Antony was beaten, but escaped across the Alps to Lepidus.

Both consuls were killed in the course of the fighting, so that Augustus was left sole commander of all his and their legionaries. He promptly marched on Rome and compelled the Senate to acquiesce in his appointment to the consulship (he was only twenty years old) and to consent to the repeal of the amnesty granted Cæsar's murderers and their fellow conspirators.

Thereafter he entered into negotiations with Antony, who had won over the legionaries of Decimus Brutus and put him to death.

Antony and Lepidus had, together, seventeen legions, which greatly outnumbered the forces loyal to Augustus.

In November of 43 B.C. they had a conference near Bononia (Bologna) and formed the Second Triumvirate, not a tacit verbal gentlemen's agreement like the First Triumvirate of Cæsar, Pompey, and Crassus, but an arrangement for joint public office to be formally ratified by the Senate and People of Rome, under which they were to have all the authority needed to reorganize the government in all respects and put it in good working order.

They agreed that Cæsar's clemency to his private enemies and his antagonists in the war with Pompey's faction had turned out to be very injudicious and that they had best do what they thought necessary to assure their personal safety. So each made out a list of the persons he wanted put to death, not on the model of the promiscuous massacres revelled in by Marius, but patterned on Sulla's retaliatory proscriptions. Their proscription lists included all the conspirators against Cæsar, whether participants in his murder, accomplices, or merely associates. Also, whatever individuals had antagonized Antony or Lepidus or whose future opposition the triumvirs apprehended. Cicero, after his fourteen cascades of oratorical vituperation of Antony, was, of course, included, as were many wealthy men not vigorous partisans of any of the triumvirs.

By the executions and confiscations following the posting of their lists the three provided for themselves individual security and amassed funds with which to pay their legionaries and carry on the government.

The triumvirs had agreed that Lepidus was to have all Spain as his province, Antony all Gaul, and Augustus Africa and Sicily—apparently a poor bargain for Augustus. He and Antony were to deal with the assassins, the other conspirators and their associates, and Lepidus, meanwhile, was to keep Italy in order.

Brutus had gotten control of all Greece, Macedonia, and Thrace, and had five legions. Cassius was in Syria with twelve legions, with which he had attacked in Asia Minor and worsted Cæsar's henchman, Dolabella, who committed suicide.

Cassius then crossed into Europe and joined Brutus. At Philippi in Thrace the two pitiful caitiffs were defeated and both, very properly, ended their contemptible lives.

The survivors of their beaten armies promptly enlisted with Antony and Augustus.

Antony marched into Asia Minor and Syria, rewarded the fidelity of all cities which had been loyal to Cæsar and had endeavored to assist his avengers; and imposed punitive fines on all nations which had sided with the traitors.

Augustus returned to Italy, where he set about punishing the communities which had taken sides against him and his colleagues or had failed to support them. Sixteen towns were the chief offenders and their citizens were evicted from their farms, which were parcelled out among the legionaries of the triumvirs.

In the course of these allotments, Fulvia, Mark Antony's wife, and his brother Lucius, who was consul, got up a cabal against Augustus, recruited considerable forces from persons evicted from their lands and other malcontents, and seized Rome, from which they were driven by Agrippa, one of the ablest subordinates of Augustus. Lucius was then besieged in Perusia (Perugia) by the troops of Augustus with some reinforcements from Lepidus. This futile local war further devastated Italy.

After Lucius had surrendered and Fulvia had conveniently died, the triumvirs made a new division of the Empire. Antony was to have full control of everything east of Scodra in Illyricum (Scutari in Albania), including Egypt and Cyrenaica; Augustus of everything west of it; and Lepidus had for his lesser share only Africa from the frontiers of Cyrenaica to the Atlantic Ocean.

Antony married Octavia, the sister of Augustus.

This was in 40 B.C.

Meantime Pompey's able son, Sextus, one of the handful of refugees from the battle of Munda, since which he had lived by guerilla warfare in the Spanish mountains and by free-booting at sea—for he was a born mariner, commodore, and admiral—had gradually augmented his tiny squadron to a great fleet, had allied himself to Cæsar's murderers, and had gotten possession of all Sicily. With Sicily as a base he cut off grain shipments to Rome and threatened the city with starvation. He forced Augustus to make with him, in 39 B.C., a treaty by which he was to have unrestricted control of Sicily, Sardinia, Corsica, and the Peloponnesus.

But the war broke out again and Sextus was the best admiral alive. He defeated Augustus in a great naval battle in 38 B.C., just after which a storm destroyed every warship Augustus had left. He at once began the creation of a great naval base near Naples and the building of a new fleet.

In 37 B.C. the triumvirate was extended for five years more. Augustus lent Antony two legions for his war with the Parthians and Antony lent him a hundred battleships. With these and his own Augustus had a fleet of 300 sail under the command of Agrippa. Although many of them and a vast number of men were lost in a storm from which Augustus barely escaped, yet he persevered and in 36 B.C. Agrippa finally defeated Sextus in a great sea fight off Mylæ on the north coast of Sicily.

That finished Pompey's faction forever.

At this juncture Lepidus, whose help had been asked and who had landed in Sicily with a large army, demanded that island for himself. When they heard of this his legionaries refused to obey him and went over to Augustus, who spared Lepidus, allowed him to retain the office of Pontifex Maximus, and permitted him to enjoy his revenues and live out his life in dignified retirement under strict surveillance at Circeii on the seashore of southern Latium, where he had a magnificent villa.

Augustus then assumed the administration of Africa. This made him absolute over the western part of the Roman world as Antony was over the eastern portion. For five years thereafter Augustus labored ceaselessly to consolidate his power and solidify the prosperity of his dominions.

Spain and Gaul were weary of war and recuperated rapidly. So did central and southern Italy. Augustus initiated a series of vigorous campaigns against the Alpine tribes, by which he carried the authority of Rome to the watershed of the Alps and established it permanently by founding a colony in each valley, a strongly fortified town as far up the valley as was judicious, defended also by a fortress higher yet, at some suitable point. This policy extended Italy to the chine of the Alps.

Augustus also made the Adriatic safe by trouncing the Dalmatians and Illyrians, after which they largely ceased to be pirates and became rather smugglers, almost as profitable an occupation and far safer.

Meantime Antony, like Cæsar before him, had fallen deeply in love with Cleopatra of Egypt. He had been in love with her before he married Octavia in 40 B.C. But after three years at Athens with Octavia she returned to Rome, and Antony to Alexandria.

From soon after the victory at Philippi in 42 B.C.—that is, for over ten years—Antony, sometimes in person, sometimes through his deputy-commanders, had been conducting campaigns against the Parthians, with more defeats than victories. Yet he still hoped to conquer Parthia.

He divorced Octavia, scrupulously fulfilling all the formalities of Roman procedure, and then publicly married Cleopatra according to Egyptian law. This made him, as it had made Cæsar before him, according to immemorial Egyptian law, Pharaoh and owner of Egypt, for, according to Egyptian law, if a daughter, niece, granddaughter or other feminine descendant of a Pharaoh became his heiress, whomsoever she might marry at once became Pharaoh and owner of Egypt and whomsoever and whatsoever was in Egypt.

Antony now, being by agreement with Augustus, and by the legislation by which the Senate and People of Rome had ratified that agreement, in possession of all the Mediterranean world east of Scodra in Illyricum and the frontiers of Cyrenaica in Africa, and being owner of Egypt as Cleopatra's husband according to Egyptian law, purposed cutting loose from Rome altogether and ruling his dominions and what he might conquer and annex eastward, as King of Egypt and sole successor of Alexander the Great. He assumed the regalia of an Oriental potentate, exacted from all and sundry the deference traditionally due the Achæmenean Shahs of Persia, and lived with Cleopatra in regal state, pomp, and magnificence.

He had had the effrontery and the audacity, on the pretext that they had once been possessions of her ancestors the Ptolemies, kings of Egypt, to present to Cleopatra the island of Cyprus and parts of Phœnicia and Cilicia, all of which had been within Roman provinces ever since Pompey's reorganization of Rome's eastern conquests in 63 B.C., over thirty years before. What was more, Cleopatra and he had had three fine children, a girl and two boys. Both these male infants Antony gazetted as kings, assigned to them portions of his domains, legally provinces of the Roman Commonwealth, and, arrogating to himself personal ownership of those regions, made a will in which he left those districts to his two sons by Cleopatra. This, in Roman eyes, was not only treason to the Commonwealth, but sacrilege against its gods, especially against Jupiter Maximus Optimus.

Augustus, backed by the Senate, overawed the custodians of Antony's formally executed last will and testament, which was in safe deposit at Rome, and compelled them to hand it over. It was opened and proved Antony's treason.

The Senate thereupon recommended, and the people voted, the termination of Antony's commandership and governorship and a declaration of war, not on Antony, but on Cleopatra. Antony, bringing Cleopatra with him, advanced by way of Ephesus and Athens, and located his campaign headquarters at Patræ in Achaia. Augustus conveyed his troops to Epirus.

At dusk on September 1st, 31 B.C., the land and sea forces of uncle and nephew were within striking distance of each other at Actium, on the west coast of Greece, north of the Ionian islands. Augustus himself commanded his legionaries, and he had Agrippa for admiral. Next day the fleets clashed while the legions looked on. Agrippa, with 250 battleships, won a quick, easy, and complete victory over a much more numerous fleet. Cleopatra fled with her entire squadron, and Antony followed her with his. There was no land battle. Antony's faithful officers waited some days for his return, and then surrendered to Augustus, with whom they and their legionaries enlisted.

Next year, 30 B.C., Augustus took possession of Egypt with little resistance, Antony and Cleopatra both committing suicide.

In 29 B.C. Augustus returned to Rome and celebrated three triumphs. After the battle of Actium, Augustus was absolute lord of the entire Mediterranean world. To comprehend with what feelings he was welcomed by his countrymen it must be kept in mind that if Antony had won the war he would have sacked and burned Rome and governed the Mediterranean world from Alexandria as husband of Cleopatra, the heir of the Ptolemies and therefore of Alexander the Great, which made him the visible successor of the Achæmenean Shahs of Persia, in which capacity he would have left all his dominions to his eldest son by Cleopatra, who would have been heir and successor to the Persian Shahs and Alexander.

Augustus had saved not merely himself and his adherents, but Rome, the Roman Commonwealth, and the Romans.

CHAPTER XIII

THE SETTLEMENT

AUGUSTUS now, at thirty-three years of age, was the actual master of the Roman world and remained so until his death, forty-three years later.

His chief title to mastery, of course, and his strongest hold on the loyalty of his legionaries, was based on the universal and to the populations of the Greco-Roman world unescapable belief that, as victor at Actium and as having dextrously outwitted Antony, nineteen years his senior, and Lepidus, twenty-six years his senior, he was manifestly not merely the darling of the gods and the choice of Jupiter Maximus Optimus for chief partner on earth, but plainly himself a man destined to become a god on his departure from this earth and therefore already in some degree a living god while yet alive among men.

With this factor in his lasting supremacy we shall deal in a later chapter. Here we are concerned with Augustus as a mere man, but vastly superior in character to any man then alive.

He was sufficiently tactful not to repeat any of Cæsar's most ill-starred blunders. Perhaps his faculties of observation and inference enabled him to judge the temper of the Senate, nobility, and populace so accurately that he avoided repeating any of Cæsar's mistakes.

Cæsar's most unfortunate failings had been a proclivity toward too great clemency and the unsuspicious acceptance of the pledges of his former adversaries and antagonists. Augustus had no such weakness of character, nor was he ever so imprudent. As after his victory at Philippi in dealing with persons about whom there hung any suspicion of having countenanced Cæsar's murderers or their accomplices, confederates, or associates, so after his victory at Actium, in dealing with persons not free from suspicion of having favored Antony, he was bland, mild, and serene, accorded an audience to any man who requested one, listened to his attempt at self-justification, asked whether he had anything further to say, and then stated urbanely that the interview was at an end and that it was absolutely necessary that his interlocutor be put to death.

No one likely to be personally dangerous to him was left alive.

Be it noted that he was kind to all from whom he ran no risk. He permitted Lepidus to die of old age. He favored Cicero's son, who was consul with him in 30 B.C. The three children of Antony and Cleopatra were brought up with princely care by his own sister Octavia, Antony's divorced wife.

In Rome, as in his camps, Augustus was protected by the permanent bodyguard of the Prætorian Cohorts, under a trustworthy prefect.

Just when Cæsar had been acclaimed Imperator by his legionaries we do not know, probably after his victory over the Swiss, his first brilliantly successful battle; certainly long before the end of his wars in Gaul. In 48 B.C., after his victory over Pompey at Pharsalus, the title of Imperator was formally conferred on him by decree of the Senate and People of Rome. This, of course, was merely accepting and registering his enthusiastic soldiers' insistence that he was Unicus Imperator, the Unique Imperator, the only Imperator ever, the only genuine Imperator. But by the decree the title was made hereditary and one which he could bequeath. This smacked too much of kingship for Roman taste and was offensive not only to the men later his assassins and their confederates, accomplices, and associates, but to the nobility and populace generally.

Yet when, after 40 B.C., Augustus regularly styled himself, as Cæsar's heir, not Gaius Julius Cæsar Octavianus, but Imperator Julius Cæsar, all classes of Romans and the colonies and armies had become habituated to the title as a name and its use by Augustus gave no offense.

After his victory at Pharsalus in 48 B.C. Cæsar had been gazetted as Dictator for one year. Before the expiration of the term this was prolonged for another year. After his triumph in 46 B.C. he was gazetted as dictator for ten years. And after his final victory at Munda he was gazetted as Dictator for life. As the dictatorship had been customarily conferred only for a definite purpose and a very limited period, all these appointments were looked upon askance by every class at Rome.

Augustus, even after Actium, discreetly declined the title of dictator.

Cæsar had taken no care to mask his autocracy. Augustus was, after Actium, manifestly the absolute master of the Roman world, but he took great pains to veil his unlimited power behind outward observance of the traditional formalities of government of Rome and her Empire by the Roman Senate and People.

Cæsar had increased the Senate to 900 members and had incensed not only Senators of ancient Roman lineage, but all Senators, all Roman nobles, all Romans, by appointing as Senators able, successful, and loyal provincials, Gauls and Spaniards, with the manifest aim of making the Senate a council of the Empire at large. He positively outraged everybody's feelings by promoting to Senatorial rank ex-centurions and sons of freedmen.

Augustus, on the other hand, won general approbation when, by virtue of his authority as censor, he reduced the Senate to its former limit of 600 members by ejecting 200 deemed unworthy of such lofty position and setting higher the requisite income for a Senator.

In 27 B.C., as consul for the seventh time, he assembled the Senate and formally surrendered his command over all armies and provinces, his control of the revenue, and all his personal privileges.

The Senate immediately voted him proconsular authority for life as to all provinces where military forces were needed to maintain order. It then conferred on him the name and title of Augustus (revered) and changed the name of the month Sextilis to Augustus, as it had years before, in honor of Cæsar, changed the name of the month Quintilis to Julius, from which decrees we still call these months July and August.

At his own suggestion he was also voted the time-honored title of *Princeps Senatus* (leader or chief of the Senate), formerly always held by its most aged member. From this title of Princeps Senatus there naturally arose the habit of speaking of Augustus and each of his imperial successors as *Princeps Civitatis* (chief of the State), or as *Princeps Rei Publicæ* (Prince of the Commonwealth), or simply as Princeps (Our chieftain). This was never an official title, but, informal as it was, was greatly valued by all the Emperors. Just as a magistracy was called *magistratus,* so the Imperial dignity was called *Principatus,* from which we derive the corresponding English word "Principate." The time which elapsed from each Emperor's assumption of the Principate until his death was also spoken of as his Principate. And the arrangement between Augustus and the Senate, in its final form, was also called the establishment of the Principate.

In 23 B.C., after an absence of three years, during two of which he lay ill at Tarraco (Tarragona), Augustus, on returning to Rome, made his final adjustment of the administrative powers and functions of the components of the government of Rome.

He resigned the consulship, which he had held continuously since 31 B.C. Thereupon the Senate conferred on him for life a general proconsular authority, valid everywhere outside Rome and paramount over any that might be granted to any other proconsular officials. This gave him legal command for life of all the military forces of the Commonwealth, on land and sea, and so put him in paramount control of all the provinces and so of the whole Roman Empire.

The Senate also conferred on him for life the *tribunicia potestas,* the authority of a tribune-of-the-people. This gave him legal power to forbid anything whatever, and so put him in control of legislation and of all departments of civil administration.

This arrangement pleased everybody and offended nobody. Both the proconsular and tribunician powers had been conferred legally by the Senate, not assumed by Augustus on his own authority.

And whereas the populace of Rome had always looked on the dictatorship as an invention of the aristocrats for their own benefit, largely to evade control of policies and projects by the citizen body, tribunes had always been regarded as the special champions of the people.

Augustus, as Cæsar's heir, was looked upon by the people as having inherited Cæsar's personal status as champion of the populace against the patricians, the Senate, the aristocracy, and the nobility. His assumption of permanent and personal tribunician power both emphasized his acceptance of this inherited status as champion of the populace and also intensified the people's faith in him and enthusiasm for him. Not only Augustus, but every Emperor after him, as his successor, for over two centuries, was so regarded by the people, apparently so regarded himself, and to a certainty was so regarded by the Senators, the nobles, and the opulent, all of whom felt his heavy hand whenever they infringed on what was pleasing to the people. Similarly, the legionaries looked upon his all-embracing and supreme authority as permanent proconsul at large of all garrisoned provinces as a recognition and confirmation of his inheritance of Cæsar's other status of champion of the soldiery against the city mob. The legionaries now felt that they were assured of reasonably fair treatment in such matters as pay, an equitable share of booty captured by them, lands for such ex-soldiers as deserved them, and general consideration.

Oddly enough, Augustus and his heirs and successors for two centuries managed to maintain and retain this double status of champion of the populace against their betters and champion of the soldiery against the comfortable civilians at home.

This then was the Roman solution, worked out by a Roman consulting his Roman advisers, voted by the Roman Senate and accepted by the Roman people and soldiery, of the two most vexing problems of their government.

There were no more squabbles between patricians and plebeians, aristocracy and commonalty, rich and poor, nobles and populace, Senate and People. The Prince of the Commonwealth settled all such matters and settled them in favor of the multitude. Emperors, however execrated by the intelligentsia, however aspersed by their biographers and censured by historians, were mostly, with only few exceptions, even idolized by the populace.

The weakness of the arrangement lay in the impossibility at that time, with Rome's traditions and the existing state of land and sea traffic, of devising any mode of selecting an Imperator other than by the prescriptive custom of acclamation by his legionaries, or of inventing any method for ascertaining who was most acceptable as Imperator to a majority of the soldiery, except by armed conflict, if two or more commanders had been acclaimed, and by victory of one in civil war.

This weakness was not perceived and perhaps not foreseen until, by the death of Nero, in A.D. 68, ninety-one years later, the family of Augustus became extinct and no legal heir to his honors was left.

The essence of this arrangement, which endured for more than two and a half centuries, was that the legionaries, who did the work of extending and maintaining the Empire, were now preponderatingly represented in the government of the Empire and therefore felt satisfied.

In practice the man acceptable to the legionaries was endowed for life by formal vote of the Senate and People (later voting by the citizens went out of fashion) with legal command of the legionaries, as Imperator Cæsar, and with legal control of the civil government, as holding for life the tribunicia potestas.

The year 23 B.C. is generally considered the year in which the Roman Commonwealth ceased to be a democratic republic directed by citizen suffrage and became an empire directed by an autocrat.

Augustus, after 23 B.C., had included in every inscription in his honor the year from his receiving the tribunician power. So inscriptions of 13 B.C. all contain the characters, TRIB. POT. X (the tenth year of his tribunician power).

So every successor of his dated his reign as Emperor of Rome from the conferring on him by the Senate of the tribunician authority, and such characters as TRIB. POT. II, TRIB. POT. XV, appear on most imperial coins.

The provinces of Sicily, Sardinia (which included Corsica), Gallia Narbonensis (Provence, southern France from the Alps to the Pyrenees), *Hispania Bœtica* (southeastern Spain), Illyricum (Dalmatia), Achaia (Greece), Macedonia, Asia (western Asia Minor), Bithynia and Pontus (northern Asia Minor), Cyprus, Crete and Cyrenaica, Africa (Tunisia), and Numidia (Algeria), were assigned to the Senate, which governed them through quæstors and proprætors, as of old, except Asia and Africa, to which ex-consuls regularly went as proconsuls.

As Imperator, Augustus took over the administration of all the other provinces and of all provinces organized later. They were governed for him by his *legati* (colonels) with proconsular powers, or his procurators.

These provinces were Hispania Citerior (northern Spain), Cilicia (southeastern Asia Minor), Syria, the three Gauls (all France, north of Provence), Mauretania (Morocco), Lusitania (Portugal), Pamphylia (southern Asia Minor), Alpes Maritimæ (Savoy), Galatia (eastern central Asia Minor), and Judæa.

Many alterations and changes were made from time to time in respect to this division of provinces into Senatorial and Imperial.

Egypt was governed in the name of the Emperor by a prefect, because Egypt was never a province of the Roman Commonwealth, but always a personal possession of the reigning emperor. This came about as follows:

Cæsar, according to Egyptian law, by his marriage to Cleopatra, heiress of the Ptolemy Pharaohs, became Pharaoh and owner of Egypt. Later Antony married Cleopatra according to Egyptian law and became thereby in like manner Pharaoh and owner of Egypt.

At his death it was not clear, according to Egyptian law as understood by the Romans, whether the legitimate Pharaoh was Augustus, as Cæsar's heir by his will, or Cæsarion, son of Cæsar and Cleopatra and therefore by blood not only senior male heir of the whole line of the Ptolemies, but also manifestly heir to Cæsar, or the elder of the sons of Antony and Cleopatra. Augustus finally and forever settled this matter by putting to death Cæsarion, who had surrendered to him, and taking possession of Egypt as Cæsar's only legal heir.

The three children of Antony and Cleopatra he ignored as possible rivals and cherished most kindly. Selene, the girl, married Juba II, son of Juba I, King of Numidia, who, after Numidia was taken as a Roman Province, was made King of Mauretania (Morocco), where the two had a prosperous reign of over forty years, Juba gaining fame both as a ruler and as an author, for his history of Greek painters and painting was the standard textbook till the smash of the Roman Empire.

CHAPTER XIV

THE EMPIRE

AFTER the establishment of the Empire, Augustus had the ill luck to lose first his nephew Marcellus, whom he had intended to make his heir and who promised well, and then his two grandsons Gaius and Lucius, whom he had chosen as his heirs after the death of Marcellus.

Between 29 B.C. and A.D. 10, chiefly through the great military abilities of his two stepsons Drusus and Tiberius, Roman armies subjugated all the inhabitants of Mœsia, Pannonia, Noricum, and Rhætia, corresponding to modern Bulgaria, Servia, Hungary west of the Danube, Austria, and Bavaria. This carried the frontiers of the Empire up to the Danube and Rhine.

After the death of Gaius Cæsar in A.D. 4, Augustus formally adopted Tiberius and named him as his heir.

He became Emperor in A.D. 14, then already fifty-six years old and a much embittered man. Augustus had compelled him, in 11 B.C., to divorce his beloved wife Vipsania and to marry Julia, the daughter of Augustus and widow of Agrippa, a woman to the last degree obnoxious and unendurable as a wife. Along the Danube and Rhine from 15 B.C. to 7 B.C., first as colleague of his brother, Drusus, later succeeding him, Tiberius had shown himself a great general. Yet at Rome in 6 B.C. he was so manifestly out of favor with Augustus that he was permitted or bidden to withdraw to Rhodes, where he spent seven years in a retirement suggesting exile. When he was recalled on the death of Lucius Cæsar he was disgusted by the renewed fawning of those who had paid court to him until he had fallen under the displeasure of Augustus in 7 B.C. and who had neglected, ignored, flouted, and snubbed him in the interval.

In the conquest of the lands bordering on the Danube, Tiberius had had under his immediate command more legionaries than had ever been under the direct personal leadership of any Roman general. Amid the not wholly undeserved but not fully

THE PROVINCES OF THE ROMAN EMPIRE

deserved vilification of him by his biographers and historians, this notable fact and his felicitous conduct of them have largely been lost sight of.

Also he was the man for whom the phrase "Your Majesty" was invented. Officers under his command were so awed by the stateliness of his bearing that to write or say "you" was less natural than to write or say "your majesty."

Besides the lands he had conquered along the Danube, which were organized as provinces during the lifetime of Augustus, during his reign he had organized as new provinces Cappadocia (western central Asia Minor), Germania Superior (Upper Germany) (Alsace, Lorraine) and Germania Inferior (Lower Germany, the left bank of the Rhine below Coblenz with much of modern Belgium and Holland).

His reign, much more than that of Augustus, consolidated and perpetuated the autocratic government of the Roman Emperors.

During his Principate voting assemblies of the populace of Rome went out of fashion and laws were ratified by the Senate only.

He was Emperor twenty-two years and so able that while in retirement at Capri he divined and foiled a conspiracy against him contrived by Sejanus, his hitherto completely trusted minister, whom he had left at Rome in command of his guards and in charge of all departments of the government.

He was ruler in fact as well as in name up to his death in A.D. 37, in his seventy-eighth year.

The grandnephew of Tiberius, Gaius Cæsar, his successor, nicknamed Caligula, was a competent ruler only in the rare lucid intervals of his long fits of insanity. He was assassinated after an extravagant reign of less than four years, during which the Empire largely ran itself and the provinces throve.

His uncle, Claudius, who succeeded him, was at his accession fifty-one years of age. Apparently he had in childhood barely recovered from a severe attack of poliomyelitis (infantile paralysis), for descriptions of his appearance, attitudes, gait, and behavior all point to that conclusion. He dragged one foot, walked awkwardly, even lurchingly, made grotesque and apparently purposeless and unintentional movements when seated, and not only stuttered or stammered, but uttered his words in a blurred and mumbled fashion, so that he did not seem or look Imperial.

But during his Principate the conquest of Britain was begun and the southern part was organized as a province, as were Mauretania (Morocco) as two provinces, Lycia in southern Asia Minor, Thrace, and Judæa, which last had been an allied kingdom for some years. His military and civil appointments were mostly very judicious. Many great public works were undertaken and not a few completed within the thirteen years of his Principate, as notably a magnificent new harbor at Ostia.

After him the Principate was held for fourteen years by his grandnephew and adopted son, whom we call Nero. He was eighteen years old when he became Emperor. During his reign there was a revolt in Gaul and a war with the Parthians, but for the most part the Empire prospered. He had the artistic temperament far too highly developed. His talents as a poet, singer, musical composer, and virtuoso on the organ, into the making of which he introduced improvements of his own invention, were of a high order. But his vanity and the flattery of his associates led him to overrate his talents and he made himself ridiculous. Also his passion, as an amateur of all arts, for painting, sculpture, and architecture led him into great extravagances. He expropriated much of the central parts of Rome from the Palatine to the Esquiline and had built a palace of vast extent, complexity, magnificence, and costliness, called, from the quantities of gilding in it, *Domus Aurea,* the Golden House. The expropriations and the insensate prodigality of his disbursements and self-indulgence alienated the very great personal popularity he had enjoyed when he came to the throne. His family troubles and personal antics do not concern us. It is characteristic of Roman folkways and conceptions of decency, decorum, propriety, and respectability, that when, in a transitory fit of rage, he kicked his adored wife, then pregnant, and caused her death, his people were shocked but shrugged their shoulders. When he in person and in broad daylight drove his own chariot team in sight of any and all through the streets of Rome, all classes at once made up their minds that he was unfit for the Principate. Within a brief time he was dethroned and dead, in A.D. 68.

So far, for more than half a century after his death, the heirs of Augustus had kept the loyalty of the legionaries on the frontiers, of the population throughout the provinces, and of the Senate and people at Rome. Nero was the last of the Claudian house.

He had perished as a result of a revolt in Gaul. There Gaius Julius Vindex, propraetor, too disgusted with Nero to serve him longer, formed a conspiracy against him and offered the imperial dignity to Servius Sulpicius Galba, one of the Empire's most distinguished generals, then at seventy-two years of age proconsul of Spain. His legions immediately saluted him as Imperator and he was promptly supported by the propraetor of Lusitania (modern Portugal) Marcus Salvius Otho, a distinguished general, whom Nero had compelled to divorce his beautiful wife, Poppaea, in order that she might marry him.

But the revolt in Gaul led by Vindex got beyond his control and became a general movement for Gallic independence, upon which Verginius Rufus, who had been consul five years before and was then propraetor of Upper Germany, moved on Vindex and crushed the insurrection.

It was after this that the Praetorian Guards at Rome declared for Galba, whereupon Nero, who might easily have rehabilitated himself by decision and vigor, fell into a panic, vacillated, and attempted negotiations. As a result the Senate met, declared Nero no longer Emperor, and proclaimed him a public enemy. Whereupon he had himself killed by one of his attendants. Galba was thereupon accepted by the Senate as Emperor and came to Rome. But he was enfeebled by age and very parsimonious, wherefore he rapidly became unpopular and after a reign of only seven months was killed while attempting to suppress a mutiny of his Prætorian Guards. This was in January of A.D. 69.

Otho was at once accepted by the Senate as Emperor. But in the meantime, since news travelled slowly in those days, the legions of lower Germany had already, at Cologne, on January 2nd saluted as Imperator their commander, Aulus Vitellius. He assumed the imperial regalia and sent against Otho his two most capable subordinates, Fabius Valens and Aulus Cæcina. Otho marched from Rome to meet them and was at first handsomely victorious over Cæcina. But Cæcina was joined by Fabius Valens and a terrific and lengthy battle was fought at Bedriacum between Cremona and Verona. By a strange combination of adverse accidents, mischances, and coincidences Otho was defeated. His legionaries were for continuing the war, but Otho, horrified at the carnage, declared that he didn't deserve to have Roman citizens butchered for his sake, and killed himself. So much was he loved and revered that more than 10,000 soldiers and officers who had served under him committed suicide on the news of his death, vowing that life without Otho was not worth living. He was a great man and his accidental defeat and death a great loss to Rome. He had maintained his precarious claim to the Imperial Dignity only from January 10 to April 16, A.D. 69.

The oath of allegiance to Vitellius was taken by almost all the legions of the Empire. He reached Rome in July, and while he had put to death some of Otho's partisans, he confiscated no one else's property and was accepted as Emperor by the Senate. He occupied himself chiefly with amazing indulgence in heavy eating of the costliest delicacies and is remembered most for his insensate gluttony and his remark amid the mounds of carrion on the battle field near Bedriacum that a dead enemy smells good and especially a dead fellow citizen.

But the legionaries in Egypt, Syria, and the East generally were far from satisfied with the way things were going in Europe. Their favorite general was Titus Flavius Sabinus Vespasianus, then sixty years of age. He came of a family of poor Sabine farmers near Reate and had served in the army from early manhood, beginning as an officer of the lowest grade and working his way up. In A.D. 66 there had broken out in Judæa a very general and formidable insurrection of the Jews. To cope with this Nero had put Vespasian in supreme command of ten legions or more, and with this large army he had crushed the revolt and was besieging Jerusalem.

At Alexandria in Egypt, on July 1, A.D. 69, Vespasian was proclaimed Emperor, and soon throughout all the East. Licinius Mucianus, the governor of Syria, with whatever legionaries could be spared from the siege of Jerusalem, set out at once overland by way of Asia Minor and Thrace to oust Vitellius from Rome and the Principate. The news of his approach and of the general revolt of the East ran before him and the legions of the Danube declared for Vespasian, and, led by Antonius Primus, they marched into Italy and arrived before Mucianus. With the forces of Vitellius, only half-heartedly led by Cæcina, who was ready to declare for Vespasian, they fought a second battle at Bedriacum, not a year after the former, this time by moonlight. The Vitellians were defeated. Primus and Vitellius then entered into lengthy negotiations, during which fighting broke out in Rome between the Prætorian Guards and Vespasian's brother Sabinus and his partisans, who had gotten possession of the Capitol. Primus marched on Rome, entered with his troops, and Vitellius was killed in December of A.D. 69. Mucianus arrived soon afterward and Vespasian himself not much later.

Vespasian had left his son Titus in command of the armies besieging Jerusalem and he and his men made a clean job of the rebels by September 8, A.D. 70. Next year he returned to Rome and entered it in a triumphal procession.

Meanwhile, during the fighting between the forces of Vitellius and Vespasian there had broken out in Gaul a second general insurrection, led by a Batavian, Julius Claudius Civilis. Civilis defeated Roman army after Roman army, and for a time there was talk of a Gallic Empire. But Batavians, Germans, and Gauls could not long coöperate and the revolt was crushed by one of Vespasian's deputies in A.D. 71, the year of the Triumph of Titus.

Vespasian reigned ten years and was succeeded by Titus, who died within two years, years notable for the eruption of Vesuvius which buried Pompeii and Herculaneum. Though it is not certain or even likely, it has been widely believed that his untimely death was caused by his chagrin at the impossibility, in view of Roman prejudices, Roman customs, and Roman law, of his taking as his wife a Jewish princess, Berenice, with whom he was desperately infatuated.

Titus was succeeded by his younger brother, Domitian, who was then thirty years old and reigned fifteen years, during which there was almost continual trouble along the Danube with the Dacians, who often crossed the river and even attempted to gain a foothold south of it. Otherwise the Empire prospered everywhere during his Principate. The capable general Agricola had already, before Vespasian's death, been commissioned to complete the conquest of Britain. Domitian prudently forbade him to waste men amid the dreary moors and glens of the highlands of northern Scotland. Agricola, however, subjugated the island as far as the Clyde and Forth, and built a line of forts from one firth to the other.

The construction of the *Limes Germanicus,* a stupendous line of fortifications protecting the frontiers of the Roman Empire beyond the upper reaches of the Danube and Rhine, from near Ratisbon to near Coblenz, projected by Vespasian, was begun or continued by Domitian.

In Rome he saw completed the Colosseum, which his father had begun on the site of the great ornamental pond of Nero's unpopular Golden House, which he had had largely torn down. Likewise the Baths of Titus, a magnificent public building contrived from remodelled portions of Nero's Golden House, with additions, were completed by Domitian. Also other splendid monumental structures begun by Vespasian or Titus.

Domitian seems to have been a capable ruler who became completely unnerved by repeated attempts on his life. He is credited with the remark that no one ever believed in the reality of a conspiracy against an Emperor unless it succeeded. Certainly the executions he ordered in the course of investigating various alleged conspiracies made him very unpopular, and as he grew more timorous, morose, retired, and suspicious, particularly of Senators and nobles, his unpopularity increased. He was assassinated by one of his Prætorian Guards.

As Domitian left no legal heirs, the Prætorians and their Prefects deferred to the Senate and left to the Senators the choice of an Emperor. They selected Marcus Cocceius Nerva, then over sixty years of age, a nobleman distinguished personally as a scholar and poet, and publicly for services to the State both as a military commander and as a civil administrator. He designated as his heir and successor Marcus Ulpius Traianus, styled later, as Emperor, Imperator Cæsar Nerva Traianus Augustus, whom we call Trajan.

Trajan, already associated in the management of the Empire with his adoptive father, succeeded him as Emperor in January, A.D. 98, for Nerva died after a Principate of less than two years.

Trajan is often spoken of as a Spaniard. Indubitably he was born in Spain and was the first Roman Emperor not born in Italy. But he was born in A.D. 52 at Italica, near modern Seville. Italica was the first Roman colony in Spain, founded by Scipio Africanus in 206 B.C. Thus Italica had been a Roman town for 258 years before Trajan was born and he was a Roman of the Romans and, as a great Roman, surpassed only by Julius Cæsar. His Principate lasted nineteen years, during which the Empire attained its acme of extent, population, wealth, and prosperity.

He fought two wars with the Dacians. After the first he left them humbled but independent under their king, Decebalus. As Decebalus at once prepared to renew the war, Trajan built a permanent stone and brick bridge across the Danube below where Belgrade now is, crossed it, and abolished the Dacian kingdom. Dacia was then colonized from the Theiss to the Carpathians and over most of modern Rumania, and was held as a populous and prosperous province for more than a century and a half.

At Rome, Trajan, all about a newly cleared open square named after him the Forum of Trajan, built some of the most magnificent structures mankind ever beheld, and midway of his Forum set up the great column, round the shaft of which winds a long series of relief carvings depicting the chief occurrences of his Dacian Wars. Under this column Trajan was later buried in the tomb he had had prepared for himself.

Besides Dacia, there were organized as new provinces of Rome during his Principate Arabia (the rocky region southeast of Palestine), which one of his governors had annexed, and Armenia, Assyria, and Mesopotamia, all of which had been conquered and subjugated by Roman armies led brilliantly by Trajan in person in wars against the Parthian kings, whom he overwhelmingly defeated in battle after battle, capturing both their capitals on the Tigris, Ctesiphon and Seleucia.

After these exploits and the organization of his new provinces Trajan fell ill, set out for home, and on his way to Rome died in Cilicia in August of A.D. 117.

Publius Ælius Hadrianus, whom we call Hadrian, was a cousin of Trajan and married to his grand-niece, Sabina. He had served with distinction in many civil and military capacities, was with Trajan during the last months of his life, and claimed to have been adopted by him. Certainly, on Trajan's death, the Syrian legions acclaimed Hadrian as Emperor and the Senate at Rome acquiesced and clothed him with all the usual powers of the Prince of the Commonwealth. He was of a cautious disposition and at once made peace with the Parthians, and abandoned Trajan's new provinces of Assyria, Armenia, and Mesopotamia, turning them into semi-independent buffer-states under kings nominated by him, friendly to Rome and acceptable to their subjects. The Euphrates was again, and remained, the eastern boundary of the Empire. He quieted seditions in Egypt and Palestine and went to Rome, where he made himself popular by remitting vast arrears of unpaid taxes. After putting the Rhine-Danube frontier in a good state for defense he spent more than ten years in a general peregrination of the Empire, during which he visited every province. In Britain he had built a continuous wall, with a broad, deep ditch north of it, across the island from Solway Firth to near the mouth of the Tyne. This, for 290 years, kept all Roman Britain south of it safe from raids and forays from the Scotch Highlands and insured its great and increasing prosperity.

From A.D. 132 he had to deal with a general insurrection of the Jews in Palestine, Egypt, and Cyrenaica, which it required three years hard fighting to quell.

Hadrian died in A.D. 138, at the age of sixty-three, after a prosperous reign of twenty-two years.

He had adopted as his heir and successor Titus Aurelius Antoninus, known as Antoninus Pius because of his filial devotion to his adoptive father. The adoption was conditioned on Antoninus' adopting as his sons and naming as his heirs Lucius Commodus Verus and Marcus Annius Verus, the son and nephew of Lucius Ælius Verus, whom Hadrian had previously adopted and named as his heir, but who had died. When adopted by Antoninus Pius, Marcus Annius Verus took the name of Marcus Aurelius, by which we know him.

Antoninus Pius was Prince of the Roman Commonwealth from his fifty-second to his seventy-fifth year, from A.D. 138 to A.D. 161, twenty-three years, during which the entire Empire was at peace and was prosperous. The only fighting was along the Caucasus and along and beyond the Danube and Rhine, and to quell a brief insurrection in Britain, the suppression of which resulted in the extension of Roman occupation of the island to the Firths of Forth and Clyde, between which he had built a new frontier wall, held for more than half a century.

Upon his death Marcus Aurelius and Lucius Verus became co-Emperors and reigned conjointly for eight years, without any disagreement or friction between them, until Verus died in A.D. 169.

From A.D. 161 to 165 Verus had been in charge of a war against the Parthians, which he had waged by his deputies, while he revelled at Antioch. His deputies won the war handsomely, stormed and burned Ctesiphon and Seleucia, the two Parthian capitals on the Tigris, and captured Axtaxata, the capital of Armenia, where they established a king friendly to Rome.

The soldiers of Verus, returning victorious from this great war, spread all over the Empire the Great Pestilence of A.D. 165, 166, 167, which carried off half the population, chiefly in the cities and particularly the upper classes. From this catastrophe the Empire never made any approach to recovery.

This terrible calamity so weakened Rome that Aurelius with great difficulty succeeded in maintaining the Danube-Rhine frontier against incessant attacks of the Marcommani and Quadi. Also there was a formidable insurrection in Syria under Avidius Cassius, after quelling which, as the rebel had had the help of swarms of Arabs of the desert, Aurelius entered Rome in triumph in A.D. 176. After more wars along the Danube and Rhine, while they still continued, Marcus Aurelius died in A.D. 180, after a Principate of fourteen years.

For more than a century, since Vespasian had assumed the duties of the Principate, the Empire had been ably and carefully governed, for, while Domitian was malignant, suspicious, and inexorable toward the nobility of Rome, he administered public business competently. After his death, for eighty-four years, good government had been assured by the happy device of having each Emperor adopt as his heir the man considered by the Senate the most promising candidate.

Marcus Aurelius, unfortunately, had a son whom he loved and overrated. So he was succeeded in the Principate by Lucius Aurelius Antoninus Commodus, then just grown, whom we know as Commodus.

Commodus was even more misplaced on a throne than Nero, the all-round artist, for he was chiefly an all-round athlete. He spent most of his twelve years as Emperor at Rome, displaying feats of skill as a charioteer, wrestler, boxer, archer, beast-fighter and gladiator. Every department of governmental administration deteriorated under the venal mismanagement of a series of unworthy favorites to whom, as Prefects of the Prætorian Guard, he committed all the cares of the Empire.

He was murdered by his associates in dissipation during the year A.D. 192.

After the death of Commodus the Senate chose as Emperor Helvius Pertinax, an elderly general of admirable character. He was accepted by the soldiery, but within three months was murdered by his own Prætorian Guards, by whom he had come to be regarded as a niggardly martinet. Whereupon the Prætorians, largely because he promised them a handsome cash bonus, chose as Emperor Didius Julianus, a Senator, who was at once accepted by the Senate.

The news that the Prætorians had failed to protect Commodus, had murdered Pertinax, and, as their disfavorers phrased it, had practically put the imperial dignity up at auction and sold it to the highest bidder, so incensed the frontier garrisons that the army of the Danube at once urged their commander to lead them to Rome to avenge Pertinax and chastise the Guards. After some hesitation he accepted, was saluted Emperor, and promptly marched on Rome, where Didius Julianus was put to death before he arrived.

This new Emperor was Lucius Septimius Severus, the first man not of Roman stock to become Prince of the Roman Commonwealth, for he had been born near Leptis (modern Tripoli) in north Africa of mixed Berber and Carthaginian ancestry, Punic was his native language, and to the end of his days he spoke Latin with a strong Punic accent.

Severus disarmed and disbanded the disloyal Prætorians, executed the murderers of Pertinax, expelled in disgrace from military service all their accomplices, and created a new Prætorian Guard. Till then the Guards had been recruited from Italy and the most completely Romanized of the colonies, and Prætorians had been always full-blooded Romans from old families in those towns which had been longest constituted as Roman or Latin colonies. Severus mustered his new Guards from the pick of his frontier legionaries.

He moreover disqualified all persons born in Italy for military service, as a punishment on the whole population for the unreliability of the former corps of Imperial Guardsmen.

He also had much less respect for the Senate than any previous emperor, ignored its advice, and filled it up with capable men from all parts of the Empire.

Before Severus had reached Rome the Syrian legions had proclaimed Emperor their adored commander, Pescennius Niger. Between him and Severus there was fought a costly civil war with several bloody battles, before Niger was finally defeated and killed in Asia Minor.

Severus had yet to dispose of a second rival, Clodius Albinus, who had been proclaimed Emperor by the legions in Britain, and whom he had at first accepted as his heir. But while Severus was occupied in the East, Albinus mobilized all available troops and the two clashed in A.D. 197 near Lyons in a terrific and bloody battle.

Thereafter Severus was Emperor for fourteen years, during which the Commonwealth and the Empire prospered.

He twice crossed the Euphrates, in A.D. 195 and 198, and showed himself a brilliant general. In 195 he overran and reannexed Mesopotamia. In 198 he annihilated the Parthian Empire, occupied, unopposed, Babylon and their capital, Seleucia, and stormed and sacked their other capital, Ctesiphon.

Ten years later he went to Britain, where he abandoned the northern province of Valentia, between Hadrian's wall from the Solway to the Tyne and the northern wall of Antoninus Pius from the Firth of Clyde to the Firth of Forth, and built a mighty wall just north of Hadrian's wall, which wall, named after him the Wall of Severus, protected Roman Britain, more populous and prosperous than England till the days of Queen Anne, for two long centuries.

He died at York in A.D. 211.

Severus was no statesman. Byzantium had sided with Pescennius Niger and held out even after his death. Severus took the city by storm and pettishly destroyed it. Now it had been sound policy for Rome to destroy alien foreign cities which had been treacherous or had insulted Roman envoys. The lesson that treason to Rome was injudicious and that Roman envoys must be respected was worth while. But the destruction of Byzantium by Severus taught no lesson except that it did not pay to side with the loser when two generals were competing for the Principate, and everybody knew that already and was eager to back the winner. What was more, Byzantium was one of the most important and vital of the frontier fortresses of the Empire and its demolition opened the Mediterranean to the calamitous irruptions of vast fleets of Gothic pirates half a century later.

The decline of the Roman Empire began before the Principate of Septimius Severus, but was not noticeable till after his time. From his death in A.D. 211 to the vanishing of the last vestiges of Roman Imperial rule in western Europe in 476 A.D. 265 years elapsed. During this period there were fifty-six acknowledged emperors, of whom twenty-seven were murdered, mostly by their guards or legionaries, and seven abdicated. There were also thirty-eight unsuccessful pretenders to the Empire, all of whom died violent deaths. Between the various aspirants to the Principate there were fought fifty-two civil wars.

For our purposes there is no use in going into the details of the precarious reigns of half-emperors and quarter-emperors. We shall mention only those important for us.

During the six years' Principate of the brutal and extravagant son of Severus, known to us by his nickname of Caracalla, Roman citizenship was conferred on all inhabitants of all the provinces of the Empire.

From 222 to 235 A.D. Severus Alexander governed the Empire well.

Aurelian, during his brief reign of barely four years, A.D. 270-275, measurably restored the power of Rome. He abandoned the province of Dacia which Trajan had conquered and annexed 160 years before and which had filled up with Roman colonists and prospered greatly for more than a century. From Aurelian's time the Danube was again the northern boundary of the Empire. From Wales to the Euphrates, from the Danube and Rhine to the cataracts of the Nile, Aurelian established peace and justice.

Recognizing the weakness of the Roman Commonwealth and the probability, even certainty, of serious invasions, he girdled Rome with fortifications enclosing as much as possible of its vast extent, fortifications which protected the city for 135 years.

Augustus had sedulously masked his absolute power by preserving the forms of the obsolete republic and by leaving to the Senate as much authority as was consistent with the safety of newly-annexed provinces and the Empire's frontiers. Most successors of Augustus had honored the Senate, though the powers of the Emperor inevitably and steadily increased and the authority, prestige, and importance of the Senate concomitantly waned.

Trajan, Hadrian, and Antoninus Pius had made every effort to strengthen the Senate and utilize it to relieve the Emperor of the crushing burden of his duties, and with much success.

Septimius Severus, being un-Roman by race and a soldier and nothing else by training, ignored the Senate, and his successors followed him and outdid him.

In A.D. 284, 270 years after the death of Augustus and 73 years after the death of Septimius Severus, the Principate was assumed by Diocletian, who apparently began life as a slave, certainly on a very low social plane. He had risen from the ranks in the army and was a capable general. But he was a Dalmatian, seemingly without any Roman blood, and he had Asiatic instincts as to government. He regarded anything which impaired or qualified the autocracy of the Emperors of Rome as a nuisance to them and as detriment to the Commonwealth and its Empire. He was in Rome only seldom and briefly. Mostly he resided at Nicomedia in Asia Minor, which had become the most important city near the Bosporus after the destruction of Byzantium by Septimius Severus. From there he completely reconstructed the entire Empire and established wholly new administrative divisions.

He reorganized the army and all the departments of the government and created a sort of Oriental despotism, strongly centralized.

He organized about him a court like that of the Shahs of Persia, wore silk robes, jewelled regalia, and an imperial crown. All persons admitted to audience with him prostrated themselves before him.

He made a belated attempt to extirpate Christianity, the most general, most severe and most notable of the persecutions of the Christians.

After he had ruled the Roman world for twenty-one years he abdicated in A.D. 305.

Within a very few years Constantine had adopted Christianity. After being a colleague of Diocletian and after wars with other colleagues and ex-colleagues he became sole emperor in A.D. 323 and lived fourteen years longer.

Gratian, who was Emperor from A.D. 367 to A.D. 383, and Theodosius, who was Emperor from 379 to 395, suppressed Paganism in A.D. 381, and their persecution of the Pagans outdid all the actual Pagan persecutions of the Christians, collectively and added together.

Throughout the two and a half centuries from 241 B.C. to A.D. 14 the Romans were building their Empire, from A.D. 14 to A.D. 117 they were extending and consolidating it. The acme of its prosperity lasted from A.D. 98 to A.D. 164. After A.D. 217 Roman power weakened and prosperity declined, but the Empire was fairly well maintained until A.D. 378. After A.D. 381 it rapidly crumbled and had evaporated by A.D. 476.

The Roman Empire, in the largest view, may be evaluated as resistance by the Mediterranean world, successful for over seven and a half centuries, to the increasing pressure from the populations of the plains, grass lands and steppes of the interior of the Great Continent, unsettled by the progressive desiccation of their native soil.

CHAPTER XV

ROME'S ACHIEVEMENT

ROME'S most conspicuous achievement was to win wars by vigor in preparation, judgment in attack, valor in battle, tenacity after defeat, and justice after victory.

The Tatars under Jenghiz Khan and Tamerlane could win battles and campaigns, and did. They expressed their joy after victories by pinioning prisoners, burying them up to the neck, and then bashing out their brains by bowling stone balls or spheroidal rocks at these living ninepins. Also they erected huge cairns of newly severed heads or of skulls.

The Assyrians won battles and campaigns. Their delight was to peg out their warrior prisoners, stripped naked and face down, each ankle and wrist lashed to a tent pin, and when they had them fast and helpless, to split their skins down the spine from nape to crotch and flay them at leisure, as hunters with us take the pelt off a dead bear. A strong man flayed, except head, hands, and feet, might be two days and nights before death released him, in agony in the bitter night wind or under the scorching Arabian sun, with the blow-flies buzzing over him till he was half hidden under writhing maggots.

The Carthaginians won battles and campaigns and gloated at rows of stakes or crosses, each supporting an impaled or crucified prisoner.

There never existed conquerors more efficient than the Turks from 1365 to 1665. They won battle after battle, campaign after campaign, war after war. Resistance they overwhelmed. All surviving non-Mohammedan inhabitants of subjugated regions they, as had the Saracens before them, dubbed "ra'iyah," which Arabic word means "flock," "herd," "human cattle"; and they reduced them to the condition of peasant serfs. Their human cattle they dealt with as ranchers of early days in Argentina or in our West dealt with their semiwild herds, as creatures to be mostly let alone and left to themselves except at round-ups. The Turks concerned themselves not at all about their subject populations, provided they hatched no insurrections, paid their taxes or tributes in coin or in kind, and handed over yearly their allotted quota of healthy male children not too young to thrive when separated from their mothers, to be brought up as Mohammedans and made into Janizaries.

Far otherwise was it with the Romans. After genuine submission they treated subject populations not merely fairly, but with sedulous care for their material and social welfare. Roman taxation was very light and always adjusted to the conditions of agriculture, woodcutting, mining, fisheries, or other productive activities of the population taxed or paying tribute.

The relief from local warfare afforded by subjection to Rome enormously increased the productivity of any district annexed, and the cost of provincial administration by a Roman proconsul or proprætor was but a small fraction of the expense of any form of local government any conquered region had ever had before the Romans acquired it. Except as to racial pride, every subjugated population was better off, as part of Rome's Empire, than it had ever been previously.

Probably no soldiery on earth was ever so acutely dreaded by adversaries as were the Romans. They did not paint their faces, nor stick feathers in their hair, nor jump up and down and whoop, nor chant what they meant to do to their victims. They were either married farmers or young men dumbly eager to marry and settle down to farming. Campaigning they took as a matter of course, and, as everybody had to campaign, nobody grumbled. But, though capable, even when laden with a sixty-five-pound outfit, of marching fifteen miles day after day, of ditch digging for hours after each march, and of standing a watch four nights out of each five, and still keeping fit, yet they did not enjoy it any more than we should. Campaigning was a nuisance to be gotten through with so as to get back home. Winning battles was the visible means of getting back home. Finding and killing enemies was their vocation. When they found the enemy they went out to kill with the impersonal efficiency of a modern mowing machine harvesting alfalfa. Usually they were no more angry with their adversaries than a boy weeding a garden is wrathful at the weeds.

There were the enemy to be killed and they went about it in a matter-of-fact, unemotional, grim, businesslike manner. The even, steady, deliberate, and confident advance of a Roman battle line always awed their antagonists and often dazed them. The unexcited thoroughness with which they abolished resistance had in it something uncanny, even superhuman.

Once resistance was at an end they were mostly the reverse of ferocious. The rank and file generally obeyed their officers, spared their prisoners of military age, refrained from looting and burning, and were kind to the population at large.

If indignant at what they considered treachery, they were quite capable of butchering all fugitives, even ladies and their little daughters, as Cæsar's men did after their defeat of the Germans under Ariovistus in 58 B.C., or of slaughtering some four hundred thousand human beings in one morning, as the same army did three years later to the Usipetes and Tencteri. If infuriated by their hardships during an obstinate resistance, they took it as a matter of course to massacre the inhabitants of a captured city, to the last infant, as the same army did at Avaricum in 52 B.C.

But habitually, once the campaign was over, the survivors were well treated. Cæsar mildly ordered the remnants of the Helvetians to return to Switzerland, rebuild their burnt farmsteads, villages, and towns, and settle down to farming, and he saw to it that their neighbors doled out to them the minimum of grain necessary for seed and to keep them alive until their next crop was harvested.

The Romans, not only the Senators and nobles, but the commonalty, the townsfolk, the rustics, the legionaries, had an hereditary inborn feeling that there were universal principles of equity applicable to all men of all races. They dealt with beaten foemen according to their innate instincts of equity and, in general, won the respect and esteem of subject peoples everywhere at all periods of their domination.

Virgil, in setting forth the high destiny of Romans in line 853 of the Sixth Book of the Æneid, uses the words, *"Parcere subjectis et debellare superbis*" ("To spare those made subjects and to war down the haughty").

As a Roman characteristic he puts clemency toward the conquered even before vanquishing the insolent. Any people felt to be potentially dangerous to the Roman Commonwealth and its Empire was ruthlessly annihilated. Others besides the Carthaginians might be cited as examples, and Carthage was not the only city utterly wiped out as a measure of prudence for the future. But such cases were rare and few in comparison with the many instances of Roman clemency.

Whether held in check by colonies in their chief towns or accepted as allies, conquered populations mostly developed a heartfelt and abiding loyalty to the Roman Commonwealth. Most of the conquered Italians were steadfast to Rome, for all of Hannibal's victories and wily cajoleries. This was no accident, but the miraculous effect of their perhaps reluctant and unwilling, but certainly general and inevitable, recognition of the fact that they were not only no worse treated than they deserved and better treated than they had any right or reason to expect, but that the Romans had standards to which they conformed as to what was proper toward even their most hostile adversaries, and that these standards were fair and rational. Creating such a state of mind among populations long their foemen, beaten only after hard fighting, and instilling it into them and their descendants, was perhaps Rome's greatest achievement.

Subjects, tributaries, and allies, in their degree, were generally well treated and mostly prospered under Roman rule, government, domination, or suzerainty.

Many recent histories of Rome write glibly of Roman maladministration. It may be stated categorically that Roman maladministration was so unusual that what Roman maladministration did occur was a negligible percentage of all Roman administration.

The most glaring instance of misgovernment of a Roman province was, of course, Sicily under Verres as proprætor as depicted in Cicero's five orations against Verres, never delivered, but published as prepared for delivery and as they would have been delivered had Verres stood trial. We may be quite sure that Cicero, as the best lawyer alive, made therein no statement which he could not have proven to the prospective jury by unimpeachable evidence. But we should be vividly aware that Cicero, as a lawyer out to win a case, omitted everything that might have been cited to Verres's credit and blackened everything that could be cited against him. Reading these orations in the light afforded by comparing Burke's attacks on Warren Hastings with what we know of the magnificent competence of his conduct of affairs in Hindustan, we may very well conclude that while the Sicilians were indubitably robbed and ill treated by Verres, even he may have conferred on them great benefits in many respects, carefully kept out of sight by Cicero.

Even Verres was not so ruinous as Agathocles or Hamilcar Barca before him, or as Gaiseric or Richard Cœur de Lion after him.

The Romans, in fact, governed Sicily far better than their predecessors the Greeks and Carthaginians, or their successors the Vandals, the Saracens, and the Normans.

So of all the other provinces. Sardinia and Corsica were semisavage islands until the Romans acquired them. When under Roman governors they prospered and throve for more than six centuries. Since A.D. 439 it was not until long after Corsica was acquired by France in 1768 that the island was as well governed as under the Romans, nor did conditions in Sardinia again become comparable to those under Roman domination until after 1862.

Government did not exist in Spain before the Romans introduced it. There was nothing there before them except internecine strife. And never, since the Roman power collapsed, has the Iberian Peninsula been so populous, prosperous, and well governed as it was under Roman rule.

Greece, Macedonia, Thrace, Asia Minor, Cyprus, Syria, Palestine, and the other lands which Rome wrested from the descendants of Alexander's successors were never, while independent communities or while kingdoms under Greek dynasties, as prosperous, populous, happy, and well governed as they became under the Romans, especially from 27 B.C. to A.D. 193. Nor have they ever been as well governed since.

Besides other proofs too numerous to be cited here, the most notable are three outstanding occurrences of identical character.

In 133 B.C. Attalus III, King of Pergamum in western Asia Minor, died, leaving no heirs. He bequeathed his kingdom to the Roman Commonwealth on the ground that his people would be better off as subjects of Rome than if independent, and were certain to be better governed than they could hope to be by any native of his realm.

Thirty-seven years later, in 96 B.C., Ptolemy Apion, King of Cyrene in north Africa, on the coast of the Mediterranean west of Egypt, made a will of like tenure.

And in 74 B.C., fifty-nine years after the death of Attalus and twenty-two after the death of Ptolemy Apion, Nicomedes Philopator, King of Bithynia in northwestern Asia Minor, did precisely what Attalus and Ptolemy had done, and for like reasons.

These three wills of earnest and conscientious rulers solicitous for the welfare of their subjects prove not only that Roman provincial administration was admired by non-Romans, but also that the results of the first and second bequests were happy, as otherwise Nicomedes would not have imitated Attalus.

If Roman provincial administration be compared with some theoretical ideal of provincial administration, it is easy to make out a horrifying list of Roman shortcomings, errors, blunders, and outrages. But if, on the other hand, Roman provincial administration is compared with the actual management of conquered territory and subject populations by any other dominant race, Roman provincial administration outshines almost all.

In fact, in general, a Roman provincial governor was a marvel and a prodigy to alien races and peoples. They were used to government by caprice of an individual despot or of the leaders of a dominant oligarchy. A Roman proconsul or propraetor was a novelty, was a ruler of a kind of which they could not have conceived, was a portent.

Be it admitted, parenthetically, that some provincial governors were incompetent, some few even cowardly, some indifferent to their duties, some merely eager to enrich themselves, some venal and prone to give judgments in civil or criminal cases for gain rather than according to the facts, some brutal, some cruel, some even malignant; yet all such cases together were a very small percentage of the Roman provincial governors at any one time and an insignificant fraction of all Roman provincial governors of all periods.

Mostly, Roman provincials found themselves confronted by a man who put general equity and fairness first, Roman customs, laws, and precedents second, advantage for the Roman Commonwealth third, and self-interest only after these. At first most localities were incredulous and amazed. Later they came to realize that a Roman governor could never be defied with impunity, that his edicts could seldom be evaded, that he was ruthless in avenging an affront, relentless in pursuit of evildoers, stern to criminals, open-minded to evidence from both sides in any suit in court, and what was much more, that every Roman governor had approximately the same standards as to what was incumbent on him and that he would not swerve from what he conceived to be his duty for any consideration of personal peril or personal advantage. Moreover, that each governor, to a great degree, continued his predecessor's methods.

(To interject a quotation: "As witness let us appeal to the high character, the sincere kindliness, the sense of serious accountability, which mark the Roman official in the somewhat hostile documents of the New Testament."—F. W. Bussell. *The Roman Empire:* Vol. I, page 31.)

Gradually there grew up throughout the Empire the conception of a typical Roman governor as a man hard-headed and clear-headed, who knew what he wanted done and how to get it done, well-intentioned, impartial, grimly ruthless towards rebels or conspirators, mild when not affronted, sympathetic to plain folk in trouble, a man who could not be intimidated, wheedled, fooled, or bribed, who felt keenly his responsibilities towards the population under his charge and yet more keenly his duty to the Roman Commonwealth.

There was something awe-inspiring in dealing, through such men, with the vast, pervasive, impersonal, sustained, invincible power of the Senate and People of Rome.

The bias of most modern writers on the Romans has generally blinded them to the fact that not the Roman Commonwealth, but the Roman Empire, was the great exploit of the Romans and that the Empire was a benefit not only to the Romans who ruled it, but to the provincials who were ruled chiefly because it was an Empire, because the Romans gave orders and the provincials obeyed orders.

Pax Romana, Roman peace, the kind of peace which the Romans created and maintained, has usually been considered their greatest exploit, and it was achieved by the spread and maintenance of their Empire. By peace the Romans meant that pacified races, nations, or communities had ceased to fight or to try to fight either the Romans or each other. Wherever a Roman province was organized Pax Romana existed on land. After Pompey's suppression of piracy in 67 B.C. the entire Mediterranean was adequately policed until the Goths forced the Hellespont in A.D. 263, during the troubled reign of the Emperor Gallienus, a period of over three centuries.

Throughout the more than three and a quarter centuries between A.D. 43 and A. D. 375 the Romans maintained peace and created and conserved prosperity from the Euphrates to Anglesea, from the Rhine, Danube, and Caucasus to the Cataracts of the Nile.

They had brought about peace over most of this vast expanse of territory as early as 61 B.C. and they protected much of it until as late as A.D. 442, when the Vandals' war fleet swept the Mediterranean and ended maritime traffic.

And Pax Romana was created and maintained by an amazingly small military establishment. Proofs of this might be demonstrated in many ways, but one is enough. Under Trajan the Empire attained its greatest extent and the Commonwealth its acme of prosperity. In A.D. 117 he was succeeded by Hadrian, who was fond of putting aside his dignity and enjoying informal jollities with his cronies, many of whom were scholars, and with them he conversed, chatted, and disputed at such times almost on a footing of equality.

He disagreed with the grammarian Favorinus as to a word, and the two had an argument about it in which Hadrian had the best of him.

Favorinus was afterward twitted by his friends for having argued weakly, and retorted that they were giving him bad advice in suggesting that he ought to argue vigorously against a man who had thirty legions.

Manifestly, thirty legions was the normal army of the Empire, for, to drive his point home, Favorinus was certain to emphasize Hadrian's power by naming the largest number of soldiers he could truthfully allege.

As a legion was normally of about 5,000 effectives with their officers, this proves that the Roman Commonwealth maintained peace throughout its extensive possessions with a maximum military establishment of 150,000 infantry privates and their quota of officers, engineers, artillery, cavalry, and auxiliaries.

By estimating the auxiliaries as equalling in numbers the Roman citizens who manned the legions, not a few writers have calculated the normal strength of the Roman Imperial army at 300,000.

Some have even reckoned each legion at 6,000 Romans, taking its full roster as equivalent to its effective fighting strength, which never, in fact, is the case with any military force in actual warfare or even while on garrison duty. This fantastic notion leads them to compute the normal Roman army of the Empire as 372,000 men of all arms.

Even this inflated overestimate, if true, would still leave us amazed at the efficiency of Roman organization and the quality of Rome's fighters.

It can safely be asserted that before Rome's Empire was created and since it vanished, there has not been a day when fewer than 3,000,000 men have been under arms in that same area of the earth's surface; and little of it has, in the interval, ever enjoyed such peace as the Roman Emperors gave it.

This may convey some inkling of what miracles Roman efficiency could achieve. To have created and maintained such peace and prosperity over such a vast region for so long with so trifling a total of men under arms was a feat surpassing anything recorded of any other people.

True to their ancestral custom of relying more on the spade than sword or spear for winning wars and maintaining peace, the Romans protected their northern frontier by that stupendous fortification called the *Limes* beyond the upper reaches of the Danube and Rhine.

It extended more than 350 miles from the east bank of the Rhine near Cologne to across from Ratisbon (Regensberg) on the Danube. The details of this gigantic series of protective defenses do not concern us.

But as conveying some inkling of Roman thoroughness, it is worth while to particularize as to the Wall of Septimius Severus across Britain from the Tyne to the Solway, seventy-three miles, just north of the fortification constructed there under Hadrian more than half a century before.

The continuous wall was of large blocks of stone, massive, eight feet thick and sixteen feet high, flanked northward by a fosse ten feet deep and forty feet broad, so that any attacking Pict or Scot in the fosse was twenty-six feet below the Roman defenders. Behind the wall, to southward, ran a military highway twenty feet wide and stone paved. All along, barely one hundred yards apart, were watch towers; about a mile apart were castles fifty feet square; every four miles was a rectangular camp, stone-walled and a formidable fortress.

Throughout their Empire, from the organization of Sicily as their first province in 241 B.C. to the accession of Caracalla in A.D. 211, a period of more than four and a half centuries, the Romans, in general, by force of instinct, habit, and intention combined and working together, held to their guiding principle of doing as little governing as possible and leaving their allies, tributaries, subjects, provincials, and colonists as much as possible to their own devices. At all times and in all places the Senate, the consuls, all officials, the emperors, the generals, the governors, and all their subordinates, were ceaselessly on the lookout for symptoms of insurrection, sedition, conspiracy, or disaffection. Activities or behavior likely to lead to any of these or causing any suspicion of such perils to the Commonwealth and Empire were peremptorily suppressed or severely reprimanded. The Romans were not gentle when alarmed. Their habitual method, for instance, for dealing with riots and diminishing the tendency towards rioting was for their soldiery to attack the brawlers and massacre them indiscriminately until the fighting ceased and the throngs vanished. Whereafter, following a cool and impartial investigation, the ringleaders or persons held accountable for the disturbance, usually on both sides of the riot, were, as a mere matter of course, publicly crucified as a conspicuous warning to all and sundry. But whatever seemed to have in it no potentiality of danger to Roman supremacy was freely permitted. In some form, every city, every town, and many districts and villages had genuine local self-government, and there existed in the Empire at its acme an amazing diversity of local religious cults, customs, usages, and laws, with which the Romans never interfered or thought of interfering. They respected and even deferred to local religious peculiarities and national traditions, and, in so far as they understood them, avoided contravening racial prejudices.

When Rome's Empire was at its height of prosperity and most extensive there existed, south of the Rhine, Danube, and Caucasus, from the Euphrates on the east to Anglesea on the west, as far south as the Cataracts of the Nile, no frontiers.

There were no governmental obstacles to travel and traffic such as our modern custom houses and import duties. Imperial couriers and officials journeying on government business were regularly provided with a *diploma,* a sort of passport which entitled them to preferential treatment as to changes of horses, lodgings, meals, assistance of all kinds, and other aids to rapid travel. Persons of importance, if they possessed enough influence, found it advantageous to procure for themselves such official diplomas to expedite their journeys. But while a diploma was a convenience, and was always honored on presentation, none was required or expected, nor was there ever any enactment enjoining travellers to have passports or forbidding travel without them.

Anyone domiciled within the Empire could set out for any destination within it without hindrance or question. As long as a traveller paid the very moderate customary charges for food and lodging, progress was not interfered with.

Because of the never ceasing alertness of the emperors and their deputies as to anything which actually or potentially menaced the Emperor, his authority, supremacy, and tenure, or the welfare of the Commonwealth, because of the promptness with which all persons even suspected of treasonable intentions were pounced upon and abolished, much has been written about the despotism of the Roman Emperors and little about the genuine freedom of most of their subjects.

During the six hundred years of its domination, the Roman Senate enacted fewer than two hundred laws affecting personal conduct and behavior. The Emperors, down to the accession of Caracalla, were equally sparing in this regard.

From the accession of Tiberius in A.D. 14 to the accession of Caracalla in A.D. 211 all free persons born within the Empire were free to please themselves as to what they ate or drank, according to their abilities to pay for what they craved.

Mating was a matter largely ignored by the government and mostly left to the individuals or families concerned.

Everyone was free to worship according to any racial tradition, national custom, family habit, just as each had been brought up, following the usages of any cult.

Any inhabitant of any part of the Empire might go anywhere, and anywhere had the right to buy and sell, lease or buy a house or piece of land or estate, settle, and marry.

Persons who aroused no suspicion of being dangerous to the government were never interfered with if they did not misbehave according to local expectations as to conduct.

The material achievements of Rome involved the conquest of a vast expanse of territory, extending northward to the Rhine and Danube and even, in places, beyond both; to the Caucasus and Euphrates, northeastward and eastward; to the Arabian desert, the Cataracts of the Nile, and the Sahara southward; and westward to the Atlantic Ocean, including Great Britain to the Firths of Forth and Clyde.

Throughout this domain Rome planted many hundred colonies.

In the early days from 328 B.C. to 83 B.C., in the times of Sulla, a Roman colony, as has been set forth in Chapter VII, was practically a resident, self-perpetuating garrison in a district subjugated but not regarded as trustworthy.

Whether the Roman or Latin colonists built a new town or took possession of an entire conquered town and all its territory, or, as was most usual, received permanent possession of the city government and of one-third of the area within the town walls and one-third of its farm lands, pasture lands and woodlands, they and their descendants became a dominant aristocracy among the descendants of the former townsfolk or of any later immigrants.

After Sulla rewarded his faithful soldiers by allotting to them as colonists portions of the land of those Italian towns which had sided with the Marians, even, in some cases, entire towns with all their territory, this became a normal method of providing for old soldiers who had earned an honorable discharge in civil war and of chastising recalcitrant communities which had taken the losing side. Such colonies were numerously founded up to the pacification of the Commonwealth by Augustus, and occasionally after later civil wars.

After the accession of Tiberius in A.D. 14 colonies were mostly of two kinds. There were actual military garrison towns laid out and fortified at strategic points along and near the frontiers of the Empire. Besides, in regions thinly populated, depopulated, or inviting to Roman settlers, as in Dacia after Trajan's conquest of it, colonies were a sort of joint-stock investment enterprise. The nature of the approved district and its possibilities as to farming, stock-raising, wood-cutting, mining and what else were carefully canvassed. It was calculated beforehand how many persons the colony would need in each occupation, as farmers, herdsmen, millers, bakers, tanners, saddlers, carpenters, smiths, masons, and otherwise and the determined number was arranged for in advance, so that the colony was complete and functioned smoothly even before the temporary ditch, earthwork, and stockade about it could be replaced by its permanent stone city walls, towers, gateway towers, gate-houses, and wide and deep dry moat.

Beginning as early as 312 B.C., the Romans surveyed, laid out, graded, and built roads connecting Rome with her colonies, subject towns, and allied cities. No such roads had ever been seen on earth before and no better have been laid since.

Roman roads were approximately fourteen and one-half feet wide and were made lasting by skillfully devised foundations of stone and concrete, usually amazingly thick. In road making the Romans heaped up across valleys and hollows long embankments, often of impressive height; they clove deep cuts through hills; they dug or hewed roadways out of mountain sides, and they bridged countless rivers, streams, and gorges, usually with arches of stone, brick, or concrete.

For seven centuries Roman road-building activity never ceased as to either maintenance or new construction. Altogether, they built fully 350,000 miles of their magnificent highways.

The outcome was, at the height of the Empire's prosperity, between A.D. 69 and A.D. 180, and even on until A.D. 275 or later, a network of roads by which anyone might journey in any direction with ease and comfort never before known anywhere in this world.

These roads connected the hundreds of cities and the many thousands of walled towns which housed the bulk of the Empire's population. Each had its aqueducts and sewers, its paved streets, its public square and basilicas.

Nothing in our modern world corresponds to the countless basilicas of the Greco-Roman cities. In origin a basilica was an oblong hall for the holding of law courts, large enough to accommodate not only the magistrate, his apparitors, the litigants, and their advocates and witnesses, but also to afford abundant space for the usual gathering of onlookers. Greco-Roman architects vied with each other in devising means for creating basilicas as large as possible. They were used not only as law courts, but as merchants' exchanges and as places of assembly for any gathering not so large as to require a public square to accommodate it. As purposive assemblies, merchants' exchanges and lawsuits did not occupy any basilica at every hour of every day, basilicas came to be natural resorts of idlers and persons at leisure and were utilized as places in which to pass the time. By the accession of Trajan every Roman town had its basilica, most had more than one, cities had many, and a basilica was practically a walled and roofed public square, well lighted, adequately protected, according to the habits of those days, against snow and rain, wind and weather, heat and cold, and therefore satisfactorily comfortable almost every day in the year. During the Empire's prosperity basilicas were a convenience that had come to be felt as a necessity of life.

The inhabitants of the Greco-Roman world passed much less of their time indoors than we, and much more in the open air. From the early period of the development of Greek civilization every town had at least one colonnade where the townfolk might transact business, discuss news and politics, chat and idle, sheltered from the rain, wind, or sun, and the vogue of porticoes, as such colonnades were called by the Romans, antedated the similar vogue of basilicas.

As the fashion took and became universal in the Greek world, all sorts of variations of plan were tried out. Usually, the colonnade faced so as to receive the maximum of sunlight for most days of the year. This made it comfortable, for people of their habits, almost all winter. When a town had two or more colonnades, they often faced different ways, so that they would afford shelter from rain at all times, and from cold winds, or from hot sun, according to the season of the year.

Often colonnades were built on all four sides of an open square, as in mediæval cloisters later, so that frequenters of them could be assured of comfort in any weather at any time of year, congregating on the shady or breezy side in summer and on the sunny or sheltered side in winter.

Rome itself, at the acme of its glory, was gridironed by a network of colonnades under which anyone could walk for miles, even as far as two miles in one straight line.

A dozen of Rome's larger porticoes occupied, with their enclosed garden-garths or courtyards, over 100,000 square yards and protected fully 25,000 square yards from sun and rain. In proportion to their population and wealth all other Roman towns and cities were almost as lavishly provided with these useful and sensible public resorts.

Concomitantly with the possession of an adequate sewerage system and an abundant and unfailing water-supply from judiciously constructed aqueducts every Greco-Roman city and town was blessed with many public baths.

During the period of the germination and burgeoning of the Mediterranean civilization soap was unknown. The populations of the Mediterranean world were of a cleanly disposition and, not yet having learned how to saponify the greasy film on a dirty human body, they steamed or sweated themselves clean. The primitive apparatus consisted of a small cell, barely large enough to accommodate the bather, a jar of water, a dipper, and a pan of pebbles heated red hot over a brazier and carried into the cell by a slave, who closed the door on the naked bather, who then poured a dipper of water on the pebbles and was at once enveloped in steam, and repeated the process until steamed enough.

Often the bather stood, often sat on a stool. Various devices, usually a hole in the door, fitting the bather's face, saved the bather from suffocation in the steam. Out of these beginnings developed countless cheap bath houses of the Roman Empire, to which, in every town, any man or woman could resort for a fee absurdly trifling and enjoy and be refreshed by a cold shower, a cold plunge, a tepid shower, a tepid plunge, a steam bath (what we call a Russian bath), a hot, dry, sweat bath (what we call a Turkish bath), or any combination of these in any order preferred.

Out of these in turn developed the Roman Thermæ (hot baths), which were institutions more or less analogous to our country clubs, casinos, and suchlike, places where the aristocracy of a town or city gathered for pleasure, diversion, and amusement, bathing being a pleasure mightily relished by the upper classes.

In the Thermæ of Rome, and to a lesser degree in those of Capua, Aquileia, Roman Carthage, and other cities of the Empire, and in thousands of towns, the conveniences of the ordinary public baths were afforded on a large scale and with every luxurious concomitant which ingenuity could invent. There were hosts of slave attendants, and bathers were massaged and otherwise catered to in every conceivable manner.

Every well-to-do town had its amphitheatre for gladiatorial exhibitions, beast-fights, and like spectacles, its circus or hippodrome for horse-races, its theatre for performances of dramas; every Greek town had its stadium for the viewing of athletic contests and competitions and its odeon for audiences eager to listen to the public declamations, lectures, readings from the poets, recitations from memory of celebrated poems, and extempore composition of poems, in all of which the Greeks took endless delight.

From soon after the pacification of the Mediterranean world effected by Augustus shortly after the battle of Actium in 31 B.C. until after the death of Aurelian in A.D. 275, except when interfered with by civil wars, famous lecturers, declaimers, and readers travelled all over the Empire—at the acme of its prosperity from Aquæ Sextiæ (Bath) and Eboracum (York) in Britain, to Nisibis in Mesopotamia—enchanting enthusiastic audiences and growing wealthy on their gains. Similarly, troupes of tragic actors, what we should call grand-opera companies, gave performances not only in Greece, Asia Minor, and Sicily, but also in Africa (Tunisia), Gaul, Egypt, and even beyond the limits of the Empire in the Greek or semi-Greek cities of the Bosporani, north of the Black Sea in the Crimea and east of it, and in the semi-Greek cities of the Parthian Empire.

Libraries, picture galleries, museums of curiosities and oddities, usually created and endowed by public-spirited men of wealth, abounded in Italy and in Greek lands, and were universal even to Britain, Dacia (Hungary), and Mauretania (Morocco), and often attached to the public porticoes.

The fashion of decorating temples, public buildings, public squares, streets and even private houses with life-size statues of loved or admired persons who deserved acclaim in life or remembrance after death spread from Greece into Italy and later all over the Empire. It is impossible for us to conceive of the universality of the custom, of the infinite number of statues and groups of statuary which adorned the cities and towns of the Empire, or of the general appreciation and admiration of them by the townsfolk who took pride in them and in dwelling in a city fittingly ornamented by such works of art. There might be thousands of out-of-door statues in any small town.

Idolatry means the cherishing of images. Not only in religion, but in life at large, the pagans of the Greco-Roman civilization were idolaters. They cherished images. From early times the makers of statues of the gods and the makers of statues of human-beings (two trades regarded as quite distinct) were among the busiest and best paid artisans throughout the Greek world. One practitioner at least of each of the two branches of the statue-making art was to be found in every Greek city, even in most small towns.

The Etruscans acquired the habit from the Greeks or improved their native art by adopting Greek methods. The Romans imitated the Etruscans and Greeks. Everyone who could afford it had made a statuette or statue of every beloved kinsman. Poor folk had little figurines of fig-wood or willow-wood, the cheapest materials. Others could afford terra-cotta. The well-to-do had life-size statues of terra-cotta, marble, or bronze. Opulence vaunted itself in life-size statues of silver or of gold. From the mingled influences of private and public use of statues resulted their universal vogue. The mere artisanship of the earlier period burgeoned into an art of marvellous originality, astonishing good taste, exquisite delicacy, and bewildering variety. This art did not lose its momentum until after the death of Domitian.

Magnificent as was the material achievement of Rome, of the Romans and of their Commonwealth and Empire, their immaterial and spiritual achievements were still more marvellous and amazing.

The Romans were a hard-headed, level-headed, and practical breed, singularly free from self-deceptions or from any tendency toward them. They kept both feet on the ground and their heads out of the clouds.

From first to last, by instinct and intuition, they conceived of a government as an organization for diminishing the number of homicides within the domain controlled by it, and kept this cardinal aim constantly in view. Prolongation and safeguarding of the lives of Roman citizens, their wives and children and slaves, and of their allies, tributaries, and subjects, by protecting them from the horrors of invasion by external enemies, was the paramount concern of the Roman Senate and People and of their Emperors at all periods of their domination.

Next after that came the suppression of insurrections, revolts, conspiracies, and plots, the squelching of riots, and the prevention of banditry and brigandage.

As creators and maintainers of a government chiefly devoted to the protection of life and property and the dispensing of even-handed justice, the Romans came nearer to ideal success than had any of their predecessors.

And since their day they have seldom been surpassed and not often equaled.

In evoking among communities and races under their sway feelings of hearty acquiescence in Roman supremacy and of enduring loyalty to Roman leadership they outdid any suzerains before or after them.

It has often been stated that the Romans, after acquiring control of the Mediterranean world, lived in affluence and luxury on the profits of mere robbery and extortion; that Rome imported everything and exported nothing.

Certainly Rome was not, like Antioch, Alexandria, or Capua, a city with a multitude of skilled artists and artisans producing vast quantities of jewelry, cutlery, pottery, statuary, embroideries, tapestries, carpets, textiles, and other valuables, the export of which brought in, as a return for their skill and labor, sums many times exceeding the cost of the materials imported and worked up into their output. Roman artisans never produced a tithe of what Rome herself consumed.

Into Rome, up the Tiber to her quays, or into Ostia or Puteoli and thence overland by road, came wheat, other cereals, wine, and olive oil from wherever they were produced in quantity, whether in Spain, Sardinia, Sicily, Africa from the Atlantic Ocean to Egypt, Syria, Asia Minor, or Macedonia, and even from many ports on the Black Sea.

So with cotton, linen, and wool, even with silk fetched by caravans from China to Antioch and from there on to Rome. So was it with gold, silver, copper, tin, lead, and iron, with all woods valued for making into furniture, utensils, and vehicles, or for use in building. So also with other building materials, especially beautiful and even precious marbles and other highly decorative minerals, as porphyry, alabaster, jasper, onyx, and all sorts of gems, especially pearls, emeralds, turquoises, opals, and amethysts.

For new colonnades there was an unremitting traffic in columns hewn from all acclaimed materials and a steady inflow into Rome of such from quarries along the south coast of the Mediterranean, far up the Nile, and along the Black Sea.

It has often been stated that Rome exported nothing in exchange for all these commodities, but took them in tribute as the spoil of conquest or paid for them in bullion paid her as tribute.

The Romans did export from Rome in exchange for their imports full value and overvalue.

For more than four centuries they exported brains, the best brains in the world, the best brains the world had ever known.

It has been truly said that the Roman brain, in its day, was the most efficient engine of government the world has ever produced.

In exchange for what she received Rome diffused genuine all-round welfare over all her domain. Roman governors created and maintained in her provinces such peace, such prosperity, and such a density of population as no region that came under Roman control had ever attained when independent and such as few have regained since Rome fell.

CHAPTER XVI

POLYTHEISM

WE have in the preceding fifteen chapters made a cursory survey of the general and local conditions out of which Rome arose, of the characteristics of the early Romans, of the rise of Rome, and of Rome's achievement. There naturally presents itself the question, "What was the paramount factor amid all those which conduced to Rome's emergence, advancement, success and long domination?" The obvious answer, in accord with open-minded and unprejudiced survey of all the records, is that the preponderant factor among those which brought about Rome's progress, invincibility, grandeur, and supremacy was the religion of the Romans and its relation to their scheme of government and of their government to their religion. That was what made the Romans' miraculous achievements possible and actual.

To understand the religion of the Romans and its relation to their government and life it is necessary to attain a reasonable degree of comprehension of Greco-Roman Polytheism and of the religious beliefs, notions, instincts, customs, and habits of the peoples of the Mediterranean world at large and of polytheists in general.

As was remarked in Chapter III, except the peculiar and unconformable Hebrews and the intrusive Persians, all the peoples of the Mediterranean world, of the Iranic Plateau, and of the Indus and Ganges Valleys and the Peninsula of Hindustan were polytheists; and, numerous and striking as were the local variations of ritual and observances, there were diffused among them very similar conceptions as to religion and a very similar attitude of mind toward religion and toward its relation to government.

It may well be observed parenthetically that there is a recognizable, even an unmistakable, kinship between the ancient polytheism of the Greco-Roman Mediterranean world and the present-day polytheism of Hindustan, often loosely called

Brahmanism, which centers about Puri in Orissa; but that, while Greco-Roman polytheism and Hinduism indubitably derived from a common origin, yet they had, even at the time of our earliest records of either, diverged widely, and their specific differences and contrasts are much more conspicuous than the generalized resemblances underlying both; so that their manifest cousinship is very distant.

If there is in print in any modern European language a fair valuation and veracious presentation of Greco-Roman polytheism, it is unknown to the present writer. All accessible and well-known authors who have dealt with the religion of the Greeks and Romans and of the other peoples of the Roman Empire and the Mediterranean world have been earnest and convinced monotheists and have written with an overmastering monotheistic bias, as a result of which they have been absurdly prone to emphasize everything in ancient polytheism which had in it any suggestion of monotheism or showed the faintest hint of a leaning toward monotheism, and to undervalue, underemphasize, or ignore the idiosyncratic features of the polytheistic attitude of mind and to write as if polytheists in general and the Greco-Roman polytheists in particular were, somehow, all the while, at the back of their minds, unconsciously monotheists in reality, which they were not in fact. This queer delusion has led these writers, one and all, grossly to misrepresent polytheism at large and Greco-Roman polytheism specifically.

Also most Christian writers on paganism appear to assume as axiomatic that the monotheistic conception is, somehow, more logical, plausible, rational, natural, and probable than the polytheistic conception, a proposition which no polytheist would for a moment admit or even entertain.

In its widest sense the polytheistic attitude of mind may be adumbrated by some such summary of its chief assumptions as follows:

In the ponds, streams, lakes, rivers, and seas of the world are fish and other under-water creatures, living the life of fish, whatever that may be, for what human being comprehends the life of a shark, tunny, octopus, porpoise, or whale?

Partly under water, partly in water, partly on land, live such creatures as turtles, crocodiles, hippopotami, and seals, mostly water livers, but resorting to the land at times.

On earth live quadrupeds such as cattle, horses, sheep, goats, deer, antelopes, swine, hares, dogs, wolves, bears, lions, tigers, panthers, elephants, rhinoceroses, camels, giraffes, apes, monkeys, and others; living lives fairly intelligible to mankind, since mankind also lives on earth and on food not dissimilar to the food of many quadrupeds.

In the air are birds, living the life of birds, whatever that may be, for much of their life is incomprehensible to mankind.

Higher yet than the birds live the gods, living the life of gods, whatever that may be, for the concerns, occupations, and doings of gods are, largely, as unknown and incomprehensible to men as the concerns of sharks, tunnies, fish in general, migrant birds, winging their way high up in the air, or of other such unhuman creatures.

Just as turtles, crocodiles, hippopotami, and seals occasionally come out of the water onto the land, just as birds alight upon trees or upon the ground, so also gods at times condescend from their lofty abodes and spend a time upon earth among men.

The gods can assume any form, shape, or appearance they please; and, when on earth, generally, if they deign to allow human beings to behold them, appear to such fortunate individuals in human form.

Fish and quadrupeds occasionally display an interest in the welfare of human beings, sympathize with them, and render them assistance. A fable tells how the poet Arion was overboard far from land, but was saved from drowning by a kindhearted dolphin which carried him to shore on its back. Another fable tells how the twins, Romulus and Remus, infants left to starve in a waste place, were succored, suckled, and saved by a kindly she-wolf. And there are other such.

As animals and fish sometimes take an interest in human beings, so, and much more frequently and notably, mankind may, from time to time, attract the notice of the gods, kindly and sympathetic beings, whose feelings toward the human race are much like the feelings of the nobility, aristocracy, and gentry of any country toward its populace, commonalty, and peasantry; in general they ignore them, but individuals of the aristocracy may be keenly sympathetic and beautifully helpful toward plain folk in trouble or distress.

As a rich man may be immersed in his pastimes, yet might become deeply and helpfully interested in a peasant who had had some misfortune, whose wife was ill or whose cow had died or whose promising crop had been ruined by a sudden hail storm and if the unfortunate happened to attract his notice and arouse his commiseration, might, for the time, put aside his pleasures and give thought chiefly to the needs of his protégé, so a god, if a votary succeeds in engaging his attention and eliciting his compassion, may devote himself to the necessities or hopes of a suppliant.

As, often, a noble or opulent family, from generation to generation, takes a special interest in one or more families of peasants and aids them with advice or counsel at any time and with assistance in time of need, so a clan or coterie of gods may, from year to year, even from age to age, favor, watch over, and protect a family, tribe, community, city, or nation.

For such a community the favor of its gods is its chief asset and most precious possession.

As a poor client family expresses its gratitude to its patrons by occasional gifts of whatever it happens to have to spare, as eggs, fruit, flowers in season; fowls, a fat goose, a lamb, or from more prosperous clients a brace of hunting dogs or even a saddle horse—gifts pitifully inadequate to requite the benefits received but suitable for conveying to the protectors a sense of their dependents' thankfulness—so men may signify to the gods their acknowledgment of reverence and veneration at all times and of gratitude for favors bestowed by offerings of flowers, fruits, and other produce, and especially by burnt-offerings of incense and of other perfumes and of portions of the flesh of cattle, swine, sheep, goats, fowls, and other living creatures offered in sacrifice.

The gods in their lofty abodes enjoy the savor of all burnt offerings made as propitiatory sacrifices; yet, just as with nobles, it is not the actual sight, smell, or taste of the eggs, fruit, fowls, or other gifts eaten which causes most enjoyment and makes most impression, but the presentation of gifts as thank-offerings and as tokens of deference and loyalty; so, far more than by the savor of burnt-offerings, the gods are pleased by the sacrifice itself and the acts and words accompanying it as tokens of allegiance, fealty, devotion, homage, and gratitude.

A community can best engage and retain the favor of its gods by asking their help, taking their advice, and acknowledging their beneficence.

Prayer is not an enterprise to be undertaken rashly or heedlessly. True, any individual may utter or whisper or wordlessly formulate a prayer to any god for help before or during any undertaking or in any difficulty or danger, and in all such cases the kindly divinity addressed will condone the informality of the manner in which the petition is offered, in view of the impossibility of mere formality in the circumstances. But, at large, just as a poor man venturing to ask a favor of a rich man washes himself clean, puts on decent garments, and generally makes himself presentable, so anyone purposing a prayer to any god or goddess bathes, arrays himself in his best, and otherwise does all he can to show his respect for the deity whose aid he seeks.

And as it is best for a plain man, setting about making a request of an overlord, to have his petition dexterously and properly presented by someone at home amid the etiquette of such matters, so it is far better for any individual to offer his prayers to any god or goddess not directly in person, but through a priest or priestess adept at all that conduces to effective prayer.

For the gods, from time to time, reveal to favored individuals the methods by which their notice may best be attracted, their sympathies engaged, their attention held, and their assistance ensured. Such persons are the natural intercessors between mankind and the gods, become accredited hierophants, and teach their lore and transmit their skill to their descendants. A wise votarý seeking the favor of any god will approach that god through a capable, competent, proficient and expert hierophant.

For the gods, while kindly toward mankind, are easily affronted by any failure to accord them what they regard as their due. Therefore a prayer improperly presented may arouse their anger instead of winning their aid.

It is therefore most important that petitions for the welfare of a community should be presented to its gods by an accredited priesthood observing the prescriptive ritual traditionally effective for the purpose.

The gods give advice to mankind in many ways, but chiefly in four:

In sacrifices;

Through birds;

Through oracles;

And by omens and portents.

When accepting from an individual or community the sacrifice of a bullock, sheep, goat, hog, or other living creature, the gods will give any question put to them a yes or no answer by the appearance of the liver, heart, kidneys, and lungs of the sacrificial victim, especially by the pattern of the veins on the outside of the liver as they look when taken out of the newly sacrificed animal, as their significance is interpreted by the chief sacrificant.

The gods live up aloft and the birds come from high up. Earth-dwelling or tree-nesting birds, birds which inhabit the same district all the year, have no significance whatever as messengers of the gods, or very little. Birds absent during part of each year, but returning each year at the same season, sometimes do not bring a message from the gods; oftener they do. Birds winging their way high in the air, birds alighting from high in the air, birds uncommon, rare, and seldom seen, are manifestly messengers of the gods and by the direction, elevation, speed, and manner of their flight, by their cries or notes, by their behavior or attitudes, may convey to men messages from the gods intelligible to such experts as are proficient at interpreting their significance.

There are places on earth, in caves and caverns, in lonely glens, by pools deep in dense pine-forests, up rock-gorges in bare mountains, amid sandy wastes, where lone listeners may hear vague voices, the voices of gods or of minor divinities, speaking direct to men, and intelligible if the hearer be adept at their interpretation. But mostly the gods prefer to speak to men not directly in person, but through an acceptable consecrated priest or priestess, devoted to the service of the gods, inspired by them and uttering their wisdom from human lips. Such utterances of hierophants, like the voices heard in isolated holy places, are called oracles. By oracles the gods answer questions, give advice, foretell the future, and comfort the afflicted.

At times, when men do not ask of any oracle nor through any sacrifice the questions most important at the time for them to have answered, the gods make them aware that something momentous is impending by prodigies: comets, eclipses of the moon or sun; the birth of monstrous calves, lambs, or foals; the appearance of rare wild animals in or near cities, and other such unusual occurrences. Also they admonish mankind of some neglect or error in ritual worship, and express their displeasure by such disasters as volcanic eruptions, earthquakes, floods, tidal waves, pestilences, conflagrations, famines, droughts, and the like. These are omens or portents. The significance of an omen may be ascertained from an oracle or through sacrifices.

The most vital concern of any community is the ascertainment of the will of its gods through the indications of it which they give by sacrifices, birds, oracles, and omens as interpreted by their accredited hierophants. The art of divination is the most important of human arts and is a highly technical art, requiring years of apprenticeship before a practitioner of it becomes adept enough to be dependable as adviser to a community faced by the urgent problems of administration, diplomacy, and warfare.

The propitiation of the gods by thank-offerings is even more than prayer to them, an occult, mysterious, and highly technical matter. The hierophants engaged in this occupation are among the most valuable members of any community.

These were the chief assumptions instinctively made and implicitly believed by polytheists throughout the Mediterranean world and the regions east of it.

As bears, wolves, and stags range over Europe; as elephants, giraffes, antelopes, hippopotami, rhinoceroses, are characteristic animals of Africa; as tigers are confined to Asia—so it was conceived that some gods frequented one part of the earth and others others; that each locality had its characteristic local gods, these local coteries mostly respecting each other's prescriptive domains, but occasionally clashing when neighboring communities were at war and the gods of each favored their votaries and so became hostile to the gods of their votaries' foemen.

It never entered the minds of typical polytheists to conjecture how many gods there might be or to set any limits to their probable numbers, any more than to the numbers of herring, sardines, wild fowl, hares, flies, mosquitoes, or other living creatures.

Nor did any natural and primitive polytheist even assume that all mankind collectively, far less they themselves, knew by manifestation all the gods or even any considerable fraction of them.

A few speculative philosophers made conjectures as to the possible or probable numbers of gods and as to whether all gods or only some few manifested themselves to mankind, but these philosophers were a negligible percentage of the population and their ideas were not widely known or of any general influence.

It seems to have been generally assumed that the gods collectively greatly outnumbered those who concerned them-

such deities as Febris (the goddess who protected from fevers), Robigo (the goddess of blight on grain), Concordia (the goddess of political harmony), Honos (the god of repute, esteem, reputation, distinction), Virtus (the goddess of manliness, valor, worth, excellence), Mens (the goddess of thought), Ops Consiva (Resource that comes from sowing, a goddess of grain).

But very early, certainly long before the expulsion of the kings in 510 B.C., the Romans began to feel the influence of the Greeks, at first through the Etruscans, who seem to have employed many Greek artisans and artists, later by contacts with Greek colonies in Italy, and so imitated Greek ways and came to represent their deities by cult-statues wholly human in form, as their religious conceptions were clarified and their religious emotions ennobled by assimilation of Greek ideas.

For emphasis it is well to recapitulate here what we have already written, that for any polytheistic city, or other organized community, the favor of its gods was its most valued asset, and that the definition of a Greek city-state, "A religious and military confraternity encamped round a church," applied more or less aptly to any city-state of the Mediterranean world, fairly well characterized any community holding a fortified town in Italy, and so fitly described Rome.

Most Greek city-states were of a homogeneous racial stock closely related in blood, often manifestly descended from one family even, sometimes indubitably from one man and wife.

Rome was a far looser confraternity, made up certainly of two stocks, Latin and Sabine, probably of more, very likely of three and not impossibly of five or six. But by the time of the expulsion of the Kings and the organization of the Republic about 510 B.C., the components had been welded into a genuine confraternity, religious and military.

Italian city-states in general, and Latin towns in particular, were, mostly, more tenacious of their home soil and town citadels than Greek city-states, and there is no conspicuous historic instance of an Italian community abandoning its hereditary lands and fortress, migrating as a body and locating elsewhere. Yet there is no doubt that after the sack of Rome by the Gauls in 390 B.C., a considerable minority of earnest Romans urged that the entrance of armed enemies into the *pomerium* of Rome had permanently desecrated that holy enclosure, had vitiated for all time its consecration, had indicated the withdrawal from Rome of the favor of the gods of the Romans, and made it advisable that the Roman community abandon Rome and migrate to Veii, recently captured from the Etruscans.

The majority urged that Jupiter and the other gods of Rome had protected Rome's citadel on the Capitoline Hill and that its successful defense demonstrated the continued favor of Jupiter and Rome's other gods.

For the Romans had long ago come to regard Jupiter (The Sky Father) originally merely a god of thunderstorms, of weather conditions in general, and of the sky at large, as "Father and King" of all their gods, and for centuries had represented him by a statue portraying a dignified man in the late prime of life, which statue was housed in their chief temple (community church) on one of the twin summits of the Capitoline Hill. On one side of him, for centuries, had been placed the statue of his daughter Minerva, goddess of brains, of intellect and so of all intellectual activity in peace or war, on the other the statue of a goddess regarded as his wife.

Juno was originally the chief goddess of Veii in Etruria, the nearest to Rome of the Etruscan cities. In 396 B.C., after an exhausting siege of nearly ten years' duration, the Romans captured Veii. They had a great respect for Juno as a mighty goddess, since she had protected her city so long. No sooner were they in possession and the dead buried, all traces of conflict removed and themselves ceremonially clean, than they reverently approached her temple, already put under adequate and sedulous guard at their first irruption, and besought her favor. As, manifestly, her former votaries had proved incapable of cherishing her fittingly, would she deign to accept them as liegemen? And, on the finest vehicle available, under a magnificent canopy, along roads newly swept and flower-strewn, through throngs clad in their best, among which choirs chanted hymns and censers diffused fragrant smoke, they conveyed her cult-statue to Rome and placed it in a new temple on the Aventine Hill.

Within no very long time Juno had come to be regarded as identical with Jupiter's wife, and in the passage of time it came to be forgotten that she had not always been so regarded and that Jupiter's wife had ever had any other name than Juno.

Rome's chief cult-temple, housing the great cult-statue of Jupiter Maximus Optimus flanked by the cult-statues of Juno and Minerva, was called the *Capitolium,* which word in English is Capitol, and was always the most valued possession of the Roman Commonwealth.

This Roman Commonwealth, which styled itself *Senatus Populusque Romanus* (The Rome Senate and People), was always conceived of by its citizens as a corporation constituted by the association of six classes of partners:

1. Jupiter Maximus Optimus.
2. The Other Major Gods and Goddesses.
3. The Minor Gods and Goddesses.
4. The Roman Senators.
5. The Roman *Equites* (nobles, "knights").
6. The Mass of Roman Citizens not noble.

Jupiter was conceived of as chief partner and the permanent head of the Firm of Senate, People and Company of Rome, Italy, in the War-business. The gods collectively were conceived of as a permanent board of directors, each supervising his or her special department. The Magistrates were conceived of as a sort of board of shop-foremen to ascertain the will of the gods and the wishes of the mass of the citizens and to evolve from them workable policies. The Senate was conceived of as a sort of shop-council of veteran experts whose chief duty was to advise any magistrate perplexed as to any point of policy.

Be it noted and noticed that no polytheistic city-state, least of all Rome, ever had any inkling of the possibility of government apart from religion or of religion apart from government.

For all of them, for the Romans, for Rome, religion was government and government was religion.

Excavations in the Tigris-Euphrates Valley have revealed to us clay tablets, inscriptions, wall tiles, bas-reliefs, and other carvings which demonstrate that in more than one city-state of Sumer, Akkad, Babylonia, and other neighboring districts, all the lands and buildings of the city and of its territory were conceived of as being the personal property of its chief deity, Sun-god, Moon-goddess or what else; the entire population as being servants of that presiding divinity; the priests and magistrates as merely representatives of that divinity; the King, however absolute over his family, ministers, advisers, generals, and other subjects, as merely vicegerent on earth of the city's chief divinity; the revenues of the state as the income of the divinity to be disbursed and utilized strictly in accordance with the declared will and expressed wishes of the supreme divinity.

Not so explicitly, but just as definitely, positively, and unequivocally, was it implicitly assumed by the Romans that the will of their gods and especially of Jupiter was paramount to all else, that following it led to prosperity, success, and victory, failing to follow it to defeat, disaster, and ruin.

Roman public worship of their gods had the specific objects of ascertaining their will, appeasing their displeasure and conciliating their favor.

For these purposes the state maintained a college of Flamens, each of whom was the priest of a specified god, and whose wife, in some cases, was *Flaminica,* or special priestess of the corresponding goddess. (The senior Vestal was practically Flaminica of Vesta and the other Vestal Virgins maidens in training to assist her with her ceremonial duties and to succeed her on her demise.)

The state also maintained a College of Pontiffs, who were priests competent to invoke, consult, or propitiate any divinity; moreover, a College of Augurs, experts at interpreting the will of the gods as indicated by the appearance, flight, or notes of birds; likewise a College of Fetiales who presided over all relations between Rome and other cities, states, nations, or peoples.

In the matter of interpreting the messages from the gods conveyed by birds the Romans esteemed themselves indubitably the superiors of all mankind. Their College of Augurs, existing from the earliest period, believed, indeed, to have been instituted by Romulus, endured until the forcible suppression of paganism between A.D. 381 and 394.

Nearly everyone who has read of Roman augury cannot help recalling the witty jeer of a skeptic who said he didn't see how one augur could look at another without laughing. This, and one or two other similar gibes, make up all that most persons know of Roman augury.

Alone, they are most misleading.

In fact, the art had the implicit confidence of the entire population, commonalty and intelligentsia alike, for over eleven centuries, and while private unofficial augurs came to be looked on as usually impostors, the members of the official College of Augurs retained the respect of the Romans throughout the period of Rome's rise and greatness.

Augur means "bird shower," "gur" being an Etruscan word. An *augur* was often called *auspex* ("bird watcher"), and the two words were used almost interchangeably. The indications of the will of the gods conveyed to men by birds, as interpreted by the augurs, were called *auspicia,* from which we derive our word "auspicious," an "auspicious day" being originally a day on which the Roman augurs announced that the omens betokened by the birds observed prognosticated the favor of the gods.

We still use the word "inauguration," which, to the Romans, meant the proper hallowing of an important enterprise, as an election of public officials, by the declaration of the officiating augur that the auspices were propitious and the matter in hand was assured of the favor of Rome's gods.

Members of the College of Augurs were always Romans, believed themselves unsurpassably adept, and consulted no outsiders.

It was otherwise with the more important method of ascertaining the will of the gods by inspection of the liver, heart, gall, kidney, and lungs of a newly killed sacrificial victim (what we might call the giblets, though we do not use the word of these organs when taken from quadrupeds), what the Roman called "*exta*," and the Etruscans, apparently, "*haru*."

Mostly any Roman pontiff and almost any Roman official, when commander of an army or governor of a province or what else, felt himself competent to interpret the *exta*.

But when a momentous occasion necessitated the impeccable accuracy of the widest knowledge and most expert skill, when any *exta* seemed unintelligible, the Romans invariably called in as consultant an Etruscan haruspex or two or more haruspices, professional interpreters of *exta*, respositories of the traditional ancient lore of Etruria concerning divination.

As they derived from the Etruscans the insignia of office of their magistrates such as the *fasces* and the curial chair, and also Chariot-racing in circuses, gladiatorial shows, military triumphal processions through the city, the art of building roomy stone sewers, massive city walls, and imposing public buildings, so the Romans had imported from Etruria this phase of the art of divination.

It must be noted, because few moderns could realize it, that, although in fact the pattern of the veins on the outside of a liver promptly taken from a freshly killed quadruped has endless variations and it is almost impossible to find two livers with vein-patterns precisely identical, whereas we assume that this is the result of the interaction of countless factors in the heredity and growth of the animal, ancient polytheists in general and the Romans in particular were dominated by the naïve notion that the god to whom the sacrifice was offered, after the sacrificant's question was put to him, arranged the veins in the pattern found as an answer to that specific query.

The art of interpreting the divine answer given in this fashion was developed in the Tigris-Euphrates Valley as early as 3000 B.C. We have found there many terra-cotta models of the livers of cattle and sheep and a few of those of other animals, and in Etruria very similar bronze models, models used in the instruction of neophytes at the art of haruspicy. Apprentices to this art spent years acquiring it before they were esteemed reliable adepts.

Haruspices of Etruscan origin or training were also consulted as adepts at the interpretation of the messages of the gods conveyed by *prodigia,* portents, such as the striking by lightning of any sacred locality or building or any cult-statue, an eclipse of the moon or sun, the birth of a two-headed foal or pig or calf, a notable aurora borealis, incursion in broad daylight of a wolf into a thronged town market-place, or any other strikingly unusual occurrence.

More and more, as time went on, oracles were consulted as to the significance of portents, and since there were few accredited oracles in Italy and those of little repute, as the Roman power grew and Rome's Empire enlarged, Rome's government more and more frequently sent deputations to consult the oracle at Delphi and other far famous and highly esteemed Greek oracles.

For the purpose of averting the wrath of the gods, if any prodigy was held to signify their wrath, of expiating any sacrilege, profanation, impiety, blasphemy, affront, irreverence, disrespect, or other action or behavior displeasing to the gods, or any neglect, omission, default, oversight, shortcoming, informality, negligence, or slight in respect to their worship, the Romans pursued what seems to us naïve methods based on very simple-hearted conceptions.

They conceived of the gods, in general, as liking what human beings liked and enjoying what mankind enjoyed; so, if the gods were angry, they sought to placate, propitiate, and conciliate them by displaying for their enjoyment and incidentally for the enjoyment of their worshippers the Romans, chariot races, gorgeous processions, lavish sacrifices, stage-plays, tragedies, comedies, farces, banquets, and other magnificent and splendid spectacles and performances.

A banquet of the gods, called a *lectisternium,* appears to us a very naïve proceeding.

At any crisis, when the state seemed threatened by a menacing peril, causing panic, terror, apprehension or concern, or after any dazzling success, when all classes were wrought up with relief and gratitude, it was usual to proclaim a solemn holy-day or series of days called a *supplicatio,* which word meant both atonement and thanksgiving. During a *supplicatio* images of the chief gods, carved in a reclining posture, were laid on magnificent sofas like those of a rich nobleman's dining table, but provided with gorgeous upholstery and cushions beyond the means of the most opulent individual, and before these reclining gods were set platters, salvers, dishes, and plates heaped with the choicest and rarest delicacies and viands, and bowls and goblets of the best wines. Before the gods at feast the populace filed in throngs, awed and reverent.

This appears to us ridiculous. But a rite so closely the counterpart of it as to be almost a replica of it is now in vogue in Hindustan, and millions of pious Hindus fervidly believe it as propitiatory and efficacious as did the Romans of long ago.

Implicitly, but indubitably, the idea back of their very costly and expensive methods of worship was, "These things put us in a good humor, therefore they will put the gods in a good humor."

It is very difficult for moderns to realize that every chariot race ever run in any Roman circus, in Rome or throughout the Empire, every official governmental public procession, every tragedy, comedy, farce, mime, or pantomime performed at the expense of the government, just as truly as every banquet of the gods and every sacrifice to the gods, was an act of homage to Rome's gods and an act of worship to Rome's gods whether performed for invocation, conciliation, or thanksgiving, and that every participant, every spectator, so regarded every one of these public pleasures from first to last, for centuries, and all pagans felt so about them even after paganism had been forcibly suppressed.

Two of these forms of homage, propitiation, conciliation, and thanksgiving, *venationes* (beast fights), and combats of gladiators, both developments of Rome's prime and exhibited in the amphitheatre, never in a circus, we shall explain further on.

The Romans believed that their gods habitually signified to them through consultation of the *exta,* through observation of birds, through notice given by prodigies, as interpreted by experts, indications of their will, advice as to public policy in war and peace and as to private and personal concerns at all times, and warnings against inadvisable courses of action. All classes of Romans except a trifling, microscopic minority of skeptics such as develops in any community, felt an abiding sense of the ceaseless guardianship, solicitude, vigilance, readiness, kindliness, helpfulness, and puissance of their gods.

The polytheists of the Mediterranean world, and the Romans among them, had nothing resembling our periodic Sundays, Sabbaths, and other holy days recurrent at definite intervals. Nor had they any such customs as our sermons, preachings, and other exhortations and our congregations assembled to listen to them. Nor did they have any such habits as morning prayers on rising, grace before meat, or night prayers before composing themselves for sleep, family prayers or anything else of the kind.

Yet, at large, they prayed oftener than we do; one might say that their intervals of prayer took up almost as much time as the intervals between praying. Throughout the ancient world, whether in Greece, Rome, Egypt, Babylonia, or wherever else from Spain to India, of whatever race or language they might be, individuals were, with some local exceptions, generally in the habit of uttering or wordlessly emitting little prayers at any time of day before almost every action contemplated. Every warrior spoke or whispered to his war-god a petition for success before he hurled his lance; every hunter as he nocked and aimed his arrow, in the act of drawing his bow, before he loosed his bowstring and let fly his shaft, breathed a prayer to Apollo or Artemis or Diana or whoever was his local god or goddess of the chase; every milkmaid similarly breathed a brief orison before starting to milk each cow. So every housewife similarly before setting about kneading her dough; every fisherman before casting his hook into the water, every rider before mounting, every woodcutter before laying ax to tree-trunk. So anyone before walking up or down a stair recited or formulated a brief prayer. So before any action anyone prayed somehow to whatever god or goddess presided over the particular act contemplated.

A failing swimmer shaped a wordless prayer for help to Triton or Leucothoë or whatever sea god or sea goddess most had his confidence. So anyone in trouble, perplexity, or peril.

But, unless urgency made it impossible, no Roman uttered a prayer without fitting preparation. Romans did not visit their temples at stated intervals as our sects go to church on Sundays. A Roman felt it unmannerly and presumptuous to intrude upon a god with prayers concerning trifles or to pester a divinity with too frequent petitions of whatever nature. But when he felt he had something for which he needed divine aid and as to which a divinity might be expected to give aid, he meticulously bathed, clad himself suitably, usually in his best, and, already assured that he had chosen a lucky day, went to the temple of the god most likely to assist and there preferred his petition, seldom without the advice of an accredited hierophant and usually through such a priest. The more important the hope or fear, the more careful was the behavior of any Roman. The illness of a child, wife, or relative was a very frequent reason for such formal prayer.

If any private care, anxiety, perplexity, misdeed, or success appeared to necessitate a sacrifice of invocation, conciliation, or thanksgiving, only the head of a family might prepare for, superintend, and offer such a sacrifice. Everybody in Rome knew whether he was rated head of a family or member of a family, and acted accordingly. In general, only through the heads of families as to private matters, only through the representatives of the state as to public matters, did the Romans invoke their gods.

And the Romans not only begged for the help of their gods, but also asked their advice.

Haruspices were consulted as to every conceivable private concern, uncertainty, or affair. *Auspicia* were felt requisite for any such undertaking as purchasing land, building a house, arranging or celebrating a marriage, or setting out on a journey. Unofficial augurs, despite the sneers at them, throve and prospered, as did haruspices, seers, soothsayers, fortune tellers and all such claimants to occult powers. Thrifty as were the ancients, money spent on such mages was accounted money well spent.

Officially, augury was trusted by all save a few occasional skeptics. The College of Augurs retained, until the suppression of paganism, control of the *auguraculum,* a place on the Arx, Rome's citadel crowning one of the twin summits of the Capitoline Hill. No edifice might encroach on the auguraculum nor might any building be erected which would cut off or interfere with the view from that consecrated spot.

In early times, when Rome's territorial possessions were insignificant and her wars were fought nearby, not only did every commander have auspices taken for him before setting out on a campaign, but, if he suffered a disaster, defeat, or setback, or matters came to a deadlock, he judged that he had "lost his auspices" and returned in person to Rome to reassure himself of the countenance of Jupiter for his enterprise by asking and receiving fresh auspices, clearly demonstrating Jupiter's approbation.

When Rome's conquests made such a return to the Capitol impossible, Rome's experts hit upon the device of having formally consecrated in the temple of Jupiter some fowls, hens and cocks, begging that Jupiter would be so good as to deign, from day to day, to signify countenance or discountenance, approbation or disapprobation, sanction or condemnation, of any project or intention, by the behavior of the consecrated fowls. They were put under the care of a special officer, taken along wherever an army or fleet went, and their behavior observed by an expert augur, who made each morning a report to the commander of the expedition. The Romans had many stories of victory following heed paid to the omens taken from the behavior of these holy birds, and other tales of disaster ensuing upon disregard of their warnings.

The sense of partnership with the gods, and of accountability to them, was with a Roman so ingrained that it seemed instinctive, even innate. Exceptions were few in early days.

On the voting fields the voters' feelings as to the participation of their gods in the proceedings varied according to the nature of the business in hand. Always auguries were taken and the assemblage assured of the favor of the gods before voting began.

But if voting on a law, during debates on the proposal and while the balloting was in progress, the voters had a very vague and scarcely perceptible sense of their free will being influenced by Jupiter directly and positively.

At elections it was far otherwise. From first to last an election appeared to a normal Roman as a process for ascertaining which candidate was most acceptable to Jupiter as his associate holding that particular office, and that a majority vote demonstrated Jupiter's choice through his immediate influence on the preferences of the voters; that, for each office, especially for the higher offices, an incumbent acceptable to Jupiter be selected was the more important, since it was not only no part of a Roman citizen's duties to pray for the safety of the state, but presumptuous of any ordinary citizen to venture so to pray; prayer for the safety of the state could avail only if properly offered by an adept at the highly technical art of using the complex ritual necessary for conciliating Rome's gods. Therefore elections were, to all pious Romans, doubly momentous occasions.

On enrollment into the army each Roman soldier took oath of obedience to his commander. This oath contained an imprecation upon himself and his kin of terrific retribution if he broke his oath. And each Roman soldier believed that his failure to keep his oath would infallibly entail upon himself and his dear ones the imprecated retribution. He believed it, as Browning phrases it, "as he believed in fire that it would burn." It is very difficult for any modern to realize how vivid was this robust faith. It cannot be demonstrated; it can only be adumbrated by analogies.

Almost any peasant of the west coast of Ireland will, under oath in court, swear to anything favorable to his own side and unfavorable to the other side, regardless alike of truth and of his oath on the Bible. But get him up a church tower with his hand on the church bell, and he will speak the exact, complete and unvarnished truth, no matter how harmful or shameful it may be to his friends, his relations or himself. For he believes that if he departs ever so little from the precise truth that bell will ring and brand him as a perjured liar.

So a peasant of any one of the Greek islands or of any valley of rural Greece will lie jauntily under oath in court as may be convenient. But get him to put his hand on a portrait of Saint Trophimus and he will, while gazing at the pictured saint, tell the unmodified truth, for he believes that, if he prevaricates, Saint Trophimus will open his mouth and audibly convict him.

A Roman soldier stood in awe of the gods by whom he had sworn just as Irish peasants today stand in awe of a church bell or Greek peasants of the portrait of Saint Trophimus.

Even as late as the times of Augustus this faith had hardly begun to wane. Sometime between the murder of Julius Cæsar and the battle of Philippi, Antony's legionaries mutinied. After a very short period they repented, returned to their allegiance and reaffirmed their loyalty. Antony forgave them. They refused to accept pardon without punishment. The prescriptive penalty for mutiny was decimation, the summary execution of every tenth man during a drawing by lot of the names of all concerned. Antony asserted that he needed more men than he had and could not afford to deprive himself of one-tenth of his best soldiers. The men argued that such a reduction of their numbers would be far less of a drawback in the campaign than would the unescapable curse that would overwhelm them all for ignoring the certain indignation of the gods outraged at the violation of the oath taken in their names. After a long wrangle a compromise was agreed on by which one man out of every twenty was butchered in expiation of their guilt. And every one of them, privates and centurions alike, knew beforehand that the drawing of the lots might result in his being one of the victims.

That shows the sort of respect Roman legionaries felt for an oath sworn before their gods and for the gods before whom such an oath was taken.

Officers, generals, commanders, magistrates, governors, and all officials of the Roman Republic, Commonwealth, and Empire, felt a similar responsibility toward the Gods of Rome.

This was what held together the Roman State, gave it its coherence, created its power, won its Empire, and maintained its dominance, the deep and abiding sense, vividly felt by every Roman, of partnership with Rome's gods, countenance from them and responsibility to them.

CHAPTER XVIII

GRECO-ROMAN POLYTHEISM

FOR the sake of clarity and emphasis we have postponed to this point the mention and exposition of one of the fundamental assumptions of ancient polytheism, universal throughout the Mediterranean world and its extensions, but with numerous local variations.

It may be adumbrated as follows: "Our gods are very busy gods and it is difficult to attract their notice and harder to keep their attention. We have had revealed to our holy men all the intricate complexities of the ritual by which, and by which alone, their attention may be caught and their favor conciliated. You must be decently reverential to our gods, but you must not show any curiosity as to the details of the ritual which insures us their countenance. Of course, while you must not pry into our hierarchic mysteries, you must not insult our gods, deride them, flout them, ignore them, or disregard them, for they would be wrathful with us for permitting such impiety from anyone, even from aliens among us. You must, therefore, be respectful to them at all times. Equally, of course, we must reciprocate by being decorously reverent to your gods and concomitantly by sedulously refraining from any approach to trying to learn your formularies of worship and conciliation."

Thus might any inhabitant of any city-state from Ireland to Annam have spoken to any native of any other at any time between 4500 B.C. and A.D. 380.

This polytheistic instinct was always vividly present to the consciousness of the Romans, but, in war and conquest, their conformity to it varied, according to circumstances, from the completest observance of it to total disregard.

Some phases of these diversities are explicable.

Sometimes the Romans conceived of the gods of a race with which they were at war as not only hostile to the gods of Rome, but as wholly dissimilar to Rome's gods and not in any way related to them or the counterparts of them. In such cases they not merely fought their foemen without quarter, parley, or truce, but, after victory, sold all survivors into slavery and abolished their state and religion by destroying their city, walls, dwellings, citadel, and all, burning even the temples and with them their cult-statues.

To whatever extent the Romans felt that they descried resemblances between their enemies' gods and their own, to that degree they were less ferocious and harsh toward their human foes, more inclined to negotiations, milder, and concomitantly, in victory, more mindful and heedful of their foemen's gods.

When a Roman army entered the territory of an allied city or the city itself, no matter whether they regarded that city's gods as wholly alien to them and wholly unrelated to the gods of Rome or as more or less analogous to Rome's gods, resembling them, akin to them, cognate with them, counterparts of them, they were not only meticulously respectful to all that city's cult-statues, shrines, temples, and consecrated or hallowed enclosures, but also regarded every object in any way dedicated to the city's gods as holy and sacred and to be reverenced and protected in every way as the property of gods whom they respected and whose favor they sought.

But if a Roman army took such a city by storm their practice varied. Usually they regarded every enclosure, temple, votive offering and cult-statue as deconsecrated by their victory, since that victory was not only a defeat of their human foemen by Rome's military, but a subjugation and abasement of the captured city's gods by the gods of Rome, so that everything previously the property of that city's gods and sacrosanct to all men, became fair loot for Rome's legionaries, handed over to them by the favor and assistance of Rome's gods.

Sometimes the Romans regarded the gods of a captured city as practically identical with Rome's gods, but as having manifestly turned against their former protégés, the inhabitants of that city, as if they had become wrathful with them for some impiety, and as having therefore disfavored their local votaries and favored the attacking Romans. Therefore, most logically, they conceived that those local divinities had abandoned to the victors all their consecrated enclosures, temples, shrines, cult-statues, and votive offerings, and that all such had become de-consecrated and the property of the victorious Romans.

In such cases their practice varied from completely looting the enclosures, temples, and shrines, but leaving the buildings unburned and unharmed, to respecting every sacred enclosure with all its contents precisely as if they had peacefully entered an allied city. This last was the behavior of Marcellus and his troops when they stormed Syracuse in Sicily in 212 B.C. during the Second Punic War, although they plundered all other buildings.

The Romans were by nature domineering and overbearing, bluff, blunt, direct, downright and forthright, not in any way considerate of the feelings of aliens and notably devoid of tact and finesse; yet, as overlords, they had amazingly sound governmental intuitions. Instinctively, after conquest, subjugation, or negotiations, they did everything possible to reconcile to their domination, suzerainty, or supremacy their allies and vassals, and inhabitants of their *municipia,* præfectures, colonies, and provinces.

One of the most efficient means was through the identification of the ancestral local gods of subjected populations with the gods of Rome. To have been subjugated to overlords whose gods were the same gods as one's own was far less humiliating than to have had one's local gods abased by utterly dissimilar gods fostering the armies of their votaries. Moreover, such a result of warfare in which both sides had prayed to, sacrificed to, and hoped for the favor of gods now regarded as identical inevitably evoked the conjecture and irresistibly forced the inference that the arbitrament of war had conclusively demonstrated that it was the will of the gods worshipped in common by victors and vanquished that the Romans should rule and that their subjects, vassals, clients, allies, and others, previously their foemen, should obey. This powerfully tended to abate, even to efface, any lingering resentment, rancor, vindictiveness, animosity, enmity, disaffection and pique.

At some stage of their contact with the Etruscans the Romans came to regard their deities as counterparts of or identical with their own, identifying Tinia with Jupiter, Cupra with Juno, Menfra with Minerva, Nethuns with Neptune, Maris with Mars, Velch with Vulcan, Turms with Mercury, Artumes with Diana, Ani with Janus, Fufluns with Bacchus, and Thesan with Aurora.

Even in dealing with their dreaded and implacable foes, the Carthaginians, the Romans thought they discerned analogies between their gods and their own and took Molech or Moloch to be the same as Saturn, Tanit as Venus, and Melkart as Hercules.

So they regarded the Gallic god Tarann or Hesus as the same as Jupiter; Bel or Belew as the same as Apollo; Tiv, Tir or Teutates as the same as Mercury.

Whether these identifications had any local influence on the relations between the Romans, the Gauls, the remnants of the conquered Etruscans, the few survivors from the once lordly Carthaginians, and other such scanty residues, we do not know. There are no records extant. But indubitably such results, if any there were, were local only and had no effect on the Empire as a whole.

Quite otherwise was it with the interaction between the cult of the Latin and Roman gods and the worship of the gods of Greece and of the Greek colonies in Sicily, Sardinia, Corsica, Gaul, Spain, and Italy.

Identification of the gods of Greece and Rome began early, progressed as contacts with the Greeks became ever less infrequent, more numerous, more frequent, less discontinuous and finally countless, perennial, and continuous. It came to be assumed that the gods of Greece and of Rome were the same and the identification came to be universally recognized and universally accepted. This created a religious atmosphere, diffused over the entire Mediterranean world as early as 170 B.C., constituting the spiritual background of all social and political activities therein for more than five and a half centuries.

In this universal religion of the Mediterranean world under the Roman Empire the accepted identifications of Greek and Roman gods were approximately as follows:

It was universally assumed that there were twelve major divinities, six gods and six goddesses, but the list varied. Usually, putting the Greek name first and the Latin name second, it was constituted thus:

(1) Zeus—Jupiter, god of the sky, of the weather, and supreme among all gods and goddesses, father and king of gods and men.

(2) Poseidon—Neptune, brother of Jupiter and god of the sea and all thereon and therein.

(3) Phœbus—Apollo, the god of light, health, brightness, brilliance, and so of healing and prophecy.

(4) Ares—Mars, god of war and battle.

(5) Hermes—Mercury, god of cleverness, ingenuity, trade, travel, risks, and ventures, the herald of the gods and guide of the ghosts of the dead.

(6) Hephæstus—Vulcan, god of heat, fire and of all artisans who used fire, so regarded as the artisan god and artificer god.

(7) Hera—Juno, wife and queen of Jupiter, goddess of womanhood.

(8) Pallas Athene—Minerva, the goddess of brains, intellect, wisdom, and therefore of all intellectual activities, war, diplomacy, arts, handicrafts, and the like.

(9) Aphrodite—Venus, the goddess of love, charm, joy, springtime, fertility, abundance and prosperity.

(10) Artemis—Diana, sister of Apollo, goddess of maidenhood, of the open country untouched by man, so of mountains, forests, valleys, meadows, and streams, so of the chase, of hunting, of all game, and in another phase of the moon as aiding hunters by moonlight at night.

(11) Demeter—Ceres, Mother Earth, goddess of agriculture fertility, grain, harvest, and similar matters.

(12) Hestia—Vesta, goddess of the hearth and hearth-fire and so of home and home-virtues.

But at least three other gods and three other goddesses were regarded generally as major divinities, and one or other of them was often found in a list of the twelve chief divinities, instead of one of those just given, sometimes two or more.

These were as follows:

(13) The god of the lower world, king of the shades, brother to Jupiter and Neptune, called by the Greeks Pluto or Hades and by the Romans Orcus or Dis (Hades was also a name of his realm).

(14) Kronos—Saturn, father of Jupiter, Neptune, and Orcus.

(15) Dionysus—Bacchus or Liber, god of all things pleasant and agreeable to mankind, so of tragedy and comedy as well as of all other forms of entertainment, but especially of luxuriant vegetation, of grape vines, and wine.

(16) Rhea—Cybele, Great Mother of the Gods, goddess of the fertility of animals and plants.

(17) Leto—Latona, mother of Apollo and Diana.

(18) Persephone—Proserpina (Libera), daughter of Demeter and wife of Pluto, the King of Hades.

Some twelve or more of these eighteen were universally regarded as Major Divinities or the rest of the eighteen as almost Major Divinities.

Other divinities regarded as nearly or quite Major Divinities were:

(19) Gaea—Tellus, Mother-Earth, the kindly, fostering spirit of the productive earth. (Demeter—Ceres, Rhea—Cybele and Gaea—Tellus were very similar goddesses, often confused.)

(20) Helios—Sol, the Sun-God.

(21) Selene—Luna, the Moon-Goddess.

(22) Enyo—Bellona, goddess of the fury of combat, of battle frenzy.

Important among Minor Divinities were:

(23) Pan, the god of woods, forests, forested mountains, and of all the wild life therein, identified with the Latin gods Faunus and Silvanus.

(24) Herakles—Hercules, god of strength, courage, might, endurance, doggedness, guidance, and salvation through perils.

(25) Tyche—Fortuna, goddess of good luck.

(26) Nike—Victoria, goddess of victory in battle and war.

(27) Chloris—Flora, goddess of blossoms, flowers and gayety.

(28) Hygeia—Salus, goddess of health.

(29) Irene—Pax, goddess of peace.

(30) Eros—Cupid, god of falling in love.

(31) Eos—Aurora, goddess of the dawn.

(32) Hebe—Juventas, goddess of youth, youthfulness, and youthful manhood.

(33) Eris—Discordia, goddess of strife.

(34) Asklepios—Æsculapius, god of the healing art, of medicine and surgery, of all surgeons, physicians and persons longing for cure.

This list might be considerably extended.

Each of these universally accepted gods and goddesses should be thought of not as an entity whose worship was gradually spread throughout the Greco-Roman world, but as a sort of composite of dozens, scores, even hundreds of local deities originally more or less distinct.

Jupiter, the chief god of Rome, who lived on the Capitoline Hill and conferred upon his votaries victory, domination, and Empire, was not only Sky-Father but God of Supreme Power. As the Romans conquered town after town, city after city, and nation after nation, each community subjugated had its own local Sky-Father and God of Supreme Power, and the victorious Romans identified each local chief god with their Jupiter, and the vanquished not merely acquiesced, but were convinced of the actuality and reality of the identity.

So in their contact with the Greeks they at once identified their Jupiter with the Greek Zeus of Olympus, Father of Gods and King of Men. And this process had begun long before contact occurred between Romans and Greeks.

It is generally assumed that the ancestors of the Greeks, herdsmen from somewhere north of the Danube, brought with them in their southwestwardly migration common gods, and that the Zeus of every Greek city-state was the local development of the imported proto-Greek Sky-Father, and this may be the fact.

But for us it is only a conjecture. Indubitably the city-states of the Greek world, at the time of our first records of them, had a very vague sense of having common gods, and many a Greek city-state felt its local Zeus as a god for them only, and as by no means identical with the Zeus worshipped by any one of their hostile neighbor states.

Yet, as the Greeks were more and more leagued and allied together, as general participation in the Olympian games at four-year intervals more and more made the Greeks feel themselves kinsfolk, so they more and more came to regard each local Zeus as identical with the Zeus of Olympus worshipped at Olympia in Elis.

Alexander's miraculous career of conquest, brief as was the duration of his autocracy, greatly diffused and intensified the operation of this process, so that even the Egyptian Ammon was identified with Zeus and came to be worshipped later in the Greco-Roman world as Jupiter-Ammon.

So of all the other divinities, major and minor, in our previously given incomplete specimen list of thirty-odd. Most had become well established as fairly universal deities throughout the Greek world during the wars and truces of Alexander's turbulent successors for a century after his death in 323 B.C. before they began to be identified with Roman deities from 230 B.C. onward.

The early Romans were dull-witted and unimaginative folk. We have no record of any race whose deities were so concrete and specific, yet so impersonally abstract and vague. Take for instance their gods and goddesses of birth and childhood.

Carmenta, the goddess who protected women in childbirth, invoked as Carmenta Porrima or Antevorta or Carmenta Postvorta, according to the presentation of the fœtus at the beginning of birth; Parca, the goddess protecting the child while being born; Rumina, the goddess helping it to learn to suck;

Levana, the goddess of rising up or of getting raised up, who favored its acknowledgment as his child by its father; Cunina, the goddess who protected it in its cradle; Educa, the goddess who helped the weaned child to learn to eat; Potima, who did the like for drinking; Ossipaga, who helped its bones to harden; Carna, the goddess of muscle; Cuba, the goddess who watched over the child when its cradle was disused and it slept in a bed; Levana again, who helped it to rise; Statanus and Statilinus, gods and Statina, a goddess, who helped it to stand; Abeona, the goddess who helped it to walk away from anything, and Adeona who helped it to walk toward anything; Fabulinus or Farinus, the god who helped it to talk.

Indubitably, the Romans of Rome and the Latins of its neighborhood seriously and implicitly believed in every separate one of this detailed list of the divinities fostering the growth of each child, and meticulously invoked, conciliated, and thanked each and all for at least a thousand years.

They had more important deities equally abstract and impersonal: Janus, god of all beginnings, so of opening doors and gates; Tutanus and Tutulina, god and goddess of safety; Robigus and Robigo, god and goddess averter of blight on grain; Febris, goddess averter of fevers; Orbona, goddess averter of childlessness; Sancus, god of good faith and oaths, also called Deus Fidius and Semo Sancus; Virtus, goddess of manly valor; Honos, deity of honorable conduct; Mens, goddess of intelligence; Concordia, goddess of political harmony; Viriplaca, the goddess who helped wives to please their husbands; the very vague goddesses Dea Dia and Bona Dea, whose nature and specialties were unknown to uninitiated women and must not even be inquired about by men; Libitina, goddess of burial and funerals, later variously identified with Venus, Diana, and Proserpina; Bubona, goddess of cattle breeding; Epona, goddess of horse breeding; Pales, goddess of sheep breeding; Vertumnus, god of the changing seasons; Pomona, goddess of fruits; Terminus, god of boundaries, frontiers and boundary stones; Forculus, god of doors; Limentinus and Limentina, god and goddess of sills, lintels, and thresholds; Cardea, goddess of door hinges. All equally abstract and impersonal.

The Romans even deified occurrences and happenings. There was a story that a voice had been heard giving warning of peril to the state some days before the Gauls overwhelmed the Roman army at the Allia and consequently sacked Rome. For centuries afterward, on the spot where that voice was supposed to have been heard, ceremonies of gratitude and propitiation were held yearly for the god, Aius Locutius (the voice that spoke). And the Romans offered many thanksgiving sacrifices to the God Rediculus (Go Back!) who was believed to have caused Hannibal, after his victory at Cannæ, to go back instead of swiftly advancing on Rome, which was the obvious and natural thing for him to do and was universally dreaded and expected.

The Romans venerated also many classes or varieties of minor deities as contradictorily at once explicitly defined and nebulously indefinite.

The Lares were house gods protecting homes from danger from outside. Characteristically they were classified as *Lares Familiares,* protecting families; *Lares Urbani,* protecting cities; *Lares Rustici,* protecting country districts; *Lares Compitales,* protecting crossroads; *Lares Viales,* protecting highways; *Lares Marini,* protecting men at sea; *Lares Privati,* protecting individuals; *Lares Publici,* protecting nations.

The Penates were the guardian gods of the storeroom and pantry of a dwelling who protected the house and household against danger from within.

Genii were guardian deities of each person, married pair, household, family, clan, tribe, society, association, guild, city, nation, race, house, house-site, spot, place, locality, neighborhood, or district; one genius, at least, usually more than one, for each. A protecting genius was conceived of as a sort of guardian angel; not as an emissary of any higher divinity, but as independent and self-governed. The genius of an individual was thought of as being quite distinct from and different from the same individual's Lar Privatus.

The Manes were the spirits of the dead who had been duly laid to rest with adequate funeral rites, thought of as well-disposed minor divinities, helpful and solicitous.

(Ghosts of bodies not properly laid to rest were of three kinds. The word Lares, besides designating the household gods of a family, meant also the kind of ghosts which returned to their earthly home, generally with no unkindly feelings toward the living, but gently hinting that some detail of their burial ceremonies had been slighted. Larvæ were ghosts which haunted graves, each lurking or hovering about its former body. Lemures were pauper ghosts, without home or grave, haunting crossroads and highways, wretched, uneasy, embittered, vindictive, malevolent spirits, inexpressibly formidable and menacing.)

The Semones were guardian deities of the State, Republic and Commonwealth.

It is probable that, even before they began to acquire and assimilate Greek ideas, the Romans had come to think of and represent their gods and goddesses, major and minor, as beings of human form. But they had few or no stories about them.

Greek mythology, on the other hand, abounded with tales about the gods and divinities of Greece, and the lure and charm of these exquisite myths made the Greek divinities appear fascinatingly human and real. The Romans gradually came to know, love, and enjoy the countless beauties of Greek mythology and to feel that Greek deities were also their deities. Thus they acquired a belief in and a feeling of possession of many minor divinities originally wholly un-Roman and purely Greek.

Such were Uranus, a god of Greece before the Greeks entered it, father of Kronos—Saturn; the Titans and Giants, primitive deities ousted and supplanted by the gods and goddesses of Olympus; Iris, the messenger of the Olympians, identified with the rainbow; Nemesis, Di-ke and A-te, goddesses of stern justice and unescapable retribution; Astræa, goddess of justice; Themis, goddess of political order; Æolus, god of the winds; Priapus, god of virility and fertility; the Dioscuri, Castor and Pollux, gods of horse mastery and boxing; the Cyclopes, minor artisan gods, forgers of Jove's thunderbolts and assistants to Vulcan; Silenus, a wood-god, companion to Dionysus; Nireus, Proteus, Phorcus, Palæmon, and other minor sea-gods; Amphitrite, chief goddess of the sea, wife and queen to Neptune; Thetis, Doris, Leucothea, Galatea, and other minor sea-goddesses; the Tritons, minor sea-gods whose legs, from mid-thigh, were like the bodies of serpents ending in a fish-tail.

The Greeks also had myths of semidivine beings such as the Sirens, the Harpies, and the Gorgons.

The knowledge of Greek myths, assimilation of Greek myths, and belief in Greek myths humanized and ennobled Roman religious thought and feeling.

Especially as the lively and tasteful imagination of the Greeks peopled all the world with minor divinities called nymphs, conceived of as kindly and beautiful goddesses in the guise of lovely young women. There were many varieties of nymphs. The Naiads were nymphs of springs, fountains, brooks, lakes, and streams; the Nereids, daughters of Nereus, sea nymphs; Oceanids, nymphs of the wide ocean; Oreads, nymphs of the hills and mountains; Dryads or Hamadryads, nymphs of the forests, troops of them anywhere, and here and there one alone cherishing one special old, large and beautiful tree; Potamids, nymphs of the rivers.

It must be understood that no Greek minor divinity ever was accepted as one of the gods of Rome invoked as fosterer of the prosperity of the Commonwealth in the course of any public ceremony conducted according to traditional Roman governmental ritual.

Nor, in fact, did any Greek major deity so become an accredited god of Rome except after formal acceptance as such by Rome's College of Pontiffs authorized by a formal vote of the Roman Senate, following careful discussion of the meaning of the oracles vouchsafed from the holy places of the highest repute, urging that Rome invoke the deity in question.

But, gradually, the Romans of Rome, as of her colonies and everywhere throughout the Empire, came to regard all Greek minor deities as having always been also their deities, to be invoked as such by anyone needing help such as they could give.

Identifications universally accepted, throughout the Greco-Roman Mediterranean world, were as follows, putting the Greek name first.

(a) Nymphs—Camenæ, since the Latin Camenæ were minor goddesses of the countryside.

(b) Muses—Camenæ, since the Latin Camenæ were goddesses of song and prophecy.

(c) Charites—Gratiæ, the three Graces, goddesses of personal gracefulness.

(d) Moeræ—Parcæ, the three dread goddesses who spun, drew out, and cut off the life span of every human being.

(e) Erinyes—Furiæ, Diræ, the furies who punished the guilty with insanity and other dooms.

(f) Daimones—Genii, minor divinities much like the guardian angels of modern mythology.

(g) Panisci—Fauns, little Pans or Fauns, boyish wood-gods, usually represented as human to mid-thigh, but with goats' legs and hoofs; conceived as companions of the wood-gods Pan, Faunus and Silenus, joyously trooping after them.

CHAPTER XIX

TENETS OF GRECO-ROMAN PAGANISM

IT must be noted that the pagan attitude of mind among the Greeks, among the Italians, all over the Mediterranean, world among its various polytheistic peoples, identified the deity and that of which he or she was deity.

This is hard for a modern to realize or conceive.

Ruskin, somewhere, wrote illuminatingly that he had known of but one modern spontaneously uttering a genuinely pagan prayer. The parents of an English child had to visit Australia, leaving their little girl in care of her aunts. They thought it best not to let her know beforehand, and, when she asked for them until an aunt told where they were going and that they were far off on the sea, the child, half dressed as she was before breakfast, ran to the wash basin, plunged her hands into it and exclaimed:

"You naughty water! Give me back my mamma and papa!"

This was completely pagan and precisely with the pagan attitude of mind.

Greco-Roman pagans did not ask what the weather was like, but what was Jupiter doing. Jupiter was not merely god of the weather; he was the weather. So they sailed on or bathed in Neptune, basked in the warmth of Apollo, cooked their food over Vulcan, ate Ceres, drank Bacchus, and spoke of a fat-witted person as with "*crassa minerva,*" for Minerva was not only goddess of brains; brain was "Minerva."

Many of the pagan gods manifestly were personifications of the powers of nature, as Jupiter, typifying the might of air in motion; Neptune, symbolizing the might of the sea; Apollo, personifying the healing power of sunshine; Vulcan, the efficacy of blazing fire; Ceres, Rhea, Demeter, and Cybele, personifying the fertility of the earth; Helios, personifying the orb of the sun, and Selene, similarly personifying the orb of the moon; Flora, the goddess of blossom time; and Aurora, goddess of the Dawn.

Some personified the influences of mankind's environment and of the conditions of human life upon mankind; as, Pan, god of everything in wild nature which affects the prosperity of explorers, pioneers, hunters, and lone crofters; and the goddesses of Luck, Victory, Health, Peace and the like.

Many personified the qualities, powers, emotions, or activities of humankind, as Mars, personifying success in war; Mercury, ingenuity personified; Juno, prototype of noble womanhood; Minerva, brain personified; Venus, typifying love; Diana, symbolizing maidenly coyness and aloofness; Vesta, personifying hearthside virtues; Dionysus, personification of enjoyment; Bellona, battle frenzy in human form; Hygeia, personified healthiness; Hebe, youthfulness personified; Cupid, personification of passionate desire; Irene, symbolizing the sense of relief upon the cessation of warfare; Eris, typifying the uncontrollable impulse to disagree.

But not a few were human beings who had helped others in life and were conceived of as undying, as living on after death, and as unceasingly invocable by human beings needing their aid.

Of this kind was indubitably Æsculapius, god of all means for the cure of human ailments, manifestly a deified physician, probably the Egyptian Im-hotep; very likely Hercules was originally a mere man of unusual strength, whose exploits and helpfulness in life led those who had profited by his aid to believe him still puissant and kindly after his death. It is not improbable that Dionysus, Vulcan, Mercury, Mars, and Apollo may have originated from the dead, or had blended with the conception of each reminiscences of the powers and helpfulness of some actual eminent and illustrious man of long ago.

In fact, from the earliest ages until the forcible suppression of paganism, the entire pagan world was permeated by the conviction that some few men became gods after they ceased to live among mankind.

This came easier to pagans, as everywhere in the Mediterranean world there was a tendency to regard all spirits of the dead properly laid to rest with adequate funeral rites as thereafter minor divinities. The Romans addressed and spoke of such spirits not merely as Manes, but usually as *"Dii Manes."* Not so definitely as among the present-day Chinese, but yet positively and without question, every Roman family conceived of all the Manes of all its ancestors as kindly minor deities watching over the family's destinies and solicitous for their descendants' welfare. And the less important the human-being had been in life, the less valuable to his clan was his aid after death; the more prominent the living individual had been, the more precious to his posterity would be his favor and help.

This attitude of mind can be seen at its intensest development in Egypt. There even the poorest family took astonishing pains as to laying to eternal rest any corpse and so insuring the everlasting guardianship and furtherance of the spirit of the dead. The cost was accounted money well spent. Well-to-do Egyptian families lavished on their dead amazingly expensive provision for the comfort of the ghost. This extravagance augmented with the rank of the deceased. For the mummy of a dead king no amount of equipment was too much, no costliness excessive. For it was the conviction of all Egyptians that the prosperity of the living depended on the adjuvancy of the spirits of the dead, the more important the spirit the more efficacious its aid, so that labor, materials, and wealth lavished on the burial of a king became the best possible investment for the surviving population of Egypt and their posterity.

In kind, but not in degree, the conceptions of the folk of the entire Mediterranean world were like those of the Egyptians.

It cannot be too much emphasized that human beings are entirely capable of taking for granted without forethought or afterthought, crediting and holding tenaciously at one and the same time beliefs mutually discordant, irreconcilable, and even directly contradictory of each other.

This is especially true as to legendary religious beliefs, the origin of which is lost in the haze of remote antiquity and which are accepted unhesitatingly by generation after generation as transmitted from their forefathers. Ancestral traditions are seldom scrutinized by anyone; and children, as a rule, absorb without question what their elders impart to them in their tender years and cling throughout life to all such beliefs as they have assimilated in childhood.

This might be illustrated by many contemporary instances. Suffice it to say that the Greco-Roman pagans held implicitly and serenely several notions as to spirits, ghosts, life after death, future rewards and punishments, and the like, which ideas were more or less mutually incompatible, but which were never, by the generality of pagans, compared, contrasted, scrutinized, and valued.

The Greco-Roman pagan conception of life after death was very different from ours, and much vaguer and fainter. Someone has neatly written that among Christian peoples life after death is a pious hope, among the Chinese of today it is an undoubted fact.

And the difference in intensity of credence in life after death among the Chinese and among European and American Christians is not so great as between the attitude toward belief in life after death among modern Christian peoples and among the ancient pagans.

It may be conveyed by contrasting the utterance of the little New England girl who said that her baby brother had gone to heaven, but the tired part of him was buried in the churchyard, with the statement in the opening lines of Homer's Iliad that the wrath of Achilles sent to Hades the wraiths of many heroes while they themselves became food for dogs and a feast for birds of prey.

The general modern conception is that of an immortal soul which *is* the individual and of the body as its temporary "muddy vesture of decay." The universal ancient conception was of the body and the human-being as identical, and of the survival after death as that of an insubstantial phantasmal image of the deceased.

Traditional beliefs are seldom clear cut or logical. So with the Greco-Roman conceptions about the spirits of the dead. No one questioned the actuality of the existence of ghosts. There were no walled-in and guarded graveyards in antiquity. Any ghost could guard its own grave. Graves, tombs, and sepulchres were put anywhere and left unwatched. Only the most irreligious, impious, and ungodly of lifelong criminals ventured to incur the doom certain to fall on those who disregarded the power of a ghost.

But just as it was held that only a few ghosts haunted their former homes, only a few wandered homeless and graveless about the open countryside; so not all spirits of the duly buried were held to become *Dii Manes*.

Whatever may have been the earlier view, the current notion throughout the Greco-Roman pagan world was that survival after death was not a matter of course and a certainty for every human being born, but was a personal boon, won by personal merit.

Any average yeoman or townsman would have scouted the suggestion that there was any life after death for a three-days-old infant. Few would have admitted any likelihood of life after death for the spirit or ghost of an aged slave, or even for that of a dull peasant freeman who had hoed clods and tended farm stock for ninety monotonous years.

On the other hand, all felt sure of the personal survival of every worthy and beloved wife and mother, still more of every citizen in good standing.

This general attitude of mind among the population at large was ancestral and was wholly unaffected by the speculations of the more distinguished philosophers and by the teachings of their disciples and admirers.

Except a microscopic minority of skeptics, no one in the pagan world would have questioned the certainty of eternal life for the spirit of any eminent and illustrious public man or of any renowned military leader. He had deserved it.

And it was generally, even universally, assumed that incomparable paragons, preëminent among their fellow men and illustrious for the benefits they had conferred upon them, were certain not merely of immortality, but of exaltation to the status of deathless godship.

This conception may have originated from and certainly was fostered by the existence everywhere of distinct classes of human beings—slaves, freedmen, freemen, citizens, nobles, and Senators; and of the belief in the existence of similar classes of divinities—tritons, nymphs and fauns, minor divinities, minor gods, major gods, and the Great Gods of Olympus; and by the coexistent universality of the belief that some men born of women, as Æsculapius and Hercules, became gods after death, survived not as ghosts or spirits, but as individuals, were welcomed among the gods by the gods as their compeers and throve forever on worship by mankind and acclaim among their fellow gods.

The selective nature of promotion for merit from one class of the community to the next higher strengthened the general belief in the possibility of some few illustrious human beings becoming gods after their decease.

As a slave might become a free man, as a freedman might become a full citizen, as an ordinary free-born man might become a noble, even a Senator, so it was believed that a mere human being might become a god by manifestly deserving such exaltation.

The belief was, with the Romans, not an importation from any foreign people, but inherited, traditional, inherent, and part of Roman primitive beliefs. One of the oldest Roman traditions was that Romulus, first King of Rome, became a god after his death; and he was invoked and worshipped under the name of Quirinus, originally the Sabine god of war, analogue of the Latin god Mars, whose cult was brought into Rome when the Roman and Sabine settlers on near-by hills coalesced into the Roman Commonwealth.

The belief that some few men became gods after death was rife among the Greeks and unquestioned, but the occurrence was considered very unusual. Like Herakles and Asklepios, all men who, by their transcendent powers and services to humanity, had become after death accredited members of the fellowship of Olympian Gods had been indeed born of women, but had had as fathers not men, but gods, and so had been demigods from birth. Therefore there was among the Greeks

So that no one, not only among the soldiers of his army, among the populations he had conquered, among his officers and generals, but even among his own kinsfolk, took it otherwise than as what was to have been expected when the oracle of Zeus at Ammon in the Libyan desert, esteemed equal in sanctity and reliability to the oracles of Zeus at Dodona and of Apollo at Delphi, declared that Alexander was the son of Zeus, not of Philip, and actually a demigod on earth and certain to be welcomed among the Olympians as their compeer after his departure from among men.

This universal estimate of him as more than a mere man, as a demigod and son of Zeus, was the chief basis of Alexander's claim to autocracy and to be regarded as accredited successor to the Achæmenian Shahs of Persia.

Throughout more than fully nine centuries after the deification of Romulus no Roman seemed to his countrymen so superhuman that it was bruited about that he was destined to deification after death. During this long period their most brilliant leaders appeared to their most enthusiastic soldiers mere men, not nascent demigods.

Yet the idea of a mere man meriting deification, while dormant for over nine hundred years, was never absent from the inner consciousness of the Romans of Rome, as of the Latins of Latium and the Italians of Italy, and was more or less implicitly believed in by every generation of Romans.

Long before his final victory at Zama in 202 B.C., in fact while he was yet a youth, a tendency developed among his legionaries to regard Publius Cornelius Scipio, later called Africanus because he conquered Africa (modern Tunisia), as a living demigod on earth among men. But this tendency worked itself off in the general belief that he was the special darling and intimate friend and confidant of Jupiter Maximus Optimus, which belief Scipio himself had held from childhood all his life long and implicitly credited.

Just about a century later, Gaius Marius, in spite of his mean, uncouth, and squalid personal appearance, after he had saved Rome from the Cimbri and Teutons, was hailed by some of his legionaries as a god on earth and had much ado, again and again, to avoid being accorded divine honors by his enthusiastic soldiery, by the populace and aldermen of this or that grateful colony or allied town, even by his political partisans among Romans in Rome. This attitude of mind toward him displayed itself sporadically, never universally, time after time during the fifteen years preceding his death in 86 B.C.

During the ensuing dozen years the like tendency appeared among the soldiery and partisans of Lucius Cornelius Sulla, victor over Mithridates, over Marius in the civil war between them and autocrat of Rome and her Empire from that victory until his death.

But neither Marius nor Sulla was ever during life openly accorded the honors due a living god on earth, nor was either officially deified after death.

Pompey, from his joining his father during the civil war between Marius and Sulla with three full regiments raised and equipped through his amazing initiative, even while a youth was looked upon as more than merely human. His continuous run of luck thereafter, in Sicily and in Africa against the Marian faction, in Spain, in the Pyrenees, in the Alps, then in Italy against the remnants of the Marian factionaries and of the Spartacan outlaws, then against the federated pirates of the Mediterranean islands and coasts, then against countless Asiatic fortresses, towns, armies, nations, and sultans, confirmed the conjecture that he was destined to deification after death and manifestly a living god on earth.

This belief, widely current among his legionaries, admirers, and partisans, greatly contributed to the deadlock between him and Cæsar which resulted in their civil war.

Cæsar was indubitably regarded as merely human by his parents, himself, his relatives and all his associates until in 58 B.C., when already over forty-four years of age, he, as proconsul, took charge of his allotted province, including Illyricum, Hither Gaul, and Farther Gaul. Even then he was regarded by his most ardent adherents as only a clever city politician, who was very likely to fail disastrously as the general-in-chief of a frontier army.

Actually he deftly surprised and butchered one-fourth of the Swiss on the Saône; defeated, vanquished, and subdued the Swiss in one hard-fought and well-led battle near Bibracte; annihilated the German power in Gaul in one equally close and neat battle near Besançon; although surprised on the Sambre by the Belgians and outnumbered four to one, he not only turned an apparently hopeless disaster into a crushing victory, but subdued all the Belgians by swiftly following up this advantage; subjugated all the many seashore states of the broken coast of western Gaul as the result of one brilliant naval victory; exterminated in one morning 400,000 Germans who had ventured to cross the Rhine not far from its delta; twice bridged and crossed the Rhine; twice invaded Britain, losing not one single private soldier on any one of the four sea voyages; stormed Bourges, blockaded and captured Alesia; and, after thus quelling a universal insurrection of all the Gauls at once, finally made all Gaul a pacified Roman provincial possession.

In the course of this hurricane of master strokes his legionaries came to regard him successively as a real Imperator, a man who could infallibly win victories; as the only genuine Imperator alive; as outclassing all Roman Imperators ever; as more than a man, as indubitably a god upon earth in human shape, destined to be a god among gods forever after he departed from among men.

And the like was felt by the populace at Rome and in every colony and allied town and city. During the seven and a half centuries which had elapsed since Rome was founded, its hallowed *pomerium* had but once been entered by armed enemies and they had been Gauls. Rome had been intermittently, almost continuously, embroiled in warfare with Gauls of some tribe or other for fully 325 weary years. Rome had won every war against Gauls, but only because Romans never gave up a war once begun, and so at last attained to a victory which would bring peace or truce. Yet, if one counted men slain on each side or battles won and battles lost, the Gauls had had far the best of it in both respects. And behold, within nine years Cæsar had killed in battle a million Gauls, with a Roman death roll amazingly small by comparison; he had taken a full million men prisoners; he had not only paid for his warfare out of the proceeds of booty captured, but had enriched himself, his men, and the treasury of Rome; he had forever freed Rome from its perennial dread of the Gauls; what was more, he had twice invaded Britain and twice bridged the Rhine, the first general to do either. This was no mere man; here was an unmistakable demigod living among men, worthy of the honors due to a god.

His victories in the civil wars and his mastery of the Roman world intensified the conviction of his legionaries and of the city mobs that he was not human, but divine, and they read his triumph over Pompey and his partisans as a clear declaration by Jupiter Maximus Optimus that this was the man he chose for his representative and vicegerent on earth, and whom he marked as a living deity among men.

Only a very small coterie of intellectuals, mostly partisans of Pompey, but also some of Cæsar's own officers, not merely scouted this general assumption, but were indignant at it as much as or far more than at his autocracy, and so conspired and assassinated him.

It should be observed that Cæsar, born as he was and brought up as he was, most likely sincerely believed in his own godhead and in his being the choice of Jupiter Maximus Optimus for coadjutor on earth, and so by him stamped as a god alive among men.

One factor in the universal acceptance of Cæsar, under the title of Divus Julius, as one of Rome's gods after his death, was the feeling among his legionaries, like that among the soldiery of Alexander after his death. In both cases the rank and file of his army had come to look on their beloved and adored leader as the source of all their successes and as endowed with superhuman powers. There was a feeling of instinctive overmastering incredulity that the personality which had been all powerful yesterday was annihilated today, gone forever, and would help them no more. They could not resist their feeling that now after his death, as then before it, Cæsar would be their chief reliance, hope, and helper. So, to them, he was a god.

From long before the foundation of Rome, all through the existence of the republic, till the instincts of paganism very slowly and gradually evaporated long after its forcible suppression, the *imperium* as conceived of by the primitive Latins, by the Romans of every period, and by their colonists, allies, and subjects, was a magical gift which consecrated its possessor and could be transmitted intact. Under the Republic the citizens indicated by their votes at each election to whom they wished the *imperium* transmitted by its then holders, but they could not confer it; only its holder could confer it.

Cæsar had been formally proclaimed Imperator for life, and he had not only adopted his grandnephew, Octavian, afterwards known as Augustus, as a son, but had made him his heir. Not a few of Rome's legionaries interpreted this as automatically, at Cæsar's death, conferring upon Augustus the *imperium* for life and an *imperium* as definitely paramount to any other as Cæsar's *imperium* had been. This feeling was the basis of his acclamation as Imperator by a minority of Rome's legionaries and the foundation of his rise to supreme universal autocratic power.

The amazing successes of Augustus in politics, intrigues, negotiations, warfare, and administration, confirmed, intensified, and steadily diffused this view, and with it created and spread the belief that he as much as his adopted father, or even more, was the darling of the gods, their chosen representative on earth, even a living deity among men and manifestly destined to be a god among the gods after his death.

Augustus never permitted any divine honors to be paid to him in Rome itself, or indeed anywhere in Italy. But he could not stem the torrent of sincere belief in his godship which inundated the Roman world and so far yielded to the general estimate of him as to permit the establishment of the cult of *Augustus and Rome* throughout the provinces, not only upon his death, but during his lifetime. Born as he was and living in the world he lived in, he himself cannot have doubted his own godship.

Practically everybody believed in it. As husband of Cleopatra, according to Egyptian law and custom, Cæsar had become, in the eyes of all Egyptians and to a great degree in the eyes of the entire Greco-Roman world, legal heir of the Ptolemies and so of Alexander the Great, who had been a god on earth, and of the Achæmenian Shahs of Persia, who had been gods on earth; and so Cæsar, not only as recognized as such by his legionaries and adherents, but as heir of Alexander and the Persian shahs, had a claim to be considered a god on earth. This opinion had been widely accepted throughout Rome's Empire. It was widely felt that Cæsar's adoption of Augustus and his heirship toward Cæsar had transmitted to him not only Cæsar's *imperium,* but his personal godship.

This feeling corroborated, in the eyes of all the denizens of Rome's Empire, the other facts, as they held them to be, which constituted valid reasons for the adherents of Augustus claiming that he was a demigod among men and destined after death to be a god among the gods.

By the end of his long Principate, Tiberius, however, hated by the Patricians and other nobles of Rome, was regarded, by the legionaries, citizens, allies, and subjects of the Roman Commonwealth and Empire as a demigod and a living god among men.

Although he was hated by the nobility and Senate to such a degree that it required all the tact and skill of so forceful a personage as Caligula to induce the Senate to permit him to execute the directions given in the will of Tiberius, and not even Caligula's dominating personality could compel the Senate to proclaim Tiberius a god after his death, yet he was regarded as a god throughout the colonies and provinces and his memory cherished.

After his time every Roman Emperor, once established in the Principate by having been acclaimed Imperator by the soldiery and clothed with the tribunician power for life by decree of the Senate, was regarded as a living demigod among men and as destined to eternal godship after death.

Claudius was always ridiculous to those about him. As a result of the disease from which he had suffered in childhood, the attack of which he had barely survived, he was awkward, clumsy, and absurd, a very unimperial and undivine figure. So, after his death, Seneca, one of the most notable public men and literary men of the time, composed a comic burlesque of a description of an Imperial Apotheosis depicting Claudius as changed not into a god, but into a pumpkin, and this *Apocolocyntosis* was a favorite humorous recitation for centuries thereafter.

Yet the belief of practically all the provincials that Claudius had been a god on earth, strengthened by the many great public works completed in the course of his Principate, was a very powerful factor among those which compelled the Senate to proclaim his official deification.

Some Emperors, as Domitian and Caligula, made themselves ridiculous by claiming that mere recognition as Emperor made them gods at once without any attainment by them of personal preëminence through military exploits or display of matchless talents.

In some cases, as after the abasement of Nero, the Senate formally voted that the recent incumbent of the imperial dignity had been chosen by mistake and was in fact no god after his death and had never been a living demigod among men.

But mostly, from the lifetime of Augustus until the death of Julian, during more than three and a half centuries, each Prince of the Commonwealth was universally regarded as not only destined to become a god after his death, but as having attained godship upon his accession to supreme imperial power and as being entitled to invocation, propitiation, and thanksgiving as a god. All pagans of the Greco-Roman world implicitly believed this and shuddered at failure to revere and reverence the reigning Emperor as horrible and shocking impiety, certain to call down on the delinquent and the entire community the wrath of all the gods of Rome.

Especially was this true of such Emperors as Vespasian, Nerva, Trajan, Hadrian, Antoninus Pius, Marcus Aurelius, Septimius Severus, Aurelian, and Diocletian. No pagan doubted their godship while they lived, and not one of them can have doubted it himself, not even Vespasian, although he joked about it on his deathbed. They were gods, and failure to recognize them as gods and to accord them the honors due them was impiety to them and to all the gods.

In extant books on the interaction between Christianity and paganism it is not sufficiently emphasized that devout pagans believed in their doctrine of the deification of preëminent men and specifically the pagans of the imperial era in the godhead of their Emperor quite as earnestly and tenaciously as any Christians ever believed their dogma of the Incarnation.

Nor has it been sufficiently emphasized that, if confronted with a request for a sincere comparison of the pagan tenets of the man made god on earth and of apotheosis after death and the Christian tenets of the god made man and the virgin birth, any average educated pagan of the millions who from generation to generation honored their Emperor as a god would have held not merely that one conception was as probable and plausible as the other but positively that the pagan conception was the more sensible, rational, and logical of the two.

CHAPTER XX

TENETS OF GRECO-ROMAN PAGANISM

(*Concluded*)

THE pagan conception of impiety, as universally held throughout the Roman Empire, is not easy for moderns to comprehend. Pagans conceived of their gods as benevolent and kindly, but as quick to take offense not only at any insult or affront, but even at any slighting, neglect, irreverence, or disrespect.

The tale of Salmoneus, who enraged the King of Olympus by imitating thunder and lightning and claiming equality with Zeus as a hurler of thunderbolts, that of Niobe, who incensed Latona by bragging of her far more numerous progeny, and the tales of some other overweening offenders in Greek mythology are extreme examples and need hardly be mentioned. So likewise Actæon, who inadvertently intruded on Artemis. Such myths merely exemplify the popular belief in the occasional wrathfulness of gods habitually kindly and indulgent, but choleric when irritated.

A most instructive illustration is the story of Ajax Oileus. None of the Olympian deities had been more consistent and enthusiastic partisans of the Greeks besieging Troy than Pallas. She had her favorites among them, Ulysses first of all, Diomede, and others. But she watched over and assisted all, not only collectively, but individually. Ajax Oileus, King of the Locrians, was one of the most capable and successful of the leaders of the blockaders. Pallas had aided him often during the ten years leaguer of Troy, and he had propitiated her with many invocations and thank-offerings.

On the night of the sack of Troy, Cassandra, daughter of Sultan Priam, took refuge in the Temple of Pallas, from which Ajax Oileus dragged her.

This was an act of outrageous impiety. As against it his years of veneration and worship and the goddess's years of protection counted for nothing. By ignoring the sanctity of her temple, by laying hands on any human being who had there taken refuge, he had merited retribution, had incurred her implacable hostility. It was incumbent upon his associates, however much his henchmen, relatives, friends, or admirers, at once and remorselessly to punish him for his transgression. He should have been then and there stoned to death, all present participating. His fellow Greeks did nothing to punish him, though some perhaps remonstrated. By failing to punish him they incurred guilt equal to his. This guiltiness affected not only the entire host collectively, but every man individually. All became, deservedly, objects of the wrath of Pallas. With the consent of Zeus she loosed upon the Greek fleet as it voyaged homeward a storm which overwhelmed and scattered it. Not only did Ajax perish, but many of the heroes guilty only as abettors of his misdeed.

The conceptions implicit in this tale existed not only in Homer's time, but as long as paganism flourished. The gods of any community were sedulous and responsive partners of men while properly reverenced, invoked, propitiated, and thanked. But any infraction of ritual, any dereliction by the priesthood, any indifference among the commonalty might incur their unmeasured wrath. What was more, the impiety of any one citizen or denizen of any country, of any member of or visitor to any community, might bring down upon the entire nation or people the disastrous indignation of its gods.

Such wrath of the gods might be appeased only by the prompt identification of the offenders and their immediate punishment by death, and by ample recognition of the past favors of the gods and of the community's desire for their continued favor by adequate services of invocation, propitiation, and thanksgiving.

At Rome and among the Romans official governmental services for the appeasement of the gods were mostly sacrifices, with the customary prayers, chariot races in circuses, and banquets for the gods with their feature of throngs of people showing respect for the gods by filing past the display of the statues of the gods reclining on their luxurious cushions with the lavish banquet spread before them. The populace came to regard the banquets and sacrifices as necessary concomitants to the chariot races, but the chariot races as the most efficient of these propitiatory observances, since, as being most enjoyable to human beings, they were assumed to be most pleasing to the gods.

Theatrical performances, tragedies, comedies, mimes, pantomimes, and farces came to be regarded as valuable auxiliary methods of propitiation of the gods, who were presumed to enjoy whatever their votaries enjoyed, and the giving of such shows along with sacrifices, chariot races, and banquets for the gods was a public concern and part of the official governmental worship of Rome's gods.

The shows of the amphitheatre, on the other hand, were not part of the governmental worship of Rome's gods, were never official, and, even if given by officials, were usually given by them as individuals, not as representatives of the Commonwealth. Yet they came to be regarded by the populace as quite as necessary to adequate propitiation of Rome's gods as chariot races in a circus. Amphitheatre shows were of two kinds, combats of gladiators and *venationes,* fights of beasts with each other or of men with beasts.

Gladiatorial combats indubitably originated among the Etruscans. In primitive times it had been a general, perhaps an invariable, custom, that upon the burial of any person of importance, prominence, or wealth, slaves or prisoners were butchered that their spirits might accompany the departed and act as servitors in the life beyond death. Also, at anniversary or other memorial services in honor of the dead, it was customary to put to death one or more human victims, the idea being that blood was life, that the dead lacked life, that an offering of blood was in some incomprehensible mystical fashion a gift of life or of some brief retaste of life to the dead and so pleasing and propitiatory to ghosts.

Somehow, somewhere, someone had the idea that instead of merely cutting the victims' throats it would be equally agreeable to the dead and more diverting to the living to set the victims to fighting each other and so shedding each others' blood. Probably at the first all were killed either by each other or by the celebrants. Later the victor in any combat was generally then spared and reserved for a future occasion. As time passed even wounding was regarded as sufficiently propitiatory to the ghosts, as blood had been shed in their honor. With the passage of time, less and less importance was attached to the honoring of the dead and more and more to the diversion of the spectators.

But it cannot be too much emphasized that every gladiatorial show given at Rome or elsewhere throughout Rome's Empire was felt by all beholders as an honor to some dead man or woman or men or women. Romans and their colonials never lost the recollection that gladiatorial combats had originally been more frequent at actual funerals than as anniversary or memorial services, and that every one was in honor of the dead.

There is no indubitable record of any gladiatorial show being given in honor of all Rome's dead collectively, as Athenian funeral orations honored customarily all the dead of Athens from her foundation to the delivering of the oration. Each and every gladiatorial show honored some specified relative of the giver of the exhibition, usually an ancestor, often a father or grandfather, or some group of ancestors, seldom all, usually those who had attained renown.

Yet, by unconscious analogy, the spectators in the Colosseum at Rome, in other countless amphitheatres throughout the Empire, as at Arles, Nîmes, Treves, Thysdrus, or wherever, came to feel that they enjoyed the gladiatorial shows as much as or more than chariot races, therefore the gods must enjoy them as much; therefore they must be as effectual means for propitiating the gods as were chariot races. This notion came to be diffused among the commonalty of all the west and then among all classes of the community. Only experts at the lore of religion distinguished chariot races as official governmental acts of public propitiation of the gods and gladiatorial shows as private acts of worship with which Rome's hierarchy had no concern and which were not only not essential to the adoration of Rome's gods, but did not contribute to that end.

Venationes originally had nothing whatever to do with worship or propitiation or any phase of religion. They originated from the desire of Roman elected officials to do whatever would please the populace and make themselves popular with the people.

Roman gentry on their estates, with much woodland, forest, or upland near by, were addicted to hunting in the customary fashion. Their huntsmen went out with nets, which they set up in the form of a V, a strong pocket net at the point, usually in a gully across which a reliable barrier net was stretched, with guard nets almost as unbreakable along the top of either bank. From the pocket net adequately strong nets extended for a sufficient distance along each leg of the V. Beyond them the V-shaped inclosure was extended, often for miles, by cords outstrung on bushes or branches, cords with bunches of red feathers at intervals. Across the wide opening of the V a sufficient force of beaters disposed themselves in a wider arc, and then, with shouts and thwacking of their staffs, with wavings of torches and hallos, drove into the V and down it into the pocket net all game before them, chiefly deer, but also hares, wild pigs, foxes, and wolves. Those successfully driven into the pocket net were there slaughtered by the gentry, as in England in our days grouse, pheasants, and such birds are habitually shot from butts by gunners who await their approach while fleeing from the line of advancing beaters.

Such battues were greatly enjoyed by all participants, not only by the gentry who did the killing, and their guests who looked on from any near point of vantage, but by the beaters and all neighborhood peasantry and slaves who could manage to get near enough to see anything of the battue, as they were permitted and even encouraged to do.

Such hunts were less frequent than fox hunts are nowadays in England, and while all the countryside participated as nowadays in England, fewer could participate and more heard of such pocket-net hunts only by report.

There was much envy by townsfolk of the country folk who had the chance to look on at such hunts, and more of the gentry able to afford them.

Some canny politician originated the idea of having beasts caught and of having them chivied and killed in an enclosure in or near a city or town where the townsfolk could gather and watch, thus making every townsman as well off as the wealthiest country proprietor, as far as concerned watching the culminating battue of a costly pocket-net hunt or its full equivalent.

The idea took and a *venatio* was first exhibited in Rome in 186 B.C. by Marcus Fulvius Nobilior, after his triumph over the Aetolians.

By the end of the republic such exhibitions of men fighting beasts and of beasts fighting each other had become frequent. Some were exhibited in the very Forum, inside temporary inclosures; others in amphitheatres of wood, also temporary. In 30 B.C. the first stone amphitheatre was built outside Rome in the Campus Martius (drill ground) by Statilius Taurus. The greatest of all amphitheatres, the Colosseum, was begun by Vespasian and finished by his son Domitian about A.D. 90. It had been dedicated and an exhibition given in it in A.D. 80, while Titus was emperor. In it, thereafter, were given the most magnificent *venationes* the world ever saw.

In them beasts occasionally fought each other, as a lion and a buffalo, a bull and a bear. Mostly professional beast fighters faced and killed beasts of every sort, as matadors in Spain today kill bulls.

Almost as frequent as killings of beasts by men were killings of criminals by savage beasts. So countless audiences beheld lions, tigers, bears, and other beasts of prey rend criminals of all sorts, which was a kind of spectacle much relished by Romans and their provincials and held greatly pleasing to the gods.

Amphitheatres, each not only with its gladiatorial shows, but with its beast fights, were built in or near every important city of the western Roman world.

The part of the Roman Empire populated by Greeks or by races with customs and habits of thought and feeling acquired from the Greeks or colored by Greek instincts, never took to beast fights or gladiatorial shows.

In most of the eastern portions of the Roman Empire gladiators were all but unknown and seldom appeared or fought; beast fights were distinctly exceptional, were shown in not many cities and rarely, and few or no amphitheatres were ever built.

Although their vogue dated only from A.D. 90 or thereabouts, within half a century, certainly long before the end of Trajan's Principate, beast fights were regarded by all the population of the Western World as just as essential to the worship and propitiation of the gods as gladiatorial shows, theatrical exhibitions, chariot races, banquets for the gods, sacrifices, or any of the other official methods of worship.

The Romans had a very positive instinct for adequacy in propitiation. It was not enough to invoke the gods respectfully, to ask their advice and follow it; it was imperatively needful also that thanksgiving be expressed commensurately with the benefits conferred on the state by the benignity of its gods and through their furtherance.

Thanksgiving (*supplicationes*) were in early times for one day; of two days only on extraordinary occasions; of three only after very noteworthy successes. In 396 B.C., after the capture of Veii in Etruria, for the first time the Senate decreed four consecutive days of public thanksgiving.

Even after that, for centuries, three consecutive days was thought enough: as for the ending of the dread of Hannibal after his brother Hasdrubal, bringing reinforcements, was defeated and slain at Sena Gallica in 207 B.C.; for simultaneous victories in Greece and Spain in 194 B.C.; for the subjugation of Liguria in 181 B.C. and of Illyricum in 168 B.C.

But when, in 62 B.C., the news reached Rome that Pompey had finally abolished Mithridates, the Senate felt that not only would the populace feel dissatisfied with a thanksgiving not outshining any preceding it, but that the gods would be affronted unless gratitude to them was manifested by unheard-of acknowledgment for unheard-of beneficence from them.

Therefore there was voted, for the first time, a *supplicatio* of ten consecutive days.

And when, in 57 B.C., the news came that Cæsar's army had overrun most of wild Gaul and had vanquished the Belgians, the most redoubtable of the Gauls, this feat appeared so much beyond even Pompey's incredible series of victories that nothing less than fifteen days' thanksgiving seemed adequate. When, only five years later, news came of the complete suppression of a general simultaneous insurrection of all the Gauls, with the amazing storm of Avaricum and the stupendous operations around and capture of Alesia, all this so far outclassed Pompey's victories in the East or Cæsar's own previous exploits, that a thanksgiving lasting through twenty consecutive days was felt barely sufficient for the expression of popular elation and national gratitude.

It has been assumed by many historians that these thanksgivings were mere factional juggleries, Pompey's partisans in 62 B.C. maliciously jeering at Lucullus by the lavishness with which they expressed elation at Pompey's feats, and the partisans of Cæsar similarly taunting Pompey by the extravagance of their exultation at their chieftain's exploits. But such writers totally fail to comprehend the pagan attitude of mind. A large majority of the Senate in 57 B.C. and 52 B.C. were bitterly hostile to Cæsar and would have done anything to belittle him and his campaigns. But they dared not come short of what his legionaries and the populace of Rome felt was barely commensurate with the favor Rome's gods had shown to the Commonwealth. To have skimped the services of thanksgiving would have been running the risk of affronting the gods of Rome and of having the citizenry recognize and resent the inadequacy of the ceremonials and express their dread of retribution from the gods for disrespect to them.

So of Trajan's festivals after his vanquishment of the Dacians. A recent historian has hinted that Trajan (next to Cæsar the greatest man the Roman world ever produced) was a megalomaniac when he had 10,000 gladiators fight in the shows he gave after abolishing Decebalus, and had more than 11,000 wild beasts killed in those same spectacles. But to any devout pagan, as to Trajan, such lavishness appeared no more than the minimum due Rome's gods as an adequate manifestation of the gratitude of the Commonwealth.

Throughout the Greco-Roman world in its prime the popular conception of the gods was of beings in human form, handsome, dignified, and stately, living forever, forever free from disease, pain, or discomfort, and unhampered by any limitations of time and place. Any deity, as Venus in the fourth book of the Æneid, was conceived of as able to go from Carthage to Cyprus and back in the twinkling of an eye, and even farther. It was generally believed that the gods, among themselves, were of superhuman size and so magnificent and glorious to behold that the sight of any deity, as they appeared to each other, so overwhelmed a human being, that the shock caused instant death. It was believed that it lay within the power of all deities to appear in their habitual guise to any human being and yet save that beholder alive, but that such miracles were extremely unusual. Generally, any deity, before appearing visibly among mankind or to any human being, put off the Olympian guise and assumed the appearance of a regal man or woman.

During over fifteen centuries of earnest and acrimonious denunciation of idolatry it has been lost sight of how beautiful and comforting a faith it seemed to its votaries. Roman imperial worship has been called "a cold and forbidding formalism." This is merely the expression of the inability of a monotheist to comprehend that no individual Roman felt any obligation to pray for the safety of the state, that, in fact, every ordinary Roman felt it his civic duty to refrain from such individual prayer, as prayer for the safety of the state was a highly technical matter demanding the expertness of adepts.

On the other hand, monotheists have seldom been able to realize how the pagan's identification of the god and the cult-statue gave any pagan votary, when face to face with a cult-statue, the sensation of being face to face with a living divinity and a simultaneous feeling of awestruck reverence and intimate sympathetic divine solicitude.

The pagan conception of right and wrong was definite and intelligible. Any action which conduced to the good of the state was right, and, in its degree, commendable, praiseworthy, or mandatory. As, at need, to die for one's fatherland. Any action harmful to the state was wrong and to be frowned upon, decried, and refrained from by any self-respecting person. Actions neither beneficial nor harmful to the state were mostly neither right nor wrong. But some might be looked on as wrong if they plainly injured or were likely to injure any family or individual. Others might be looked on as right as plainly benefiting an individual or family.

Philosophers discussed right and wrong as abstract conceptions, and their views had more or less influence on their disciples and those who adhered to their teachings. But not all the Greco-Roman systems of philosophy collectively made any appreciable impression on the population at large or brought about any discernible alteration of ancestral beliefs as diffused all over the pagan world.

For pagans, right and wrong were not objective realities existing of themselves, but matters of human opinion. Pagans conceived of right and wrong conduct on the part of any individual as being approximate conformity or nonconformity with what was expected of that person by the general opinion of the community of which he or she was a member.

There is in existence a mass of printed matter about the depravity of the Romans of the Empire and their debaucheries. Some few were debauchees, probably no greater percentage of the total population than are debauchees among us today.

As for Greco-Roman depravity, the talk of it merely signifies that the Greeks and Romans approved of or mildly disapproved of, or positively disapproved of, but genially tolerated, many kinds of behavior of which the early Christians fanatically disapproved and against which they frantically inveighed. Some of these varieties of behavior are now positively disapproved. But it must be remembered that many of them

it or doubted it. Except philosophers, hardly anyone discussed it. It was not thought of as a subject for discussion; it was implicitly acted on without thought about it.

What pagans had to do to fulfill their civic duties varied from age to age. In early ages it meant preparation for soldiering from childhood, soldiering throughout one's prime, farming and thrift to the end of life. For Romans this condition lasted until the expansion of Rome's Empire and the augmentation of Rome's wealth led Marius to substitute volunteering for an inclusive and selective levy and so relieved most of the citizenry of military service.

From the first, participation in the worship of Rome's gods had been, along with soldiering, among a Roman's most important civic duties. When soldiering was no longer universal it became for many Romans, for most Romans, their most important civic duty. Participation in the propitiation of Rome's gods, for an ordinary individual, consisted chiefly of making sure that public offices were filled by the men most acceptable to Jupiter as his deputies and servitors.

For some centuries this was accomplished to the satisfaction of all Romans by suffrage at elections. From 133 B.C., when the Gracchi began their turbulent public activities, achieving it came to be more and more of a puzzle.

From 88 B.C., when Marius and Sulla clashed over the question which was the accepted representative of Jupiter Maximus Optimus, the settlement of such questions, every time that they came up, grew to be more and more a puzzle.

After the battle of Actium all devout pagans felt mightily relieved; Jupiter had unmistakably proclaimed that Augustus was his chosen representative among mankind and vicegerent on earth.

Thereafter the chief civic duty of every Roman, of every devout pagan, was fitting reverence for the reigning emperor. This most of all ensured the favor to the Commonwealth of Rome's gods who had chosen and exalted the ruling Prince of the Roman Commonwealth.

To sum up: what cemented every prosperous community of the Mediterranean pagan world was the universal instinctive conviction of and belief in the tenets:

(1) That the individual existed for the state and not the state for the individual.

(2) That the partnership of the all-powerful, kindly and helpful gods was the chief asset of each state and their favor its most precious possession.

These two beliefs were the dominant factor in the creation of Rome's Empire.

And its maintenance was caused chiefly by two other beliefs.

(3) That Rome's prosperity was assured by the leadership of a demigod who had been indubitably proclaimed as Jupiter's choice as his representative on earth.

(4) That the Prince of the Commonwealth would see to it that Rome's gods were properly reverenced, invoked, conciliated, and thanked.

Their faith in these beliefs and in what went with them gave Romans of Rome's acme of prosperity their serene confidence in the permanence of their Commonwealth and of its Empire.

CHAPTER XXI

THE CAUSES OF THE FALL OF ROME LISTED AND THE EXTERNAL CAUSES CONSIDERED

Ἀλλ' ἔστιν, οἶμαι, τὸ μὲν αἰτιολογεῖν δυσχερές,
τὸ δὲ ῥησικοπεῖν ἐν τοῖς βυβλίοις ῥᾴδιον

—Polybius XII, 25, i, 9.

But I suppose that tracing causes is difficult, while stringing words together in books is easy.

E. S. Shuckburgh's translation.

FROM soon after the sack of Rome by Brennus and his Gauls in 390 B.C. to the death of Trajan in A.D. 138, for over five and a quarter centuries, Rome not merely held off the pressure from without, but steadily pushed back her enemies on all frontiers and steadily extended her Empire. From soon after the death of Trajan until the final catastrophe, Rome stood on the defensive and either barely held her own or lost steadily.

It is obvious that if Roman armies in earlier times thrust back the menacing northern barbarians, as, for instance, the Cimbri and Teutons about 100 B.C., if, 500 years later, about A.D. 400, Roman armies failed to hold off similar invading hordes, the difference can have been due only to the increase of pressure from without or to the weakening of resistance from within or to both conditions progressively worsening together.

Manifestly, the causes of the fall of Rome can all be classified as either external or internal; there is no third category. We shall consider them in the following order:

(A) The paramount external cause:
The progressive desiccation of central Asia.

(B) Contributory external causes:

(1) The Great Wall of China.

(2) The gradual diffusion northward beyond the limits of the Mediterranean world of a progressively better and better knowledge of the arts of metallurgy.

(3) Better and better generalship of the leaders of the migratory hordes, from generation to generation progressively.

(4) Better and better individual health, strength, endurance, and valor, from generation to generation, in the hordes of the steppes.

(C) Contributory internal causes:

(1) The Roman habit of civil war.

(2) The exhaustion of the soil of Italy, Sardinia, Sicily, and Roman Africa.

(3) The weakening in respect to fighting power of each community brought under the *Pax Romana.*

(4) The influx into Rome and Italy of aliens, whether free or slaves, and the dilution of the Roman stock through marriages with the descendants of such aliens and of slaves.

(5) The effects of affluence and ease on the aristocracy.

(6) Malaria and mosquitoes.

(7) Alterations in the climate of Italy and the Mediterranean world.

(8) The dispersion of genuine Romans into the colonies.

(9) The debasement of the populace in the city of Rome itself.

(10) The facilities offered by the general peace and the ease of internal communications for the spread of pestilences and of alien cults subversive of Greco-Roman culture.

(11) The mental and moral enervation caused by a government more and more centralized and often characterized by irresistible despotism and capricious tyranny.

(12) The unsoundness of general economic and financial conditions from the first and all along and the progressive debasement of the coinage.

(13) The Great Pestilence of A.D. 166.

(14) The prohibition by Septimius Severus of military enlistment in Italy.

(D) The paramount internal cause.

The weakening of military and civic morale by the spread of Christianity.

(A)

The effects of the progressive-desiccation of central Asia have been fully set forth in Chapters I and II. It should be noted and cannot be too much insisted on that the effect on the Mediterranean world, like the condition of desiccation in the far interior of the Great Continent, was progressively intensified. The pressure from the steppes outward, southward and southwestward, was more powerful in 400 B.C. than it had been in 1200 B.C. and more powerful in A.D. 400 than it had been in 400 B.C. So of any two dates at any considerable interval.

(B, 1)

The Great Wall of China was a contributory external cause of the fall of Rome. This statement may surprise some readers. But a very cursory glance at any good map of the Great Continent will remind anyone that inhabitants of the steppes, grasslands, and plains of central Asia, and of the interior of the Great Continent in general, could emerge toward warmer and more fertile regions only in three localities: in the Far East, between the mouth of the Amur and the eastern scarps of the great Tibetan-Himalayan highlands; between the western spurs of the Himalayas and the Caspian Sea; and between the Black Sea and the Baltic Sea.

Elsewhere they were barred by mountainous regions, not, indeed, impenetrable to armies or hordes, but so difficult to surmount that they were practically impassable: the Tibetan-Himalayan highlands, the loftiest region in the world; and the Caucasus.

Now the Great Wall of China was built by the Chinese Emperor Che Wang-Te with the belief, as all Chinese scholars affirm, that it, by itself, would protect China from foreign invasion from that direction completely and forever. He was as mistaken as was Justinian when he thought that his code would end lawmaking for all time and would never be added to nor modified in any manner whatever, till the end of the world.

But Che Wang-Te's fourteen-hundred-mile wall, fifteen to twenty-five feet thick and fifteen to thirty feet high, was built along a sinuous line judiciously chosen where conditions of soil and climate made all the territory to the south of it naturally fit for the support of a dense agricultural population and conditions of soil and climate to the north of it made agriculture so difficult that those regions were and are naturally fitted for human habitation only by nomadic herders of cattle, horses, sheep, goats, or camels.

The Great Wall of China at once enhanced the safety of the peaceable agriculturists to the south of it and curbed the predacious rapacity of the covetous tribes north of it. It stopped, at once and forever, casual raiding by handfuls of horsemen. No longer could a half dozen likely lads on desert ponies ride south and return driving before them rich spoil of slaves, cattle, horses, or what else, themselves riding festooned with plunder. The Wall made that impossible, made forays impossible for scanty forces and even for small armies.

Actually, in the interval of over 2,135 years since it was completed, the Great Wall of China has been forced very seldom, and each time only by an overwhelmingly large army of hardy warriors led by an unusually capable, bold, and resolute general.

The Chinese Emperor Che Wang-Te died in 210 B.C. The Great Wall of China, according to Chinese historians, was com-

pleted during his reign. He died while Hannibal was in Italy, the very year in which young Scipio, afterward known as Africanus, took command of the Roman armies in Spain.

Within a century, about ninety-seven years after the death of Che Wang-Te, and not many more after the completion of the Great Wall of China, the Cimbri had crossed the Danube and were clawing at the foothills of the eastern Alps. In whatever part of the interior of the Great Continent originated the pressure which drove the Cimbri southwestward, the waves of southwardly migration set up by that pressure had been reflected and turned back westward by and from the Great Wall of China.

(B, 2)

We know that the population of the steppes and grasslands of the interior of the Great Continent, like all the populations of the Great Continent, used at first weapons tipped with bits of stone roughly shaped by chipping, that later they used similar arrowheads, spear heads, and knives less roughly shaped by flaking, that later still their stone weapons were polished, that later still they came to use bronze weapons and later still weapons of iron and steel; we know that this progress from rough stone to smoothed stone, from stone to bronze, from bronze to iron, was far slower among populations in the interior of the continent than among the luckier and brainier stocks of the Mediterranean world.

It appears, though we are not certain, that the knowledge of the use of bronze for tools and weapons did not originate anywhere in the interior of the continent, but was gradually transmitted northward, probably from metallurgical discoveries made in Egypt. It is likely that most of the bronze used by human beings in the interior of the Great Continent was imported from more southerly lands, and that little of it, perhaps none at all, was mined, smelted, and worked among the nomads of the steppes and plains or the semisavages of the forests and swamps to south of them.

We know that, in the centuries between 800 B.C. and A.D. 1200, iron very gradually replaced bronze all the way to the Arctic Ocean. But we know very little of the details of the process. It is reasonable to conjecture, but it must be kept in mind that it is merely conjecture, that between 400 B.C. and A.D. 400 there was a slow but steady increase in the amount of iron exported northward from the Mediterranean world, and a similarly slow and steady improvement in its quality, and it may be that, during these eight centuries, more and more of the northern barbarians learned how to mine, smelt, and shape iron for their arms and armor.

This possibility or probability must be taken into account as perhaps a contributory external cause of the fall of Rome.

(B, 3)

The steppes of Mongolia, about A.D. 1200 produced that amazing bevy of paragon commanders who led to victory the soldiers of Jenghiz Khan. The notion current in Europe and America concerning these Tatar armies is that they were vast hordes of semisavages and that their countless victories were won by mere weight of numbers against foes inferior only in numbers. Actually Jenghiz led or sent out small or large armies of superlative fighters incomparably officered.

Subutai and the other generals who served Jenghiz were adepts at all that goes into success in levying, selecting, equipping, training, and leading recruits so as to make them irresistible soldiers. The men composing Jenghiz Khan's armies were individually as perfect as intelligent sifting could arrange. Each was in the prime of youthful manhood, hardy and possessed of that combination of character, instincts, and knowledge which enabled him to keep well, fit, and able in any climate, at any season of the year and in any weather. Their clothing, armor, and weapons were the best in the world in their days. And every kind of obtainable supplies was intelligently provided for by a commissariat both competent and vigilant.

Above all, the armies of Jenghiz Khan were inimitably led. In respect to ascertaining the location, strength, and quality of the enemy, discerning the strategic value of the terrain about them, choosing an objective and moving on it, usually in three parallel columns, with unerring precision, Subutai and his colleagues and associates compare very favorably with Philip of Macedon, Alexander the Great, Hamilcar Barca, Hannibal, Julius Cæsar, Gustavus Adolphus, Frederick the Great, or Napoleon Bonaparte. Equally favorable to them is a comparison with these heroes in regard to battle tactics, battlefield strategy, and grand strategy.

If, in 1200 B.C., the steppes had only semisavage hordes led by semisavages, whereas, about A.D. 1200, they sent forth the perfectly manned, perfectly equipped, perfectly led armies which owed allegiance to Jenghiz Khan, it is probable that the improvement in leadership was not sudden and late, but continuous and slow, and that the leadership of the hordes which attempted the invasion of the Roman Empire between 100 B.C. and A.D. 400 was progressively better and better. This, however, is mere conjecture, but worth setting down and emphasizing.

(B, 4)

Whether the quality of the individual warriors who composed the fighting forces of the invading hordes also progressively improved as time passed can only be conjectured. But it seems likely that it did. For conditions on the plains, grasslands, and steppes of the interior of the Great Continent were such that only robust and sturdy infants could live, so that the parents of each generation were very possibly sturdier and tougher than their own parents and so on from age to age.

CHAPTER XXII

THE CHIEF INTERNAL CONTRIBUTORY CAUSES OF THE FALL OF ROME

(C, 1)

OF THE internal contributory causes of the annihilation of the Roman Commonwealth indubitably the most potent was the pernicious Roman habit of civil war.

Here it must be observed that there seems no justification for the very general assumption of an alteration or change in the Roman character about 133 B.C.

Time and again from the very establishment of the Roman Commonwealth in 510 B.C. records or traditions describe internal dissensions during which civil war was very narrowly averted, even while the Volscians, Æquians and Hernicians were in arms within ten miles of the gates of Rome.

If only a miracle of sagacity and eloquence kept the Romans from rioting or civil war when redoubtable and rancorous foes were near at hand, why conceive any alteration in Roman character when, in later times, with no enemy in sight, no formidable foes anywhere, the Romans ultimately settled controversies among themselves as they and their forebears for thousands of years had settled all controversies with aliens, by fighting to a finish?

Rioting is a kind of spontaneous and informal civil war and some of the riots inside Rome resulted in very heavy loss of life.

Tiberius Gracchus was killed in a riot in 133 B.C. Theodosius defeated Eugenius at Aquileia in A.D. 394. Within the 526 years that elapsed between these two events, what with riots in the city and battles outside, hundreds of thousands of Romans perished in conflicts with other Romans. Ignoring insurrections, revolts, and rebellions, and counting only struggles for the mastery of the Commonwealth and her Empire, it would be easy to make out a list of more than forty civil wars, disturbing more than seventy different years, about one year out of every seven.

The most important were: those fought by the factions of Marius and Sulla (100-72 B.C.); Cæsar against Pompey and his faction (49-45 B.C.); Augustus, Antony and Lepidus against Brutus, Cassius, and their fellow conspirators (44-36 B.C.); Augustus and Antony (31-30 B.C.); Otho and Vitellius (A.D. 69); Vitellius and Vespasian (A.D. 69); Septimius Severus against Didius Julianus, then Pescennius Niger, then Clodius Albinus (A.D. 193-197); various pretenders throughout the general confusion during the "reign" of Gallienus (A.D. 260-268); Constantine against his rivals (A.D. 306-314); and Constantine and Licinius (A.D. 323).

The list of battles fought, numbers engaged in each, and total slain would make an impressive showing. But it is unnecessary to tabulate the total of the Romans who died untimely deaths in riots, proscriptions, and battles in the course of their many civil wars and other civil strifes. Without such a tabulation it is manifest that the loss to the Commonwealth was very great, in mere numbers of citizens dead before their prime. And the loss was far greater. For the dead were mostly the very pick of the Romans of their day, and their loss not merely diminished the number of Roman citizens in their generation, but still more for the next generation, and impaired the quality of the succeeding generations even more positively than it lessened their numbers.

The probability is very strong that, if the Romans had been able to settle their dissensions without mutual slaughter and had been able to utilize all their military man power against foreign foes, they might very well have conquered and colonized Europe to the Niemen and the Bug and have held it indefinitely, might very well have subjugated and kept not merely the valley of the Tigris-Euphrates, but the Iranian Plateau, and the valleys of the Oxus, Jaxartes, Indus, and Ganges. The enormous waste of Roman lives in civil conflicts and internecine butchery cannot be exaggerated.

Probably the pernicious habit of civil war did more harm to the Roman Commonwealth than all the other contributory internal causes of the ruin of Rome collectively.

It is generally assumed that the quality of the individual Roman soldier deteriorated steadily and increasingly. This is most likely true, but it is by no means a certainty. Studied without prejudice, it is very difficult to perceive any discernible difference in the fighting qualities of the Roman legionaries at different periods.

Consider the subjoined series of events.

First, cities taken by siege and capture: Veii (396 B.C.), by Camillus; Syracuse (212 B.C.), by Marcellus; Carthage (146 B.C.) and Numantia (133 B.C.), by Scipio; Athens (86 B.C.), by Sulla; Avaricum (52 B.C.), by Cæsar; Jerusalem (A.D. 70), by Titus; Sarmizegethusa in Dacia (A.D. 102), by Trajan; Palmyra (A.D. 273), by Aurelian; Ctesiphon (A.D. 283), by Carus.

Secondly, notable Roman defeats; at Heraclea in 280 B.C. and at Ausculum in 279 B.C. by the Greeks under Pyrrhus; on the Ticinus and on the Trebia in 218 B.C., along Lake Trasimene in 217 B.C. and at Cannæ in 216 B.C. by the Carthaginians under Hannibal; at Noreia in 113 B.C. and at Arausio 105 B.C. by the Cimbri; at Carrhae in 53 B.C. by the Parthians; in the Teutoburg Forest in A.D. 9 by the Germans; at Abricium in A.D. 251 by the Goths; at Edessa in A.D. 260 by the Persians, and at Adrianople in A.D. 378 by the Goths.

Thirdly, notable Roman victories: at Trifanum in 338 B.C. over the Latins and Campanians; at Sentinum in 295 B.C. over the Samnites; at Beneventum in 275 B.C. over the Greeks under Pyrrhus; at Panormus in 251 B.C. over the Carthaginians; at Telamon in 225 B.C. over the Gauls; at Nola in 215 B.C., at Sena Gallica in 207 B.C. and at Zama in 202 B.C. over the Carthaginians led by Hannibal or his brothers; at Cynoscephalæ in 179 B.C. over the Macedonians; at Magnesia in 190 B.C. over the generals of Antiochus; at Pydna in 168 B.C. over the Macedonians; at Leucopetra in 146 B.C. over the Achæan Greeks; at Aquæ Sextiæ in 102 B.C. over the Teutons;

at Vercellæ in 101 B.C. over the Cimbri; at Chæronea in 86 B.C. and at Orchomenus in 85 B.C. over the forces of Mithridates; at Tigranocerta in 69 B.C. over the Armenians; on the Lycos in 66 B.C. over Mithridates; at Bibracte in 58 B.C. over the Helvetians; at Besançon in the same year over Ariovistus and his Germans; on the Sambre in 57 B.C. over the Belgians; at Alesia in 52 B.C. over the Gauls; at Chalons in A.D. 251 over the Huns.

The legionaries whom Aurelian led across the blazing deserts in A.D. 273 on his retributive second expedition against Palmyra seem in no respects inferior to those who captured Jerusalem under Titus two centuries earlier, to those who wore down the stubborn defense of Numantia more than four centuries previously, or even to those who stormed Veii almost six centuries before.

The legionaries mishandled by Valens at Adrianople in A.D. 378 stood their ground as doggedly and fought on as manfully as those butchered by Hannibal along Lake Trasimene or at Cannæ six centuries agone.

During the nearly two and a half centuries which elapsed between the Great Pestilence of A.D. 166 and the collapse of the Western Empire after the death of Theodosius in A.D. 395, the Rhine-Danube frontier was forced by twenty-three invading hordes of barbarians whose ravages took up altogether 59 years out of 229. Every one of these inroads was repelled, although two of them penetrated into Greece and three into Italy, and in the course of these 59 years of hard fighting Roman armies achieved many well-fought and clean-won victories, but after A.D. 166 the frontiers were never adequately manned and their defenses twenty-three several times gave way under the pressure from without.

These facts warrant the conclusion that the legionaries were still of good individual quality as fighters but never sufficiently numerous for their task.

And the depletion of the supply of recruits for the legions was due more to the slaughters of civil war after civil war than to the mortality in the years of the Great Pestilence.

It has been generally assumed that the overwhelming victory of Fritigern and his mounted Goths over Valens and his Romans on foot at Adrianople in A.D. 378 ended the use of infantry in Europe for a thousand years and made cavalry supreme by demonstrating the superiority of cavalry over infantry. It did not. Had there been enough Romans of military age to recruit the Empire's field army up to merely its old norm of thirty legions they might very well have cleared the barbarians out of all the provinces and reëstablished the defenses of the Rhine-Danube frontier. Roman legionaries, after their defeat at Adrianople in A.D. 378, vanished from the world because not enough recruits were to be had. The civil wars had swallowed up Rome's military manhood.

Even after the Empire had ceased to exist in fact and was only a name, the remnant of Roman legionaries under Aëtius were the shock troops which broke the power of Attila and his Huns at Chalons in A.D. 451; and the West Goths under Theodoric, and what Franks and Burgundians took part in that decisive battle, were mere auxiliaries of the invincible Romans.

The Roman legionaries failed their countrymen not so much in quality as through paucity. They were unbeatable, but they were too few, and of the factors which caused their scarcity, while Christianization was the most momentous, recurrent pestilences were far outranked in virulence by the carnage of the civil wars.

(C, 2)

Whether we consider China, the valleys of the Ganges, Indus, Euphrates, Nile or Ohio, ancient Italy or modern North America, wherever we have or can plausibly reconstruct the history of any region of the temperate zone originally heavily forested and ultimately thickly populated, we find approximately the same series of changes in the conditions and the environment of the inhabitants. At first there was a struggle to make some little headway against the forest growth, to fell at least some trees and to clear some land for tillage; later human communities controlled the soil and had plenty of produce, fish, game, and timber; still later human beings became even too numerous, and game, timber, and fresh-water fish grew scarce; later still crops were seldom overabundant and more and more often scanty; lastly crops failed more and more or altogether.

From about 500 B.C. to about 300 B.C. much of Latium supported a very dense population, as high as a thousand to a square mile. Livy, three centuries later, expresses his wonder as to how it came about that vast armies of Volscians, Æquians, and Hernicians were bred and supported in regions where, in his days, the only inhabitants were small, scattered bands of slaves herding their masters' sheep and cattle.

When, about 306 B.C., the Romans launched their first war fleet, the timber came largely from the hills about Latium. By A.D. 14, at the death of Augustus, timber for Roman warships was mostly cut on the Dalmatian mountains, northeast of the Adriatic, for by that time Italy had been mostly denuded of timber suitable for shipbuilding.

When, in 67 B.C., Pompey cleared the Mediterranean of pirates, Sardinia, Sicily, and Africa (Tunisia) were the chief sources of the grain from which was made the bread on which the population of Rome fed. Within three centuries the wheat shipped to Rome from Africa, Sicily, and Sardinia was a trifling fraction of the city's total food supply.

The depopulation of Italy, of Roman Africa (Tunisia), and of some other parts of the Roman Empire has, by many historians, been blamed on the creation by wealthy proprietors of vast estates (*latifundia*). The vast estates were the result of the depopulation, which was caused not so much by the arrogance of the new-rich or by the devastations of the civil wars as by the slow, steady, inevitable, and irresistible results of the gradual exhaustion of the soil in all arable areas. As long as the Italian farmer could make a bare living for himself and his family he clung to his plot of ground. Only when existence was impossible were farm holdings abandoned anywhere.

Now it is perfectly plain that when Italy, Sicily, Sardinia, and Africa produced a mighty surplus of exportable wheat they supported a dense resident agricultural population of hardy yeomen who furnished a large and unfailing supply of excellent recruits for Rome's armies.

When, later, these regions were exhausted and could raise only scanty crops, their population fell off almost to nothing and the military quality of the inhabitants deteriorated faster and more seriously than their numbers.

(C, 3)

Manifestly, the creation of the Roman Empire enhanced the collective martial power of the communities included within it, but diminished the potentiality of resistance, and the defensive strength of every individual community so included.

In 372 B.C., before Rome had any Empire, every community in the vast area later her domain was, habitually, at war with all its neighbors, and seldom did a summer pass when any one community was not at war with some other. Every adult male had to serve as a soldier. As in Abyssinia today, no lad unfit for military service, ever, to the end of his life, counted for anything among his fellows. The remorseless and unescapable operation of campaign and battle conditions inexorably eliminated weaklings, defectives, fools, cowards, and hot-heads, and those who survived to marry and rear families were mostly sound, sturdy, hale, vigorous, cool, valiant, intelligent, and capable. And every boy, lad, and man had a keen sense that the welfare of his town, of his family, of his dearest and nearest, depended visibly on his loyalty, dutifulness, courage, and skill.

These conditions waned very gradually. Until after Hannibal's departure from Italy in 203 B.C., even until after Sulla's quelling of the Italian insurgents in 88 B.C., although many men spent most of their terms of enlistment far from home, even overseas, few escaped the stern training of actual warfare. Every fortified town could man its walls and beat off any force not overwhelming.

But as early as 107 B.C. Marius introduced his highly original method of mustering an army by calling for volunteers instead of by general conscription. And, though not infrequently later, in times of urgent peril, as in Cæsar's levy against the Helvetians, and commonly in the civil wars until the battle of Actium, every available recruit was nabbed and enrolled, yet the total of men under arms was, from year to year, a lessening fraction of the total capable of military service.

After the pacification of the Mediterranean world by Augustus in 27 B.C. enlistment became more and more a selective process, and from generation to generation a larger portion of every given community lived out their lives without participating in any military activity.

The absence of any visible enemy, the distance of the barbarian foes along the Rhine-Danube frontier, the protected conditions of life within the Empire, as in Italy, Spain, Egypt, all along the north coast of Africa and on the islands of the Mediterranean, bred lads who were, potentially, far less capable of military service than their ancestors.

In evaluating this factor in the weakening of Rome's fighting strength it must not be forgotten that no matter how far from the frontier a town might be, no matter how many generations it might be since it had stood a siege or seen an array of armed foemen, yet each had its amphitheatre and its gladiatorial shows and every lad saw men fight, saw men wounded, and saw blood flow, saw men die. So that, if drafted, no Roman lad, of Rome, or of any of her colonies or allied towns or cities, had to be blooded on the field of battle. All had seen combats, wounds, and the agonies of death. All were habituated to such sights and at home with such occurrences.

The gladiatorial shows afforded no discipline to their onlookers, but they contributed vastly to the quality of the potential military morale of all youths who had regularly viewed them, and they kept up the local interest in sword play, and, all over the Roman portions of Rome's Empire, boys, lads, and youths were as keen on practice at fencing with sword and shield, on target practice with javelins, lances, and spears, and on such exercises, as now are any modern lads on their national game, be it bull fighting, baseball, cricket, pelota, pallone, or what else. Weapon play was, from antiquity centuries before, the traditional customary athletic exercise of all boys and youths of Roman blood all over their world.

But these influences were a trifling factor against the enervating effects of age-long peace and absence of visible day-by-day responsibility for the safety of each lad's home town, as before *Pax Romana* overspread Rome's domain.

The effect of inclusion within the Empire upon the supply of adequate leaders was even more adverse than upon the fighting qualities of the rank and file. Of course, any youth with an appetite for military life could find a ready welcome in the imperial army and, if capable, rose according to his capacities. But this was very different from each town's having within its walls mature men who had made good as commanders in the field, as was the case before Rome annexed her provinces, over all the territory later embraced within the boundaries of her Empire.

(C, 4)

As a factor in Rome's decline, the influx into Rome and Italy of aliens, whether free or slaves, and the dilution of the Roman stock through marriages with the descendants of such aliens, was by no means so detrimental as it has generally been assumed to have been by writers on the subject. Manumitted slaves were generally individuals who had proved their possession of capacities, abilities, and character of no mean order.

They and their descendants were, in general, valuable additions to the population of the Empire at large and of Rome in particular, and an advantage, not a harm, to the body politic.

On the other hand, they did not possess the qualities which went with Roman stamina, Roman level headedness, Roman self-reliance, Roman directness, and Roman courage; nor the Italic and Roman instinct for the appreciation of the value of the Commonwealth, of the community at large, its welfare, its peace, and its Empire; nor the Roman instinct for even-handed justice to all men, Romans and aliens alike.

(C, 5)

Every nobility known to history, whatever other influences may have contributed to its decline, has deteriorated chiefly from one and the same cause affecting all alike. This cause operated on the Roman aristocracy as on those of Egypt, Babylonia, Assyria, Persia, Greece, and Carthage before, as on those of the Saracens, Turks, Spaniards, and Manchus since.

Up to the end of the Hannibalic wars Roman women, even of the proudest patrician families, ground grain, baked bread, prepared wool and flax, spun thread, wove cloth, and in manifold similar ways did their share of the work of the community.

Roman boys, in those days, inherited competence, capacity, intelligence, and character not only from their fighting fathers and grandfathers, but from their domestic mothers and grandmothers.

After the enrichment of many of the Senatorial families by the spoils of conquest between the end of the Second Punic War in 201 B.C. and Pompey's triumph in 61 B.C., still more after the pacification of the Mediterranean world by Augustus in 27 B.C., Roman ladies tended more and more to become brainless, characterless, pleasure-loving idlers. From generation to generation Roman noblemen inherited less and less of any value from their mothers and grandmothers.

This effect of affluence and ease no aristocracy of the world's past has ever escaped. This factor, more than any other, caused the degeneracy of the Roman Senatorial and equestrian stocks, the deterioration of the efficiency of the leadership of Rome's armies, and the general demoralization of the later Empire.

CHAPTER XXIII

CONTRIBUTORY INTERNAL CAUSES OF THE FALL OF ROME

(C, 6)

FROM Naples to Genoa the entire western coastal plain of Italy has been notoriously malarious in recent centuries, notably from, say, 1600 to 1800. From 800 B.C. to 300 B.C. the arable areas of these districts bred and supported a population averaging close to one thousand per square mile and the males were fighters of such stamina, strength, and valor that we cannot escape the inference that either malaria was non-existent in Italy at that period or, if present, was of a very mild type and of merely sporadic occurrence.

Positive proof of the absence or presence of malaria in those days cannot be achieved. On the one hand the goddess of fever was early worshipped in Latium; on the other, the fevers against which her protection was invoked may not have been malarious.

The conjecture that malaria entered Italy with Hannibal's invasion is plausible; certainly it was well known within the next half century, for Terence, who died only fifty-nine years after Hannibal's inroad and only forty-four after his departure from Italy, made in one of his comedies a reference to malaria which proves that it must have been familiar to an average theatrical audience. In 220 B.C., just before Hannibal's invasion, Italy south of the Rubicon and Macra could supply to Rome's armies and navy 700,000 fighting men, of unsurpassable strength and vigor, as their battles against Hannibal's forces demonstrate. No such a soldiery, still less any such number of such paragon warriors, could have been bred of malarious mothers.

The probabilities are that infected individuals among Hannibal's troops brought the filaria of malaria to Italy in their blood, were there bitten by Anopheles mosquitoes and thus infected the mosquitoes of Italy, which in turn infected the human inhabitants. The devastation of large areas during the Hannibalic wars must have favored the formation of pools, ponds, and swamps and the multiplication of malarial mosquitoes, and so the spread of the disease.

Certainly by the times of Augustus all varieties of malarial fever were well known in and about Rome.

But we do not read of any noticeable deterioration in the quality of army recruits from Italy till long after Septimius Severus forbade natives of Italy to serve in the army. Up to his days Italy had had the privilege of recruiting the Prætorian Guards, the *élite* corps of the Imperial armies. The Prætorians, while arrogant and mutinous, had been magnificent fighters whenever led into battle. When the pressure of necessity brought about the rescinding or evasion of the edict of Severus and enlistment was resumed in Italy, the youths drafted were often unfit for military service and those enlisted of very poor quality.

The repeated statements that, during the decline of the Empire from A.D. 237 to 395 legionaries alleged that they were physically unable to carry their arms and armor have been explained as based on the malingering of Christians afraid of eternal damnation if they served in the army but too cowardly to avow their Christianity before Constantine's days or ashamed to give their genuine reason after Christians in large numbers had taken to soldiering. Such statements of historians are much more likely to be authentic records of the pleas of wretches suffering from the debility caused by malaria, either the mild form which does not display itself in fever or the after effects of severer types.

How slowly or how rapidly conditions on the coastal plain north and south of Rome altered from the salubrity of the times of Rome's wars with the Latin tribes to the horrible noisomeness of Tuscany and the Campagna from 1725 to 1850 cannot be demonstrated. But several known facts point to the inference that while malaria was prevalent in and about Rome from 50 B.C. on, the adjacent regions did not become pestilential till after the sack of Rome in A.D. 410.

For instance, the Roman Emperors had no villa from the establishment of the Principate in 27 B.C. till the reign of Hadrian, A.D. 117 to 138. Hadrian, finding the imperial palace on the Palatine irked him as an all-the-year-round residence, built a villa at Tibur. Presumably he selected the site for healthfulness, agreeableness, and lovely outlooks. Certainly in his times it cannot have been unhealthful, yet ancient Tibur was the same town as modern Tivoli, infamous in recent centuries, down to 1825, as the most malarious locality in all Italy.

As a malarious woman seldom gives birth to a live child at full term, as most children in malarious countries have the disease, as it stunts and weakens all its victims, the presence and intensification of malaria in Italy must have operated to diminish the population of the peninsula, to deteriorate its quality in all ways, and especially to weaken its fighting power both in respect to reducing the number of youths fit for military service and of impairing their quality as fighters.

And Italy was the heart of the Empire. It has been said that the Roman Empire was destroyed, not by men, but by mosquitoes. That is putting it too strong, but they were a factor in its downfall.

(C, 7)

In recent years, not a little has been published concerning the relation between climate and civilization. It has been fairly well established that there is a definite type of climate which is most powerfully stimulating to racial and national vigor and to individual originality and enterprise, and therefore most congenial to the germination and burgeoning of civilization. It has been equally well made out that other types of climate are less favorable and others positively unfavorable. It is also manifest that in many parts of the world the climate has changed greatly since the beginning of human records, that in some regions it has progressively worsened, while in others it has altered for the better.

Now if it could be proved that the climate of Italy between 1000 B.C. and 100 B.C. was ideal for the development of national greatness, that somewhere between 133 B.C. and A.D. 117 it altered for the worse, that between A.D. 117 and A.D. 166 the effects of the alteration began to make themselves manifest, and that from A.D. 166 onward to and after A.D. 457 the climate of Italy was adverse to national greatness, then it would appear that there was a definite causative relation between the climate of Italy and the rise and fall of Rome.

Similarly, if it could be shown that, from 4500 B.C. to 600 B.C. the climates of Egypt and Babylonia were positively congenial to the germination and development of civilization; if it could be shown that from 490 B.C. to A.D. 117 the climates of Greece and Italy were notably favorable to the burgeoning of racial greatness, and that after A.D. 100 the climate of the entire Mediterranean world altered for the worse until it was deleterious to national vigor—then it would be manifest that there was a definite causative relation between climate and the waxing and waning of Greco-Roman civilization.

But no such manifest and positive alterations in the climate of Italy and of the Mediterranean world at large can be proved. In fact, there is nothing now known which makes the supposition probable or the suggestion plausible. There were fluctuations, centuries of more abundant rainfall with plentiful harvests, centuries of scanty rainfall with meager harvests, but no sequential and progressive change.

Therefore, while it is worth mention as a possibility, there is no reason to believe that alteration of climatic conditions was a factor in Rome's development and senility.

(C, 8)

The notion, expounded by historian after historian, that the dispersal of the Roman stock into the colonies weakened the Empire seems unfounded. Manifestly, considering all the full-blooded Romans alive at any given date, the larger proportion domiciled outside of Rome itself, the weaker was Rome as a city; and the larger proportion resident beyond the limits of Italy, the weaker Italy was. But if the total number of genuine Romans was the same, the Empire as a whole possessed the same intellectual power of leadership and the same fighting power wherever the Romans might be located. Actually it is a reasonable view that as long as the central government was capable the Romans who manned the Empire's defenses were just as effective when born in any colony as when born in Rome itself.

As long as the policies of the Commonwealth were controlled, to however small a degree, by the voters assembled in the *comitia* at Rome, it made a great difference what proportion of Roman citizens dwelt in Rome; but after voting went out of use, during the Principate of Tiberius (A.D. 14-37) the domicile of any given Roman citizen had no effect whatever in governmental policies.

As long as the Roman citizens of unmixed Roman blood were loyal to Rome, to her gods, and to her Emperor, it mattered not where they were born, where they lived, nor where they went, their value to the Empire was uniform.

(C, 9)

When, in 211 B.C., Hannibal camped in sight of Rome, but did not venture an assault, not only did Rome's fortifications contain a population larger than that of any city in Europe, but the quality of its males as military material excelled that of any city on earth. Rome itself could supply an amazing number of legionaries matchless in every characteristic.

When Aurelian began, A.D. 271, his unwelcome task of girdling overgrown and defenseless Rome with adequate fortifications, the city mob was almost wholly worthless as military material and few men from Rome itself served in the legions.

To some extent this alteration may have been due to the introduction, crudescence, and virulence of malarious infection among the populace. But this is and must remain conjectural.

Among the known and undeniable causes of the debasement of the Roman citizenry to a rabble, the easing of their anxieties as to the cost of their food has been accounted the most pernicious by nearly all historians.

Even before the Punic Wars it had come to be regarded as a national disgrace that Roman citizens, or their wives or children, should starve or be in danger of starvation. In times of extreme scarcity the neediest families were assisted not merely by wealthy individuals acting unofficially, but by government aid officially voted.

Gaius Gracchus in 123 B.C. proposed uniform, systematic and perennial state aid to indigent citizens.

The upshot was that whereas in the first instance penniless families were supplied gratis, poor citizens at part cost, and any commoner at the current price of grain, there came to pass the subjoined sequence of government indulgences to the populace. Dates and minor details do not concern us.

First the State arranged that all citizens might purchase at the current market price the wheat necessary for the sustenance of themselves and their dependents; then it was sold them below cost; then at a fraction of its value; then it was doled out without any cost whatever to the beneficiaries of the laws. The custom reached this state of development under the Republic.

After the establishment of the Empire, while some emperors had the lists of beneficiaries rigidly revised and made sure that only genuine citizens were listed, some even required a trifling payment by all not certified as indigent, the indulgence increased steadily. First, all citizens except nobles had a right to free grain or flour for themselves and their dependents; then bakeries were established, one or more for each precinct of the city, where recipients of the dole might bake their bread free of cost; then the distribution was not of unground grain or of ready flour, but of baked bread; then the bakeries were made to serve also as free public kitchens where any recipient of the dole of bread might have any food cooked free; then, from about the times of Gordian about A.D. 237 the registered populace received cooked rations daily or twice daily, not only bread, but whatever was usual poor-man's fare.

So that, from the accession of Trajan in A.D. 98 and probably from the accession of Claudius in A.D. 41 to the accession of Diocletian in A.D. 284, during from two to two and a half centuries, a Roman citizen had to provide for himself and his family only clothing and lodging; the state fed them and they had free seats at all public race meets, prize fights, beast fights, and such entertainments.

This bred a populace vastly different from the citizenry that stood off Hannibal, men who knew that failure in frugality meant the pinch of hunger, actual famine, or even death from starvation for themselves and their dear ones.

But while the facts are indubitably as just set forth, their interpretation by modern historians does not convey the mental attitude of the Romans themselves to these regulations. Both the recipients of the dole of bread and other food and the voters, tribunes, magistrates, senators, and emperors who established, maintained, and amplified the custom, regarded the dole, so to put it, as a proper dividend to each citizen on his personal holding of one share of stock in the Roman Commonwealth. Their ancestors had conquered the Mediterranean world and had organized it into provinces, and freedom from taxation, with food that cost each man nothing, was the bequest of their ancestors to them and their natural and proper inheritance.

The dole may have debased the Roman populace, but they themselves felt no sensation of debasement, no shame in their free food, but rather took pride in their heritage.

And be it noted that the degradation of the Roman mob, while it weakened Rome, did not necessarily weaken the Empire as a whole if there were more than earlier of capable Roman citizens, counting all everywhere.

Yet, indubitably, the deterioration of the quality of the individuals composing the populace of Rome was an adverse factor in computing the strength of the Empire as a whole at any given date.

(C, 10)

Manifestly the profound peace and general prosperity of the Empire from its establishment in 27 B.C. by Augustus to the murder of Severus Alexander in A.D. 235, a period of two and a half centuries, afforded the greatest opportunity until then created on earth not merely for traffic, trade, and travel, and with them for the diffusion of wealth, prosperity, knowledge, civilization, and culture, but also for the concomitant diffusion along with the beneficial of all sorts of deleterious influences.

Conspicuously, such a disease as an epidemic of Asiatic cholera had very little chance of overspreading the Mediterranean world in 400 B.C., when, in most languages, the same word stood for "foreigner," "alien," "stranger," and "enemy." Not merely the early Romans, but the Italians, Gauls, Spaniards, Berbers, Carthaginians, and Greeks of those days, killed first and asked questions afterward, not invariably, but yet habitually. Any infectious disease carried by a wanderer mostly died with him.

But after Actium, when the Roman fleet ceased to be a defense and became a mere police force, when Augustus dismantled his five-banked war galleys (quinqueremes) since no one else had any, and triremes (three-banked galleys) were cheaper and handier, when the Mediterranean became a peaceful highway, anyone could go anywhere, and trade, traffic, and travel throve. There were no regulations calling for passports for travellers or for clearance papers for ships. Anyone with coin travelled as he liked, afoot or on horseback or by carriage, according to his ability to pay. Any ship sailed when and whither its owners or master chose.

Amid these conditions, pestilences, certainly of typhus and cholera, possibly of smallpox and influenza, spread like wildfire and took a heavy toll. Each visitation was, in general, more widespread and more virulent than any of its predecessors.

Similarly, local cults, as those of Osiris, Isis, and Serapis from Egypt, as the cult of Mithras from Asia Minor, as Christianity from Judæa, seeped and trickled into every part of the Roman world.

The pestilences were manifestly disastrous and, of the alien cults, one at least was more calamitous than any pestilence.

(C, 11)

Considering the inhabitants of the area later included within the Roman Empire as they were before Rome began to win her domain, say from 450 B.C. to 350 B.C., it is plain that each separate community consisted of capable fighters and possessed competent leaders, for, if any city-state failed in either fighting power or generalship, it was quickly annihilated by its neighbors.

What was more, individual soldiers fought amid conditions where each had to think for himself to a great extent.

And not only the officers and commanders in the field, but the town councillors and townsmen within the town walls, had to think for themselves.

Also every individual had to think for himself at the frequent and hotly contested elections and during the lengthy and acrimonious debates as to laws proposed and opposed. All this bred a race full of physical, mental, and moral self-reliance.

As previously set forth, inclusion within the Empire deteriorated the quality of the men available as soldiers, and still more of those put in positions of responsibility and power, and this by mere lack of practice in the field as legionaries or officers.

The quality of town councillors, local officials, and military leaders deteriorated even more from the concomitant effects of the habit of taking orders from the Emperor's procurators or other representatives, and of looking to them and to Rome for orders, guidance, and suggestions. At first, local self-government went on much as under the proconsuls and proprætors of the Republic. But, as time passed, the imperial chancellery concerned itself with an ever-increasing list of departmental functions. Theoretically, local self-governing communities were left to themselves except where it was absolutely necessary for the imperial authority to impose uniformity. Practically the Prefects of the Prætorium, from Sejanus on, more and more encroached on the independence of local officials.

By the time of Trajan (A.D. 98-117) mayors of cities and such officials had acquired the habit of asking advice from the imperial government on all points, even of refraining from taking any action, or from coming to any decision on any point, without previously ascertaining the views of Rome and making sure of imperial approbation or acquiescence.

By the times of Severus Alexander (A.D. 222-235) men capable of initiative were very scarce all over the Empire.

This deterioration progressed very gradually. Galba, Otho, and Vespasian, in A.D. 69, were as virile, able, and self-confident commanders as ever were any Roman generals before their days.

As late as A.D. 193 Pertinax, Septimius Severus, Pescennius Niger, and Clodius Albinus, as generals or as men, compare very favorably with Fabricius, Flaminius, Marcellus, Fabius Maximus and Marius three or four centuries before them.

But the deterioration was continuous, and worse and worse, from age to age, both accelerating and intensifying as it progressed.

Moreover, individuals possessed of the vigor of character, originality of disposition, superabundance of energy, and restlessness of spirit which produced dashing cavalry commanders, brilliant commodores, and successful generals in the early days, or of those qualities which made men leaders in politics, law, and literature, mostly worked off their overplus of energy in conspiracies or insurrections against the reigning Emperor. The suppression of conspiracy after conspiracy led to an established imperial policy of getting rid of all individuals deemed likely to become conspirators. This exterminated the very men who possessed the potentialities of successful leadership. They vanished without descendants and soon the population was brainless, apathetic, acquiescent and helpless. Such as were not suspected and abolished felt that there was no use in trying to rise to power or to modify the existing conditions and remained inactive and hopeless.

Yet these conditions must not be thought as affecting the entire population; they affected only those individuals who would have been demagogues under the Republic and malcontents under any form of government.

Steadier natures found their mutual emulation and lifelong competition for a chance to rise in the imperial service as invigorating a stimulant as had ever been open rivalry for popular favor and freemen's votes to the politicians of the Republic.

Thousands of such men in each generation prided themselves on their citizenship, gloried in their share in Rome's greatness, were as loyal as possible to the Principate and the Emperor, and gave the Empire splendid service in arms ashore and afloat, as governors of provinces, as magistrates, as judges, as treasury officials, as imperial procurators and secretaries.

Yet it is manifest that a Senate filled by imperial election, however impartial and intelligent, could never possess the capabilities of a Senate filled with men chosen by the votes of their fellows and personally proving their worth as commanders, governors, magistrates, or what else. Neither the stern selectiveness of evaluation by cool-headed fellow citizens nor the inexorable weeding out of incompetents in office had operated on the imperial as on the republican Senate.

CHAPTER XXIV

MINOR CONTRIBUTORY INTERNAL CAUSES OF THE FALL OF ROME

(C, 12)

THE wealth of any human community, race, nation, or whatever, under the control of a centralized government, may be classified in two categories as either created wealth or diverted wealth.

For example, at the present moment, all the wealth in Iceland, on the Canary Islands, the Cape Verde Islands, Madeira, or the Balearic Islands, is created wealth. So likewise all of the wealth in New Zealand, Australia, Argentina, and North America north of the Rio Grande is created wealth. No wealth existed in these areas until they were colonized by Europeans. The colonists, their descendants, whatever immigrants followed the colonists, and their descendants, have created all the wealth now in existence in those regions.

On the other hand, the Vandals, from their establishment in control of Africa, in A.D. 440, after ravaging and pillaging Gaul in A.D. 406-409 and Spain for ten years, until their destruction by Belisarius in A.D. 534, were one of the wealthiest races earth ever saw, yet all their vast wealth was diverted wealth, looted from France, Spain, Morocco, Algeria, and Tunisia; for they never created any wealth whatever.

Very similarly, the Turks, from their invasion of Europe in A.D. 1365 to long after their decline began in 1566, certainly for three full centuries, were one of the wealthiest races on earth, one of the wealthiest races ever on earth. Yet every piaster's worth of the wealth of the Turks at the acme of their affluence was diverted wealth. Their prowess as warriors had put them in possession of the created wealth accumulated through centuries of industry and thrift by the nations they conquered. So the wealth of the Assyrians and of the Achæmenian Persians from 550 to 330 B.C. was largely diverted wealth. So of the wealth of Spain after the conquests of Mexico and Peru.

The Romans indubitably created wealth on a vast scale. The wealth of Carthaginian Spain was wholly created by Hamilcar Barca and his aides and successors between 236 B.C. and 201 B.C. This wealth, what of it was not annihilated by warfare, fell to the Romans, and their administration vastly augmented it, so that when all Spain became Roman in 27 B.C., its wealth was mostly created wealth then and thereafter.

The great wealth of Roman Gaul from 27 B.C. to after A.D. 403 was wholly created wealth, created by the shrewd and far-sighted policy with which Julius Cæsar had organized the provinces he conquered and by the prudent administration of sagacious Roman governors.

From the Atlantic, even beyond the Straits of Gibraltar, to the confines of Egypt, all the coastal regions of North Africa, far south into what is now hopeless desert, became under Roman rule one vast olive orchard, dotted with patches of fabulously productive farmland wherever irrigation was possible. The resultant wealth was all created wealth.

But a considerable proportion, perhaps far more than half of the wealth of the Romans, from the beginnings of their domination in 202 B.C. to the end of their prosperity in A.D. 166, was diverted wealth, wealth accumulated throughout hundreds, even, in the case of Egypt, throughout thousands of years, and suddenly acquired by the Romans as they annexed Asia Minor, Syria, Egypt, and other Eastern countries.

Beyond contradiction, the Romans augmented the wealth of these possessions of theirs. Roman Egypt, while perhaps never so productive and affluent as under its greatest native dynasties, was certainly more prosperous than Egypt had ever been as Persian satrapy, or under the kingship of the Ptolemies. Syria and Asia Minor to an even greater degree throve under the governors Rome appointed, and attained a populousness, a peacefulness, and a prosperity vastly beyond anything they had achieved when independent or had enjoyed under the incessantly warring successors of Alexander.

The wealth of the Roman Empire as a whole, from 27 B.C. onward, was wholly created wealth, but the disproportionate share of it which the Romans enjoyed by right of conquest, subjugation, domination, bequest, or from whatever cause, was more diverted wealth than created wealth; and however it comes about, diverted wealth never has the solid permanence and enduring dependability of created wealth.

An adequate and stable coinage is both an evidence of prosperity and a powerful influence for the maintenance of prosperity, and a gold standard and a gold coinage excels any other.

The Achæmenian Shahs of Persia, from Darius in 521 B.C., till Alexander's conquest in 330 B.C., achieved and maintained both a gold standard and an adequate coinage of gold, and their darics were as highly respected and as unhesitatingly accepted in those days as ever were golden guineas and pounds sterling in modern times.

But neither as a Republic nor as an Empire did Rome ever achieve a gold standard or a stable currency.

Rome's first coinage was in 366 B.C. of clumsy chunks of copper weighing a pound apiece. This primitive unit of value was called an *as* and all Roman silver and gold coins were regarded as multiples of the *as*.

Within half a century the Roman government began to debase its coinage, and throughout its use of copper, silver, and gold as metals of exchange the bad practice of debasing the coinage was repeated at not infrequent intervals.

From 217 B.C., soon after Hannibal's invasion of Italy, all through its expansion and prosperity, the Roman world was on a silver basis and the coinage was fairly stable until the reign of Nero, A.D. 68.

After the accession of Caracalla in A.D. 211, the coinage was progressively debased by emperor after emperor.

While gold coins were minted from the beginning of the prosperity of the Republic, about 200 B.C., the Roman world never enjoyed the felicity of trade and finance on a gold basis.

Gold for coinage was always insufficiently abundant within the Empire, and there was a steady drain of gold to India in exchange for pearls, other gems, spices, and such Oriental wares.

The heavy work of the world in our days is done by machinery constructed of iron and steel, made and set in motion by heat derived from coal. Coal and iron do our heavy work for us.

The heavy work of the Greco-Roman world was done by man muscle, mostly the muscles of slaves. Slaves, therefore, formed the chief item of wealth of the Greco-Roman world and of the Roman Empire.

The Romans, whose ancestors, the shepherds of the Alban hills, had been among the poorest men on earth, continued poor until their conquest of Etruria, Samnium, and Campania was well advanced, about 300 B.C.; and they did not begin to grow rich until their annexations of Sicily, Sardinia, and Spain, 241-197 B.C., poured into Latin Italy a flood of cheap slaves, captured in warfare.

Slaves began to be cheap and plenty about 200 B.C., after the Second Punic War, and continued, with fluctuations, cheap and plenty, and even grow cheaper and plentier until the death of Trajan in A.D. 117.

After Trajan's time the boundaries of the Empire remained stationary or even receded, no new territory was annexed, no foreign conquests brought in hordes of slaves, and hard times were near.

During the reigns of Hadrian and Antonius Pius, A.D. 117-161, about half a century, the Empire was at its acme of prosperity and no dearth of slaves was felt, as Trajan's extensive conquests had glutted the slave markets. Throughout this period there were enough home-bred slaves to supply the Empire's wants and prosperity did not wane.

But the great pestilence in 166, although it took its heaviest toll of the upper classes and the town dwellers, yet ravaged fearfully even hamlets and farms and vastly diminished the numbers of slaves.

From A.D. 169 onward the dearth of slave labor was more and more acutely felt and the prosperity of the Empire steadily waned.

There were other factors in the unsoundness of the general economic and financial condition of the Empire, but the important factors were the too great proportion of diverted wealth in the make-up of Roman opulence, the condition of the currency, and the failure of the supply of slave labor.

(C, 13)

The Great Pestilence of 166 was, in fact, the real death blow to Rome's greatness, and from it dates the decline of the Roman power. It broke the tradition of civilization and culture which had grown from its small beginnings among the primitive Greeks and Etruscans more than two thousand years before. During all those two thousand years there had been a more or less continuous and scarcely interrupted development of the agriculture, manufactures, arts, skill, knowledge, and power of the mass of humanity about the Mediterranean Sea; men who fought with spears and shields and swords, also with arrows and slings, believed in approximately the same sort of gods, wore clothing rather wrapped around them than upholstered on them as with us; reclined on sofas at meals; lived mostly out-of-doors all the year round; built their houses about courtyards, and made rows of columns the chief feature of their architecture and, sheltering themselves in these colonnades, sunny or shady according to the season of the year, the chief feature of their comfort. Up to the year of the Great Pestilence that civilization had prospered, had produced a long series of generals, inventors, architects, sculptors, painters, musicians, poets, authors, and orators. Everywhere men had shown self-confidence, capacity, originality, power, and competence, and had achieved success for two thousand years.

The Great Pestilence of A.D. 166 so depleted the population of the Empire that Rome never again advanced its boundaries. Some lucky armies won victories even glorious, but Rome never again put in the field an overwhelming army for foreign conquest, never again could fully man, even defensively, the long line of her frontiers.

All classes of the people suffered, but most of all the rich, the well-to-do, the cultured and educated classes of the towns and cities. And the main point of difference between the Great Pestilence and the others which had preceded it was the universality of its incidence. For two thousand years pestilences had occurred at intervals, but previously not everywhere at once. If one country suffered, others did not; if half the Mediterranean world, even, was devastated, the other half escaped.

From immune regions competence and capacity flowed into the ruined areas and civilization was restored there. But the Great Pestilence left no district unscathed. In six months it killed off all the brains and skill, all the culture and ingenuity, in the Empire. There were so few capable men left in any line of activity that the next generation grew up practically untaught. The tradition of two thousand years was broken. In all the Mediterranean world, until, centuries later, descendants of the savage invaders developed their new civilization on the ruins of the old, no man ever again made a great speech, wrote a great book or play or poem, painted a good picture, carved a good statue, or contrived a good campaign or battle. The brains of the Roman world died that year; the originality of the whole nation was killed at once; the tradition broke off.

The Great Pestilence of A.D. 166 left Greco-Roman civilization crippled, infirm, debilitated, enfeebled, and decrepit, but not moribund.

What the pestilence was, whether Asiatic cholera, typhus, or what else does not matter. The fact of its virulence and universality is beyond question. It ravaged the Empire from Nisibis in Upper Mesopotamia to the west coast of Wales, from the Rhine and Danube to the cataracts of the Nile. Every farm, hamlet, and village suffered; in not one town did more than half the inhabitants remain alive. Few cities escaped with so much as a third of their population surviving. Famine accompanied the pestilence in all the western portions of the Roman world, and from famine perished many whom the plague had spared.

(C, 14)

Septimius Severus was so horrified and revolted at the disloyalty and arrogance of the Prætorian Guards because of their mutiny against Pertinax and their murder of the man they existed to protect, that he not only disbanded the corps and created a new Prætorian Guard recruited from his loyal frontier legionaries, but also regarded Italians as unreliable material for the Imperial bodyguard in particular and for soldiering in general.

Long before his time Romans, Roman colonists in Italy, citizens of allied towns in Italy, and residents in Italy collectively, had been freed from the obligations of military service. But it had been the prerogative of Italy to supply recruits for the privileged, pampered, and envied Prætorian cohorts, the magnificent personal guards of the emperors. Likewise, up to the accession of Severus, any Italian with a desire for military life was welcomed into the army. Severus not only deprived Italians of their cherished exclusive right to serve as imperial guardsmen, but prohibited any native of Italy from serving in the legions in any capacity. This was bad statesmanship. It at once reduced the Empire to a hollow shell of colonies and provinces, without living inner vitals.

It is worth while to recapitulate the steps in the decadence of Roman military power and national vitality.

Hannibal's invasion devastated Italy and perhaps brought in malaria. The wars with the revolted allies in Italy wrought further havoc, and the civil wars and servile wars yet more. These causes and the exhaustion of the soil diminished the population of Italy. The effects of civil war, malaria, and depopulation impaired the quality of later generations. Peace and ease accelerated the deterioration of the Romans of Rome and of her colonies. More civil wars further diminished their numbers. Centralized and capricious despotism deteriorated the quality of the nobility and gentry. The great pestilence of A.D. 166 was Rome's death blow, and Severus, when he prohibited enlistment in Italy, gave the Empire a sort of *coup de grâce.*

This was approximately the sequence of the internal contributory causes of the ruin of Rome, of her Empire, and of the Greco-Roman religion and culture.

CHAPTER XXV

CHRISTIANITY AND ITS EFFECTS

O lips that the live blood faints in, the leaving of racks and of rods!
O ghastly glories of saints, dead limbs of gibbeted Gods!
Though all men abase them before you in spirit, and all knees bend,
I kneel not, neither adore you, but standing, look to the end.

—"Hymn to Proserpina"
ALGERNON CHARLES SWINBURNE.

(D)

MOST writers on the interaction between paganism and Christianity have entirely ignored or totally failed to grasp the fact that for pagans religion and government were identical; that Roman religion was Roman government and Roman government was Roman religion.

Most of them have treated as axiomatic fully seven assumptions:

(1) That pagan beliefs were false and may therefore be ignored.

(2) That therefore paganism deserved to perish.

(3) That therefore the fall of Rome was not detrimental to humanity at large and no loss to future generations.

(4) That Christian beliefs were true and that therefore Christianity deserved to triumph.

(5) That therefore the triumph of Christianity was beneficial not only to all future generations and to mankind at large, but to the population of the Roman Empire.

(6) That, anyhow, pagans did not really believe in their beliefs nor in their gods.

(7) That primitive Christian dogmas and precepts were identical with those now current among modern Christians

(usually the tenets of the sect with which the writer was affiliated were meant, and the tenets of all other Christian sects are ignored).

Of these only the premise of the first is universally accepted by mankind; the last is manifestly false and the rest highly debatable.

In any worth-while discussion of the interaction between paganism and Christianity all prejudice one way or the other should be eliminated and there should be set forth what, in fact, were the beliefs of the pagans; what, in fact, were the tenets and teaching of the early Christians; and what were the effects of the spread of Christianity on the population of the Roman Empire and on the vitality of the Roman Commonwealth.

Chapters XVI-XX attempted to elucidate for modern readers the actual beliefs current among the pagans of the Greco-Roman world.

This chapter and the next endeavor to set forth the effects of Christianity on the Roman Commonwealth.

These effects naturally classify themselves under four heads.

(E) The effects of the diffusion of Christianity.

(F) The effects of the adoption of Christianity by Constantine.

(G) The effects of the suppression of paganism by Theodosius and Gratian.

(H) The effects on the Roman world of the Christianization of the hostile barbarians beyond the limits of the Empire.

In the consideration of the results of the spread of Christianity we have no concern with effects of Christianity on individuals except in so far as adoption of Christianity or knowledge of Christianity affected inhabitants of the Roman world as citizens of the Roman Commonwealth or subjects of the Roman Empire.

These effects of Christianity on the Roman world will be considered under six heads:

(1) The appeals of Christianity to early converts.

(2) The effects of Christianization on denizens of the Roman Empire.

(3) The effects of Christianity on waverers between belief in pagan traditions and in Christian innovations.

(4) The effects of the knowledge of Christianity on the population at large.

(5) The effects of knowledge of Christianity on devout, sincere and lifelong pagans.

(6) The effects of Christianity on the general military morale of the legionaries and of the population at large.

(E, 1)

It has been very generally assumed that from the first proselytes were attracted to Christianity because it appeared to them to promulgate a system of ethics patently superior to that implicit in current paganism. There were such proselytes, and perhaps from the first; but they were very few and were chiefly neurotic intellectuals of the upper social strata, persons of the sort which we characterize as afternoon-tea socialists, parlor Bolsheviks, and by similar descriptive labels; sentimental idlers of the leisure class, agape for any novelty. To most pagans primitive Christianity did not make any such appeal.

Indubitably, primitive Christianity made no converts in country districts. The first Christian communities arose in towns and cities, never in *faubourgs* composed of palatial mansions, seldom in well-to-do quarters, mostly in the crowded slums where the poorer classes herded and swarmed. The earliest proselytes were made chiefly among slaves, the indigent proletariat, the rabble, peddlers, street sweepers, beggars, and the like, with more than a sprinkling of thieves and other professional criminals.

Little as an average modern could conceive of it without a specialist's acquaintance with the peculiarities of ancient mentality, Christianity appeared to most of such folk as a novel and superior variety of Babylonian magic.

To illustrate: The Eskimo shamans were much occupied with taboos. One Eskimo might not eat of the meat of a seal's ribs, another might never eat of any part of its head, another never of its liver, another might plait thongs in three-strand braids or five-strand braids, but must never plait, use, or touch any four-strand braids; one must use only one special bone out of which to make spear heads, never any other bone, or two bones only, or three; and the forbidden bones varied from person to person. Often taboos applied to whole families. One family might never eat whale meat, the hunters of another might never hunt bears; one family might use only a specified material for making lamps, all other materials were to them taboo; so of a great variety of whimsical prohibitions.

When two shamans met they compared taboos and the one who knew fewer acknowledged his inferiority. In a gathering of shamans the one who knew more taboos than any other was acclaimed master of all. Especially did knowledge of or promulgation of or invention of any novel taboos earn preeminence and veneration for their proponent.

When Christian missionaries appeared among these Eskimos their preaching excited ridicule until their auditors grasped their ideas about Sunday. Then the shamans withdrew for a conference, after which they announced their ardent adherence to Christianity, for, in all the traditions of Eskimo shamanism, there was no mention of anyone's having thought of making a day taboo. The missionaries had a taboo not merely novel, but of a wholly novel kind. Therefore Christianity must be far superior to their native shamanism and so was to be embraced at once by all.

Babylonian magic was widely diffused over the Roman Empire and its practitioners were found in all cities and countless towns. There were many varieties of Babylonian magic, but one very well-known and respected type proceeded as follows:

To realize a highly desirable aim, take a very rare and precious object and treat it in some very unexpected fashion.

For instance, to prepare an infallible love potion take the tumor found between the ears of a new-born foal (actually found once in about fifty thousand foalings) and . . . But the records of the eccentricities of the treatment have been lost.

Now to persons acquainted with Babylonian magic Christianity appeared magic of this type, the prescription having been as follows:

To attain life eternal and eternal bliss, they had taken the only son of the only god and had . . . crucified him!

Now it was impossible to conceive of an end in view more worthy of desire than life eternal and eternal bliss. Surely there could not be found in all the universe any object more precious than the only son of the only god. And one could think forever and not be able to conjure up anything that could be done to the only son of the only god more unexpected and anomalous than to crucify him.

So, manifestly, this magic outclassed all other magic past, present and to come. It was unsurpassable. Therefore Christianity was to be embraced.

The promise of life eternal was explicit, not as with the vague promise of paganism, an all but unrealizable chance of attaining a sort of life after death by deserving and earning grateful recollection among posterity, by which a minority might become *Dii Manes,* and a very few might attain the bliss of the Elysian Fields, of the Fortunate Isles, or of minor godship; the Christians' promise was of individual, personal, eternal existence for all who believed the teachings and followed the precepts of the Apostles. And the fervid zeal of the early missionaries made the heaven they depicted appear to their neophytes actual and real and close; for the primitive Christians, one and all, expected the second coming of the Christ, the Last Judgment, and the end of the world at no distant date, but soon, at an interval to be measured hardly by years, more likely by months or days. Also the homilies they listened to caused hell to appear as actual as heaven and made a powerful appeal to the credulity and vanity of such slaves and paupers by suggesting that they alone of mankind had had the incredible good fortune to learn of and adopt the only true faith so that they alone would enjoy life eternal and eternal felicity in blissful heaven, while all the rest of mankind, including their pagan masters and the envied gentry and nobles, were to burn in hell forever.

This appeal was reinforced by primitive Christian equalitarianism. All mankind was equal in the sight of God. Not merely could they look forward to an everlasting self-congratulation in eternal heaven from which they would gaze down at their former betters roasting forever in flaming hell, but now, at once, the moment they became full-fledged members of a Christian society, they were the equals of all nobles, grandees, and even of Senators, consuls, and of the Emperor himself.

This contrasted mightily with the pagan tradition of slow and painful rise from the status of slaves to the status of freedmen, by proving one's merit by long years of probity, industry, thrift, and social tact; and the still slower process of a similar rise from the status of free man to the status of full citizen, from plain citizen to nobleman, from equestrian nobility to Senatorial rank.

Powerfully did primitive Christianity appeal to probationers as a cheap religion, inexpensive to a degree unimaginable before they first heard of it. No sacrifices! The only son of the only god had been sacrificed, and that one sacrifice outvalued all actual prior sacrifices and all possible subsequent and prospective sacrifices added together and so manifestly sufficed for all mankind forever. So no other outlays for sacrificial victims, not even any expenditures for fruit, flowers, and incense, were necessary for accredited Christians.

Also, while in many ways an exacting cult, it appeared in other ways alluringly easy. Its emphasis was on thoughts rather than on deeds; it was an inward rather than an outward religion. Humility, which was belauded in its homilies, most early converts, in their station in life, had anyhow. An humble and a contrite heart, love even for one's enemies, chastity and other Christian virtues, were perhaps difficult to achieve. But how much easier than the respect and esteem of one's associates universal throughout one's family, friends, acquaintances, and entire community, slowly won by years of industry, thrift, fair dealing, probity, helpfulness, tact, and courtesy!

And it was very easy to pretend to have the Christian virtues and succeed with the pretense. Most primitive Christians were fervently and zealously, even fanatically, sincere, and their faith genuine to a degree not to be exaggerated, even inexpressible. But, from very early, the sect attracted a minority of hypocrites and shams who successfully fooled their associates, perhaps even themselves. It was all but impossible for anyone to demonstrate that the claim to a contrite heart was false; a Christian could achieve a reputation for humility by claiming to be humble; but no pagan could pretend to have served through twenty summers of campaigning, to have risen from a mere legionary to being one of his legion's chief centurions, to have been personally decorated for valor in battle, and to have returned home alive and hale. Paganism, in most respects, was a more exacting cult than Christianity.

The tale of the penitent thief on Calvary and the dogma of the efficacy of deathbed repentance appealed powerfully to professional criminals. One might be a sneak thief or a highway robber all one's life and, by a sincere deathbed repentance, might escape hell and win eternal bliss in heaven if one were a Christian from long beforehand. Of course a Christian was obligated to refrain from thieving and robbery, but temptation was a valid excuse, the flesh was weak, and a genuine, heartfelt repentance cost nothing and wiped out all the effects of past sinfulness, hypocrisies, and sins.

(E, 2)

Christianization made every convert at once not only unsympathetic toward the most important current beliefs of the pagan world, but also positively antagonistic to all its most vital tenets.

From the earliest ages, throughout the entire development of the civilization of the Mediterranean world, the duties of a pagan had been conceived of as toward his parents, his family, and his commonwealth; paramount among these duties to the state, and preëminent over all the duties of military service and of reverence toward the national gods.

Primitive Christian preaching inculcated into its proselytes that, for a Christian, soldiering was a horrible sin. War must not be participated in by a Christian in any way. Still less must soldiering be taken up as an occupation or entered upon as a career; it must not even be thought of.

And primitive Christianity preached that devout Christians had no concern whatever with the welfare of the state, with the prosperity of the commonwealth, with the goodness or badness of the government under which they lived or with its survival or existence.

The concern of all Christians, their chief concern, their vital concern, their only important concern, was the escaping of the flames of hell and the attainment of everlasting bliss in heaven after death. Nothing else mattered to a Christian. Good works counted, but faith was the preponderant factor in eternal salvation. The relative importance of faith and good works was a question hotly debated among Christians for centuries.

To pagans, life after death was a vague, shadowy, hazy, nebulous, and unimportant consideration; the world in which they lived, their duty to parents, fellow citizens, and the commonwealth, were all in all; the duty of propitiation of the gods of their ancestors, the gods of their commonwealth, the most vital of all duties, for upon it depended not only abundant harvests and national prosperity, but success in war and so the protection of the state from the peril of destruction from without; military service merely put into effect the will of the gods that their votaries be victorious, won for those votaries by adequate invocation, propitiation, and thanksgiving.

Much has been written about the hypothetical effect on the vitality of the Roman Commonwealth of the diffusing throughout the Empire of alien cults, such as the worship of Isis, Osiris, Serapis, and Mithras. But, as already mentioned, the adherents of these cults continued respectful toward the gods of Olympus, participated in all forms of public worship and propitiation, and were no worse military material than before they had affiliated themselves with such cults.

Whereas Christianization made every proselyte not merely poor military material, but utterly useless for the defense of the Empire.

Again, much has been written of the deterioration of the quality of the populations of the western provinces, of Italy and of Rome, by the infiltration of Asiatics and by the dilution of native stocks with freedmen, originally slaves, from every part of the outside world.

But these outlanders were all pagans, with instincts, however inferior to Roman instincts, concordant with Roman instincts. For all of them, it was instinctive to realize and to try to fulfill their duties to their parents, families, and the Commonwealth; the duty of reverence to the gods, of course, and always; and the duty of military service if necessary and unavoidable.

The total impairment of the vitality of the Roman Commonwealth, by infiltration of denizens and citizens of alien stock and by infiltration of alien cults, was trifling compared with the effects of the spread of Christianity.

For all votaries of alien gods and all denizens and citizens of alien blood were loyal to the Commonwealth and to its gods and to their vicegerent the reigning Emperor.

Christians were hostile not only to the gods of the Commonwealth, but to it and its Emperor.

Christianity has been lauded as a religion of brotherly love. For primitive and early Christians that meant brotherly love for fellow Christians, but bitter hatred for all pagans.

The spirit of this hatred is preserved for us, among others, in many passages of the extant writings of Tertullian, Arnobius, Lactantius, and Augustine.

Every convert to Christianity, both in respect to availability for military service and as to civic duties, ceased to be an asset to the Roman Commonwealth and Empire and became a detriment.

CHRISTIANITY AND ITS EFFECTS

(E, 3)

From soon after A.D. 42, the preaching of Christianity among pagans not only made many converts, but resulted in a far larger number of pagans becoming waverers, even lifelong waverers, between the appeal of the belief in their ancestral gods and the appeal of the doctrines expounded by ministers of the gospel. These waverers were tormented by many self-questionings and confronted by many insoluble dilemmas.

What were to pagans not merely personal pleasures, but reasonable duties, incumbent on all as proper acts of worship to Aphrodite-Venus, Eros-Cupid, Dionysus-Liber, and Priapus were stigmatized by the puritanical missionaries as deadly sins, abominable in the sight of the God of the Christians, and infallible passports to eternal agonies in hell. If the Christians were wrong, failure adequately to worship Venus and her associates would incur their displeasure and resentment and the resentment of the gods; if the Christians were right, homage to Venus and her associates would incur the wrath of the Christians' God. The dilemma was insoluble.

We moderns think of Jupiter and the other gods of Olympus precisely as we think of the Lilliputians and Brobdingnagians in Swift's *Gulliver's Travels;* as figments, as imaginary beings who never had an objective existence.

But it was certainly long after A.D. 1000 before anyone thought of denying, even of impugning, the actuality and reality of the gods of Olympus. The early Christians conceived them all as existing beings, as demons in the service of Satan, commissioned by him to entice the souls of credulous human beings into the everlasting agonies of hell by the elaborate device of masquerading for centuries as beneficent gods and so inveigling whole races and nations into worshipping them and thereby incurring the penalties of their mistake in not merely failing to worship the only true God, but in according divine honors to malignant, deceptive, deluding fiends.

To all pagans who heard of these ideas they appeared inexpressibly horrible. Eternal punishment was an idea familiar to all pagans, but the Tartarus of their underworld was for the very few, exceptionally wicked persons who had merited an eternity of pain by very shocking misdeeds. Now, the suggestion that every human being was destined to eternal bliss or eternal agony appeared horrible in itself, and the notion of such beings as fiends yet more so. The custodians of the pagan Tartarus were conceived of as a sort of jailers who did the duty assigned to them, but not only did not enjoy it, but found it unpleasant. That there might exist beings whose one delight and sole eternal occupation was the torturing of their victims appeared inexpressibly horrible.

But still more horrible was the difference between the world about them as depicted by pagan myths and by the Christian missionaries. The pagan myths peopled all nature with diverse types of divinities, from the nymphs to the gods of Olympus, varying in their powers and importance, but all, while irascible if affronted, habitually and by nature kindly and helpful. The insinuation that all these divinities, for ages believed benignant and gracious, were in reality cunning fiends masquerading in these deceptive guises to ensnare mankind to appalling dooms, appeared shockingly hideous and horrific.

The suggestion that their beloved parents, respected grandparents, and revered ancestors were all burning in the Christian hell forever because they had failed to detect the snare laid for them by the fiends who masqueraded as the pagan gods, was too hideous to think of.

Yet they could not put out of their minds the horrors conjured up by the Christian missionaries. The Christians believed them. Perhaps they were true! The doubt darkened all their world.

Persons who fell under the influence of Christian preaching sufficiently to become waverers but not converts were torn by such doubts and suffered horribly.

All such persons impaired the vitality of the Commonwealth and Empire by their doubts and by the knowledge or suspicion among sincere pagans that there existed such doubters.

(E, 4)

The average denizen of Rome, of any part of Italy, of any Roman colony, of any city or town in any province of the Empire, could not but learn by personal observation or hearsay, if he knew anything about Christians at all, that they never offered sacrifice to any of the pagan gods; never participated in any public or private sacrifice, not even as bystanders or onlookers; absented themselves, not merely frequently but invariably, from all banquets of the gods, votive processions, performances of tragedies, comedies, farces, mimes, or pantomimes, games in the circuses and gladiatorial shows or beast-fights in the amphitheaters; and that they would have nothing to do with oracles, and sneered at auguries, omens, portents, and prodigies.

This, in itself, would, in the eyes of all normal pagans, convict Christians of impiety and would justify not only the general impression that they were imbued with hatred of the human race, but also the appellation of public enemies very generally given them.

The knowledge, or even the impression, that the Empire harbored a considerable number of persons characterized by what must appear to pagans only as an insane impiety, could not but cause much uneasiness.

To pagans, the presence in their midst of a society whose members denied the might of their gods and refused them their due of propitiation was certain to call down on their Commonwealth the wrath of its gods unless these blasphemers were hunted out and put to death, preferably by exposure to wild beasts in the arena of an amphitheater, as a public and solemn expiatory offering to the justly offended gods.

The hearsay report that Christians regarded warfare as wicked and considered a soldier fully as bad as any brigand, bandit, or other outlaw could not but confirm the current impression of the insanity and impiety of all Christians.

What pagans might be able to learn, if they learned anything, of the probity and other personal and family virtues of

Christians would appear to pagans by no means to offset their shocking impiety, insanity, and cowardice.

It cannot be too much emphasized that when pagans, from their seats in the *cavea* of an amphitheater, looked on at victims being torn to pieces by lions or other beasts of prey, they regarded thieves, robbers, highwaymen, murderers, murderers for hire, and such criminals as persons who had committed crimes deserving of their punishment, but as having, in committing their crimes, injured only the persons killed or robbed and the state at large. They felt no personal animosity to such victims.

But when they watched the rending of Christians, whatever their age or sex, they felt against each and every one of them an intense personal animosity. These people had by their impiety insulted the gods of the Commonwealth and rendered the Commonwealth liable to disasters, or even to total destruction, as a retribution likely to be sent upon it for its negligence in permitting the existence within its territories of sectaries so irreverent and blasphemous. These blasphemers had individually injured every devout pagan by robbing him of part of his share of the precious favor of the gods of the Commonwealth.

CHAPTER XXVI

THE EFFECTS OF CHRISTIANITY

(E, 5)

PROBABLY few cultured pagans learned anything of Christianity during the early stages of its diffusion except, perhaps, of its existence. Any new sect, the members of which were chiefly slaves and canaille, would scarcely attract a noble to learn more of it.

When Christianity began to be recognized as a danger to the state, all pagans, even the wealthiest and most cultured, could not but feel about it as did the generality of the population—that its existence was an insult to Rome's gods, and that its growth, strength, and presence could only be expiated and the gods propitiated by the extirpation of what appeared to pagans a noisome superstition, through the exposure to wild beasts of every one of its adherents.

Any sincere pagans who learned anything of the actual teachings of Christianity could not fail to be shocked at such precepts as those embodied in some of Tertullian's aggressive utterances: as, "We fear our God, not your governor," "If your law errs, I conceive it was devised by man, not handed down from heaven." To any devout pagans utterances such as these could only be characterized, as they were, as "The voice of insurrection."

And when Christians declared themselves to be "sojourners upon earth," that their home was in heaven, normal pagans could only feel such utterances as not merely evidences of lunacy, but as proofs of attitudes of mind antagonistic to the most cherished pagan instincts and subversive of all that pagans held most precious.

When Christians were brought before any Roman tribunal and interrogated, they habitually, uniformly, perhaps invariably affirmed their loyalty to the Emperor and the Commonwealth, and their obligation, as Christians, even more positively than before Christianization, to obey the laws of the Republic and the edicts of provincial governors and to fulfill all civic duties.

These bland and plausible utterances, contrasted with their obstinate refusal to have anything to do with military service or the worship of the Commonwealth's gods, the two civic duties most important in pagan eyes, produced in the pagans a profound and unbanishable impression that Christians were disingenuous, evasive, deceitful, and mendacious, and that duplicity and hypocrisy were outstanding characteristics of all Christians.

Cultured pagans knew of the Ten Commandments as the kernel of the Jewish law and, if they went so far as to acquaint themselves with the specifications of these Commandments, they derided the ninth and tenth as having to do with thoughts rather than deeds; abhorred as impious the prohibition of the worship or carving of idols, and made light of the rest as practically identical with the chief regulations of any human society.

One phase of the reaction of cultured or sincere pagans to one feature of Christianity might be adumbrated as follows:

"Credulity is one of the basest and most contemptible of human weaknesses. The Christians give credulity a name of their own and call it 'Faith,' denominate it a virtue and exalt it above all human virtues. This appeals to slaves, paupers, and the rabble generally, for they have little reasoning power and are prone to superstitions. Thus the Christians entice their gulls into putting aside rationality, which requires intellect and character to maintain it, and into steeping themselves in an infatuation for delusion, which is easy."

The austerities and asceticisms of Christian practice and preaching were to the last degree obnoxious and odious to devout pagans. It was one of the cardinal assumptions of their public worship that what was agreeable to human beings was pleasing to the gods of Rome. The Christians inculcated into their proselytes that all the pleasant things in life were displeasing to Jehovah and that what most pleased Him in His votaries was refraining from pleasures and enjoyments, abnegation of desire, and the endurance of such unpleasant conditions of existence as lifelong chastity and frequent fasting. This, if they learned of it, appeared to devout pagans a mixture of insolent impiety and odious lunacy.

The government of Imperial Rome in all its ramifications, through all its agents, was incessantly on the watch for symptoms of disaffection, conspiracy, sedition, and insurrection. Roman officials, like the Canadian Mounted Police, comported themselves in accordance with the salutary maxim that the time to stop trouble is before it starts.

On the other hand, the imperial government of Rome was to the last degree indulgent to all sorts of local peculiarities of custom, observance, and ritual. Roman officials never interfered with anything unless they sensed in it some suggestion of the possibility of danger to the Empire at large or to their provincial authority in particular.

The obscurity of the primitive Christians as individuals, their lowly station in the tiering arrangement of the classes of Greco-Roman society, the utter unintelligibility to the pagan mind of most of what Roman officials could learn about them even from direct interrogation, brought it about that they were generally looked on as harmless, though very disgusting, lunatics. Roman officials tortured Christians not because they enjoyed cruelty, but because torture was an accepted method of curing maniacs of their folly, just as within a century and a half it was a common practice in France or England to whip bedlamites to make them behave rationally.

Most moderns have a totally false impression of the disposition of Roman officials toward Christians brought before them. This comes to pass because moderns, practically universally, accept as if they were authentic and veracious records of actual occurrences the fantastic fictions of the martyrologies, which are a tissue of fabrications and inventions.

The martyrologies, as they exist, came into their present form as follows: The early Christians were so muddled-headed and illogical that they failed to realize that endurance of torture proves nothing except the victim's ability to endure torture; or, in the case of a bigot, proves merely the intensity of the fanaticism, which is the cause of the prisoner's contumacy. The early Christians harbored the comical delusion that when Christians were interrogated by a Roman official, urged to renounce their alleged beliefs, given a time within which to abjure and then tortured to bring about a disavowal, their endurance of any torture rather than recant proved the truth of the tenets of their creed; the greater the tortures endured the more convincing the proof of the Christian dogmas.

This led to all sorts of accretions on what were originally simple narratives of what actually happened. The more and severer the tortures which the martyr endured the more convincing proof that martyrdom gave of the truth of Christianity and the falsity of paganism. Therefore most martyrologists felt that they were acting for the honor of the Church of Christ and for the Glory of God when they added to the original account of any martyrdom anything that came into their heads or which they could laboriously invent depicting the Roman official as a callous, flinty-hearted, inhuman, malignant, browbeating bully, harsh, ruthless, iron-handed, cruel, brutal, and ferocious; portraying the martyr as innocent, meek, and submissive; and representing the tortures as ingenuously atrocious, exquisitely fiendish, reconditely agonizing, inexpressibly excruciating, unimaginably frightful, inconceivably terrific, incredibly appalling, and to any mere human being unsupported by supernatural aid, manifestly intolerable, unendurable, and insupportable. The more harrowing details could be foisted into the account of any one martyrdom, the better satisfied with it any martyrologist felt.

Then, after the suppression of paganism and the establishment of Christianity, any city, town, or locality where a Christian had been martyred felt highly honored by the fact that the power of divine grace had been demonstrated within its boundaries and the more horrible the tortures the greater the honor.

Wherever there were genuine and authentic records of martyrdoms these records were improved to any extent attainable by the imaginative powers of the concocters. Wherever no actual martyrdom had even taken place, martyrdoms to suit were freely invented.

Nineteen out of every twenty martyrdoms described in the extant martyrologies never took place at all, and of the tortures particularized in those narratives which have a basis of actual fact nineteen-twentieths are out-and-out inventions, such as were never endured by anyone on earth, and not only never inflicted by the order of any Roman official but never thought of by any Roman. These phantasmagoria originated in the diseased and morbid imaginations of monks cloistered in mediæval monasteries.

Roman officials dealing with Christians mostly felt sorry for them rather than indignant with them, and few discerned in their queer notions, obduracy, and crabbed or saucy impudence any germ of danger to the existing order of things.

Yet long before Christianity had been recognized by local officials or by the central government as a threat to the Empire and a peril to the Commonwealth, any cultured pagan who really made himself acquainted with the tenets and teachings of the Christians could not fail to realize that Christianity and the prosperity of the Greco-Roman world could not co-exist; that either Rome must extirpate Christianity or Christianity would ruin Rome.

Christianity, certainly from the time of Domitian, made some converts among the upper classes, the cultured nobility, even the Senators. But there were few. Not much more numerous the lifelong waverers. For most educated pagans the existence of Christianity, even a fairly complete knowledge of Christian precepts, made no difference whatever.

There is no discernible difference between the convinced belief and pious devoutness of Quintus Aurelius Symmachus and Vettius Agorius Prætextatus in A.D. 373-394 and of Publius Cornelius Scipio Africanus himself, six full centuries before.

(E, 6)

From its first manifestations in the slums of the large cities Christianity began, insidiously and imperceptibly, to impair the military morale of the Roman Commonwealth, Empire, and army.

This is manifest to any fair-minded student of the records covering the years between A.D. 41 and 451. But it is very difficult to prove succinctly and can only be indicated here. The reader must be left to draw his own conclusions from what can be set forth.

Originally, while Rome was in danger of siege every summer and its capture was by no means improbable, the immediate pressure of the nation's foes created an unsurpassable military morale. Every legionary knew that he must fight his utmost if Rome were to survive, every able-bodied man was drafted.

We do not know when it began to be the custom among Roman recruits, both to the infantry and cavalry, to bind themselves together by a formal, but unofficial, mutual oath that they would not desert each other in danger; probably after the rout on the Allia in 390 B.C. This indicated rather a resolution to maintain military morale than any waning of it, but did indicate a diminution in the daily and hourly consciousness of imminent peril to the state.

In 226 B.C., just before the battle of Cannæ, for the first time, Roman soldiers publicly took official oath to obey their officers, no matter what orders they gave, and to remain with the standards until dismissed. This oath was taken individually for more than a century.

Sometime about 107 B.C. Marius had the soldiers take the oath collectively instead of individually, and this continued the custom until the extinction of the Roman power and the disappearance of the legion as a military organization.

Thus from the times when every able-bodied man had to serve in the army and did so serve every summer, through the times when every man served, but not every summer, on through the times when every man might have to serve, but not all did serve, and on after Marius's device of calling for volunteers brought it about that only a minority of Romans had to man Rome's armies, the tradition of morale from the times when all men served was unbroken. Every Roman felt that he might be called on at need and was fit to take his place in the ranks. Every member of every Roman community, whether at Rome or in the most distant colony, felt that war was every Roman's duty and glory.

All Roman soldiers took the same oath and felt alike toward it. All felt the same enthusiastic approbation from their home communities.

Sometime after A.D. 41 it first began to be bruited about the Roman world that there were folk in the slums of the cities who regarded war as criminal and soldiers as no better than brigands or bandits. This was the turning point. The denizens of the Empire were no longer all of one mind as to war; not even all Roman citizens were any longer, on this point, unanimous. Now there had been many and bitter discords among Roman citizens ever since soon after the establishment of the Republic, but never before as to the righteousness and praiseworthiness of warfare.

For more than a century military service was looked upon as impossible for a Christian, no soldier became a Christian and remained a soldier, and no Christian entered the army. It happened more than once that soldiers, even centurions, were converted to Christianity and could not obtain their discharge from service.

Some of these declared publicly, several even in the presence of their fellow soldiers and officers, that war was wicked and that they refused any longer to participate in it in any way. These fanatics were naturally executed as mutineers. But such occurrences did not tend to improve military morale among those who saw them happen nor among those who heard of them by report.

We do not know at what date converted legionaries began to compromise with their consciences enough to remain soldiers after conversion; nor do we know at what date the pressure of many in that situation led to Christian communities relaxing their primitive strictness and retaining such persons as members of their congregations in good standing. But we do know that both conditions came to pass, that there was more than a sprinkling of Christian soldiers with the standards in all parts of the Empire, and that members of Christian communities in increasing numbers took to soldiering without losing their status as Christians and their acceptance as such among their home folks.

Such a state of affairs could not but impair military morale. In most legions, even in most cohorts, were a few soldiers who did not worship the gods of the Commonwealth and to whom their military oath was either not binding at all, or binding in a sense other than that in which it was understood by pagan legionaries.

We do not know that any talked to their fellows, tampered with them, or attempted their conversion. But such occurrences, in view of the bigoted fanaticism of the primitive Christians, appear more than likely.

And to whatever degree Christian soldiers among the pagan legionaries operated to impair the morale of the garrisons or camps, perhaps to a very small degree, the increasing numbers of town Christians who despised and loathed warfare and soldiers must, to a much greater degree, have impaired that sense of solidarity with the civilian population and of countenance from them which is one of the strongest supports of military morale.

Even before Constantine's time there were legions a large minority of whose men were Christians. Rivalries and jealousies had sprung up between legions wholly pagan and legions partly made up of Christians.

(F)

On attaining to supreme power in Italy in A.D. 312 Constantine at once proclaimed Christianity the national religion of the Empire and reinforced this decree by further edicts next year.

At this time not much over five per cent of the population of the Empire was Christian. Putting it otherwise, nineteen out of every twenty of the denizens of the Empire were pagans.

His proclamation had several effects adverse to the vitality of the Roman Commonwealth.

It dashed the spirits of all pagans and caused a dismay verging on despair. For two centuries pagans had been adread of the wrath of the gods because Christianity existed at all within the limits of the Empire, had feared that the failure of the government to extirpate this ungodly sect might result in such indignation on the part of the gods as to bring about the total withdrawal from the Commonwealth of their favor and countenance, and so its utter destruction. Now that Christianity had attained imperial recognition and patronage, their horror and alarm could not be exaggerated.

They could not but feel that the Commonwealth and the Empire were doomed.

Then, as soon as the news was abroad, there was a rush of secret-service men, hangers-on, parasites, toadies, courtiers, tufthunters, time servers, and sycophants to become Christians, because it paid. This did not improve the quality of the Christian communities nor of the imperial service.

About A.D. 315 Constantine promulgated an edict forbidding any gladiatorial combats being held outside the city of Rome. This had a very depressing effect on the spirits of the pagan populace, since they regarded gladiatorial shows as an important item in the list of performances essential to the adequate propitiation of the gods. The pagan intelligentsia, of course, knew that gladiatorial shows were no part of the public worship of the Commonwealth, but that had no effect on the beliefs of the populace. So that dejection and apprehension were general.

As the pagans were still heavily in the majority everywhere, this decree was very generally evaded. But its promulgation had an immediate and positive adverse effect on the military morale of the western world. On the east it had no effect, for there gladiatorial shows had been so unusual that one might

pagans ascribed each to the flouting of the gods of Rome by Constantine and his Christian successors; all Christians, on the other hand, attributed every calamity to the culpably weak-kneed indulgence with which paganism was tolerated. There was less and less unanimity and more and more disunion within the Empire.

(G)

The suppression of paganism began in the Western Empire about A.D. 381 after Gratian felt himself established as Emperor. It spread to the Eastern Empire within a very few years, as soon as Theodosius felt himself well established as Emperor there and had set on foot the, to him, far more important business of the extirpation of Arianism, for Christians of different sects hated each other even more venomously than they hated pagans.

The suppression of paganism was a thirteen years' orgy of confiscations and similar high-handed proceedings.

The many "persecutions" of the Christians, from A.D. 65 during the Principate of Nero till the death of Galerius in A.D. 311 had been of various kinds. Some were outbursts of mob violence on the part of populaces incensed at what they viewed as outrageous and wantonly insulting impiety on the part of a few lunatic fanatics. Some were local exercises of police authority by provincial governors. The last three years of the Principate of Marcus Aurelius (A.D. 177-180) are generally spoken of by Christian writers as the fourth persecution and the first general persecution. The evidence, however, on which this period is dubbed a general persecution is far from being unequivocal, and many historians, even many specialists, deny that there was then any general persecution. Nor is it by any means indubitable that the so-called fifth persecution (A.D. 203-211), during the Principate of Septimius Severus, was in reality a general persecution. But there can be no doubt that the persecutions during the Principates of Decius (A.D. 249-251), Valerian (A.D. 258-259), Aurelian (A.D. 270-275), Probus, Carus and Carinus (A.D. 278-285), and Diocletian and Galerius

(A.D. 311) were as general as the urgent edicts and rescripts of the emperors could make them. By the accession of Decius it was becoming apparent to far-sighted statesmen, and by the accession of Diocletian it was manifest to any average official that Christianity and the Roman Commonwealth could not co-exist, that either Christianity must be extirpated or the Commonwealth and Empire must perish.

Why Christianity survived the attempts at its extirpation has been much debated.

Among other factors which contributed to the outcome it should not be lost sight of that the earlier partial persecutions were mostly local exercise of ordinary police powers by governors very reluctant to assert their authority and therefore languid in asserting it or eager to avoid so doing; while the officials entrusted with carrying out the edicts which set on foot the later general persecutions found their duties irksome and costly rather than remunerative. Christians were mostly poor, and few were rich and fewer opulent. Persecuting Christians did not pay.

On the contrary, suppressing paganism was hugely enjoyable and very profitable.

The pagan majority was helpless against the exultant minority who abhorred every tradition of Greco-Roman culture and were intensely envious of the prosperity and elegance of the cultivated nobility.

Jubilant mobs everywhere stormed the pagan temples, tore the jewelled rings, bracelets, necklaces, diadems, and girdles from the cult-statues, overset, befouled, mutilated, or shattered the statues themselves, looted the temple treasuries, rifled the temple archives, pillaged the libraries, and made bonfires of their contents, for books on ritual, sacrifices, divination, and prophecy were particularly the objects of Christian detestation.

Many temples and shrines were demolished and all those left standing were closed, and the priests, priestesses, and hierophants driven away. Everywhere the endowments of pagan temples were sequestrated and confiscated and the pagan hierarchy beggared.

These confiscations, of course, annihilated most of the wealth, diverted and greatly impoverished the Empire; for the enriching of the few favorites who profited by the sequestrations was a trifle compared with the dislocations of economic conditions caused by the dispossessions and evictions.

The pagan majority, of course, were in despair. Their gods had apparently abandoned them. A few devotees hoped that these appalling occurrences indicated merely a severe warning from their deities, with the possibility that future expiation might regain the favor of Rome's gods. But most were hopeless and certain that inevitable doom impended as retribution on the Commonwealth for the impiety of the Christians; that the gods in their just wrath would be satisfied with no lesser punishment than the total annihilation of the Empire and Commonwealth. And when the catastrophe occurred, most pagans looked upon it as the manifestation of the wrath of the gods of Olympus for the disrespect done them by the Christians and their abettors.

The cultured upper-class pagans looked on helpless at what they viewed as the subversion of a noble and beautiful natural religion by a singularly degrading and debasing superstition which was triumphing because of its universal and subtle appeals to the credulity and vanity of the rabble.

(H)

During the brief and headlong *débâcle* throughout the twenty-odd years intervening between the suppression of paganism in the west in A.D. 382 and the smash of the Rhine frontier in A.D. 404 to 406 the edicts forbidding paganism in any form and enjoining that all subjects of the Empire become Christians had fatal effects on military morale in countless other ways and especially in one.

For almost eleven centuries Roman armies had gone to battle with the comfortable feeling that their god, Jupiter Maximus Optimus, was the greatest of all gods, that their pontifices and flamens knew how to propitiate him and secure his favor and countenance, that their enemies did not know how to win even his attention, and that, anyhow, their foemen prayed to other and less powerful gods.

Now, with the legionaries partly sincere Christians but mostly unwilling, forced, nominal converts, with all the prayers on their side Christian prayers, with their barbarian foemen mostly also Christians with Christian priests among them, the legionaries went out to campaign or battle with the deadening, the disheartening knowledge that their foemen were praying to the same God to whom they were praying and just as likely to gain his attention and enlist his aid.

No modern can realize what a difference this made in their hope of victory, in their élan, in their cohesion. No expatiation could exaggerate the adverse effect of this appalling idea.

CHAPTER XXVII

SOME AFTER EFFECTS OF CHRISTIANITY

VICISTI, GALILÆE!
(You've won! You Jew!)
Dying words of the Emperor Julian.

THERE were two respects in which Christianity exerted a powerful and highly detrimental influence on the Greco-Roman Mediterranean world, neither of which contributed much, if at all, to the collapse of Rome's Empire, but one of which was a potent factor in the extinction of the worship of the Olympian Pantheon; the other was the paramount cause of the annihilation of the Greco-Roman civilization and culture.

The former was the effect which the presence of Christianity and the exultant jeers of the Christians had toward intensifying the dismay of pagans confronted with the indubitable actuality of the sack of Rome and the vanishment of Rome's Empire, whereas one of the cardinal tenets of Roman paganism had been that Jupiter had guaranteed to his Romans everlasting domination over the whole world.

To any open-minded student comparing the two it must be manifest that Greco-Roman paganism, as a form of polytheism, was a religion vastly superior in every way to modern Hindu polytheism. Yet Greco-Roman paganism was completely subverted by Christianity, and beneath its crushing weight and the terrific impact of the barbarian invasions dissolved, evaporated, and totally vanished; whereas Hindu polytheism, though almost as completely submerged by the spread of Buddhism about 275-225 B.C. as Greco-Roman paganism had been by Christianity during the supremacy of Gratian and Theodosius, revived powerfully and is today as robust, hale, and vigorous as it was in 624 B.C. before the Buddha was born, when, according to Roman legends, Ancus Marcius was king in Rome and ruled over a coalition of unfortified hill villages and a puny township thereabouts.

A puissant factor among those which have brought about the long survival of Hinduism is the fact that it never identified itself with any one system of government, dominant race, prosperous locality, or lordly city. If the Hindu gods were ever chiefly givers of victory, they long ago became transmuted into givers of comfort and prosperity to subjugated populations and have survived as such.

But from not long after the complete subjugation of the Latins in 345 B.C., powerfully after the subjugation of all Italy proper by 266 B.C., and positively after the desolation of Carthage in 146 B.C., the belief that Jupiter had selected them to rule all men everywhere forever came to be a settled conviction among Romans, a dogma of their personal faith, and an article of their national creed.

It was universally believed among them that Jupiter had proclaimed this as his unalterable determination and purpose by many utterances of all the most highly esteemed oracles, and had ratified such proclamations by countless officially certified auguries, omens from the sacrificial *exta,* and prodigies.

Quite seriously did all cultured Romans from the days of Scipio Africanus to the days of Aurelian believe that they were the chosen people of the greatest of all the gods, Capitoline Jove, Jupiter Maximus Optimus whose temple crowned the Capitoline Hill in Rome, and that he had given them to rule all men everywhere forever.

From the time of Augustus until the contemporaneous extinction of Roman domination, Roman religion, and Roman culture not only all noble Romans, but all educated Romans of every class, learned by heart Vergil's words in lines 278, 279 of Book I of the Æneid where Jupiter says, in the course of a speech in which he prophesies to Venus the future greatness of her descendants, the Romans to be: *"His ego nec metas rerum nec tempora pono, Imperium sine fine dedi"* ("To these men I have set bounds neither of possessions nor time; I have given them sway without limit").

The Romans of the days of their greatest prosperity, during the two centuries from the Principate of Tiberius from A.D. 14 to the Principate of Septimius Severus to A.D. 211, believed this implicitly.

During the decline of the Empire from the accession of Caracalla in A.D. 211 till the final catastrophe two centuries later, their descendants clung to this belief and, after each fresh disaster in the appalling series of Rome's calamities, tried to hope that Rome's mastery of the power of victory would reappear and Rome's majesty return.

After the complete dissolution of the Empire and Commonwealth and the ravaging by invading barbarians of every part of Rome's territories, the most devout pagan could no longer hold his ancestors' beliefs as to this particular.

But, if Christianity had not been in existence, if the dominant invaders had been polytheistic heathen and not converted Christians, there would have been found some explanation, or some compromise would have been devised, by means of which the discrepancy might have been explained away; it might have been held that their ancestors were mistaken in this, but right in general, and the inhabitants of the Mediterranean world might have continued believing in their ancestral gods.

But most of the invading hordes and most of the savage new overlords of what had been the Roman world were ardent Christians, and they and the other Christian denizens of Rome's ravaged empire taunted the pagans, gibing that Jupiter had never been a god, anyhow, but merely a subordinate demon, satellite of Satan, released from hell for a time specifically that he might inveigle with his deceptions the credulous Romans to become his dupes and votaries.

The pagans who survived the barbarian inroads and the sacks of Rome for the most part died sincere and unalterable pagans, but they reared no pagan generation after them; the contrast between their ancestors' age-long implicit faith in their being Jupiter's chosen people and in his guaranty to them of everlasting dominion over all other races and their actual abasement and subjection was too great; their downfall was too hopeless; confronted with Christianity, the dogma *Imperium sine fine dedi* had killed Greco-Roman paganism.

It is true that when Justinian promulgated his code of laws it decreed severe penalties against anyone convicted of offering a sacrifice according to pagan ritual, of lighting a fire on any altar in any pagan temple, of burning incense in such a fire, of adorning the door or doorway of any temple with garlands or flowers. Penalties would not have been threatened for these actions unless they were likely to come to pass. These specifications in Justinian's code prove that during his reign, A.D. 527-545, more than a century and a half after the suppression of paganism, there were still many earnest and sincere pagans. But paganism so survived merely as the faith of an obstinately devout minority; it no longer counted as an important factor in social or military conditions.

The effect of Christianity which worked powerfully for the annihilation of Greco-Roman civilization and culture was the result of the concomitant influences of the Christianization of the invading barbarians and of the insistent, consistent and persistent preaching from most Christian pulpits that all buildings, statues, carved reliefs, paintings, or other products of Greco-Roman art, as being dedicated to the gods of Olympus, were impious toward Jehovah and abominable to all Christians; and still more emphatically that reading any book of the pagans was impiety and unworthy of any Christian.

It is infinitely improbable that Roman military power could have maintained Rome's Empire and safeguarded its vast territories indefinitely. Sooner or later the northern frontiers must have given way under the increasing and intensifying pressure from without and thereupon savage hordes of northern barbarians must have inundated all Rome's provinces, as they did. Christianity hastened the coming of the catastrophe, determined its nature, and greatly exacerbated its concomitant calamities, and so was the chief internal cause of Rome's fall as it actually came to pass. But even if Christianity had never developed, sooner or later the Roman Empire must have waned and vanished.

Yet, if Christianity had never come into existence, Greco-Roman paganism and Greco-Roman civilization and culture might very possibly have survived the Empire's overthrow.

Chinese civilization, culture, and religion have survived uncountable civil wars, many of them exceeding in extent, fury, carnage, devastation, and havoc any which marred Rome's prosperity; sundry invasions; and two complete conquests, by the Mongols about A.D. 1213-1280, and by the Manchus about A.D. 1616-1650. No matter how numerous and how arrogant the invaders, Chinese civilization assimilated them and they absorbed Chinese culture and religion, and adopted Chinese forms of worship.

Had the population of the Roman Empire been pagan, and the worship of the pagan gods, however languid and conventional, the form of worship in vogue throughout the provinces; had their temples and cult-statues been in existence, however dilapidated and neglected; had the invading hordes been polytheistic heathens, not fervent recent proselytes to Christianity—it is more than likely that the invaders would have spared such temples and cult-statues as escaped the accidental havoc of war and would gradually have absorbed more or less of the usages, practices, and observances of the indigenous races and insensibly come to be assimilated into Greco-Roman civilization, and even little by little have come to tolerate, to like, even to appreciate Greco-Roman culture, art, and literature.

While this is likely, it must not be regarded as anywhere near a certainty. The Greek myths concerning Uranus, Kronos, the Giants, and the Titans appear to indicate that the savage ancestors of the Greeks made a clean sweep of the religion which they found in vogue among the aborigines of Greece and its adjacent lands when they first entered them as invaders, extinguished the cult of the primitive deities, and substituted the worship of their own ancestral gods.

Moreover, the heathen Lombards, in Italy, were nearly as destructive as the Christian Goths, and in Britain the heathen Saxons made a clean sweep of what they found there, burning every building and butchering the inhabitants to the last infant.

But, in fact, at the time of the smash of the Roman Empire, about A.D. 395-455, and of the influx of savage northern hordes, paganism had been forcibly suppressed, few cult-statues had escaped the thirteen years' orgy of wanton destruction under Gratian and Theodosius; some temples had been demolished; confiscations had beggared the pagan hierarchy, and most pagan hierophants had been violently expelled from their temple inclosures and homes. The denizens of the cities and towns were either of that minority which had already been Christianized before the suppression of paganism began, had been ostensibly converted to Christianity under the pressure of personal advantage or dread of threats, or were pagans barely tolerated by the majority, despised and insulted and living in daily apprehension of mob violence or official animadversion.

Outside the towns and cities there were few or no Christians, for *paganus* means simply anyone dwelling in the countryside, but these pagans remained such by connivance, if they had an easy-going governor, on sufferance, if their governor was indifferent, or surreptitiously if their governor was a fervent Christian. They were peasantry, yeomanry, or, at best, gentry not much better than yokels. Not many temples had ever existed outside of cities and towns, and few of those had escaped the orgy of desecration. So that, even while the invasions had not penetrated south of the Balkans and Alps, and the Rhine frontier held, paganism was dissolving, evaporating, vanishing; its appeal and its allurements had already vanished.

The invaders were mostly Christians and they took their somewhat recently acquired Christianity and all its precepts very seriously with the habitual fervor of neophyte converts. Christians native-born inside the Empire, however bigoted and fanatical, had grown up in cities ennobled and beautified by magnificent public buildings, amphitheatres, circuses, basilicas, porticoes, temples, baths, and others. They could not help taking all these as matters of course. Occasionally, incited by some hysterical preacher, they might join a mob in demolishing a shrine or burning a temple. But mostly they moved about among the splendid bequests of the pagans of bygone days, accepting them and ignoring them almost as much as the clouds or the blue sky.

Far otherwise the Christianized intrusive savages. Their bigoted clergy reiterated that all these buildings and all their component parts had been devised to honor the pagan gods and had been consecrated to them, therefore they were an insult to Jehovah and abominable in his eyes; wherefore it was the duty of all pious Christians to burn, pollute, maltreat, gut, deface, mar, maul, batter, dismantle, wreck, shatter, demolish, and annihilate all such edifices, with their contents.

These teachings had much effect. It is recorded that, more than once, the Goths in France worked like beavers for days to stuff with firewood the cellars, vaults, openings, archways, passageways, and adits of a Roman amphitheatre, with the idea that when kindled the fierce conflagration of all this fuel would reduce to dust what they misconceived as having been the temple of a pagan idol.

Being savages, most of the invaders, however fervent in their bigotry, were desultory and unsystematic in their havoc. If Christianized, their fanaticism aggravated their inborn tendency toward destructiveness; if heathen, the example of their Christian competitors, whether allies or rivals, enhanced their innate proclivity toward mischief. But all alike—Alans, Goths, Burgundians, Franks, Saxons, Thuringians, Lombards, Huns, or Avars—were haphazard and intermittent in their casual, random, promiscuous destructiveness.

Not so the Vandals. Of themselves, without any urging by their bigoted clergy, they were, without doubt, appallingly destructive. When, about A.D. 375, they floundered out of their native swamps and forests northeast of the headwaters of the Danube and Rhine, they were bestial savages, unsurpassably ferocious, bloodthirsty, and incendiary. In Gaul and Spain in 407-410 they habitually massacred to the last infant the populace of every town and city they stormed, and burnt every building they approached.

But their deservedly bad reputation is not due to this. They took so seriously the preaching of their bigoted clergy that they went out of their way to shatter statues, carved reliefs, and similar decorations of buildings, and to hack away mosaics and frescoes, and spent much time and labor on such wanton destructiveness, setting about it in a systematic and thoroughgoing fashion. When they had not spare time or energy for total destruction of such artistic treasures, they at least left no statue unmutilated and no picture undisfigured.

After they established themselves as overlords of Mauretania, Numidia, and Africa (modern Morocco, Algeria, and Tunisia) they gradually came to appreciate the value and convenience of public baths, basilicas, and colonnades. But they had every statue smashed to atoms, had every square inch of mosaic and fresco hacked from the walls of the buildings they spared, and covered every wall with a blank expanse of plaster, stucco, or whitewash.

They could worship only when undistracted by any glimpse of beauty and made the interiors of their churches as forbidding, bleak, and hideous as whitewash could achieve.

The same sort of preaching which resulted in the zealously systematic destructiveness of the Vandals later brought into being the iconoclasts of the Byzantine Empire and issued in the rabid fury of the Mohammedans who spread the blight of their prophet's malign precepts wherever their conquests reached.

Within the Christian world, for a thousand years after the smash of the Rhine-Danube frontier in A.D. 406, it was held a meritorious and virtuous act to quarry in any of the remains of pagan buildings, yet more to obliterate all traces of any.

Still more was it held a work of merit to destroy statuary. In the general impoverishment most statues of bronze were melted down to be made into coin; but marble statues were of no value for their material and mostly went into kilns to be burnt for lime, being of convenient size to be easily broken up into blocks not too heavy for a man to carry.

Such bigoted preachments greatly increased the destruction of books. Even without them the havoc was horribly rapid and complete. Before the invasions, mob violence during the thirteen years of active suppression of paganism under Gratian and Theodosius had left few temple libraries undespoiled. In their eagerness to extirpate the art of divination the apparitors of the officials and the leaderless mobs were equally prone to carry out and burn every written roll in any temple library in order to make sure of leaving no book on augury, haruspicy, or divination unburnt.

Papyrus was extremely brittle, frail, and inflammable. Preservation of papyrus rolls required sedulous care, as water, even dampness, rapidly ruined them and they were too fragile to survive much handling or any rough treatment. In the course of the invasions, ravagings, and stormings of cities vast numbers of books in public and private libraries were destroyed by the inevitable devastations of warfare.

In the general destitution of those nightmare years of horror, despair, and misery, when a large portion of the population had perished by massacre, pestilence, and famine, when the survivors not only saw all the decencies and comforts of life swept away as the sewers were blocked, aqueducts cut, and market houses deserted, but were constantly and daily threatened by the menace of hunger and in danger of death from starvation, pestilence, or massacre, no one had surplus energy or spare income to care for libraries. Within half a century after the annihilation of the legions along the Rhine by the overwhelming tide of Suevi, Alans, Goths, and Vandals in A.D. 406, the inundation of all parts of the western Empire, even Italy itself and the islands of the Mediterranean, by these malignant savages, and the attendant ravagings and ruin, had mostly destroyed the enormous accumulations of third-rate and second-rate books; commentaries on commentaries, commentaries on second-rate and third-rate authors, fantastic romances of no literary value and popular only with the commonalty, treaties on obscure subjects, books by specialists and the writings of such feeble authors as pullulate wherever long and profound peace and prosperity breed a rabble of scribblers; and even most books of merely mediocre value or which appealed only to cultured idlers.

But here and there a town escaped being stormed and sacked, and they aggregated many score, perhaps many hundred all together. The most notable example was Amalfi, which was never entered by any party of assailant Goths, Lombards, Germans, or Saracens, perhaps never attacked by any, and remained undisturbed and kept unmarred its civic life and ancestral customs and habits until broken into by the Normans after A.D. 1015. In such towns some books remained undestroyed and perhaps also here and there in sacked cities not wholly burnt.

In such towns and cities there were families formerly wealthy and cultured, the remnants of whose vanished wealth put them a little farther from penury than their fellow sufferers and whose family traditions of culture bequeathed to some at least a hankering after learning, a relish for reading, and an affection for books, perhaps here and there even an appreciation of literature.

Also in such towns and cities the booksellers' trade and the profession of copyist survived with a continuous tradition from generation to generation unbroken from the earliest ages to the invention of printing. But what had been during the prosperity of the Empire, from A.D. 27 to A.D. 166, a vast flood of books dwindled to a scanty trickle. The impoverishment of all parts of the Empire after A.D. 211 caused the demand for books to fall off and their production to lessen.

The export of papyrus from Egypt had already developed into an important and fairly steady traffic before Alexander's time. It persisted and increased in volume and value, despite wars and pirates. After the pacification of the Mediterranean by Augustus in A.D. 29 it flourished uninterruptedly until the inroad of the Goths from the Black Sea about A.D. 264 during the Principate of Gallienus. This temporarily obstructed it, but it endured until the Vandals about A.D. 440 launched their war fleet from Carthage and swept the Mediterranean of all commercial traffic. Until A.D. 399 books had been fairly cheap and plentiful, booksellers prosperous and professional copyists well employed. From A.D. 400 invasions and ravagings diminished and then all but annihilated the demand for books and greatly increased their cost. After A.D. 440 as papyrus became unobtainable and all new books had to be written on parchment (compared with papyrus a very costly material), the cost of books was so vastly increased that few could afford to order or buy any.

Few people had books, fewer people read books, and very few wrote books, sold books, or bought books. Yet the tiny rill of book making would have preserved for all future generations all that was best in Latin literature had it not been for the hatred of Greco-Roman culture general among the Christian clergy and for their insistent, consistent, and persistent preaching that it was impiety for any Christian to read any pagan book. While many book lovers infringed, neglected, evaded, ignored, or actually repudiated these precepts, even some of the clergy appreciating and loving classic literature, such unremitting authoritative preachments had great effect in turning potential lovers of the classics into haters of them or avoiders of them, and constituted a powerful factor among those tending to aggravate the conditions adverse to the survival of Greco-Roman culture.

The conditions were adverse enough, anyhow. Until the smash of the Rhine frontier in A.D. 406 and the sack of Rome by the Goths led by Alaric in A.D. 410, Romans had been proud of their culture and of all that went with it; of their dwellings, furniture, utensils, implements, vehicles, attire, personal ornaments, food, table manners, baths, and amusements.

To sit viewing beast fights, gladiatorial shows, and, most of all, chariot races, to revel in the luxury of a hot bath each afternoon, to loll on an ample sofa, well propped among soft, embroidered cushions, when partaking of a meal, to walk abroad clad in a toga, which only a Roman citizen might wear—these had been worth while as marking one as a superior being, as one of the dominant race. After Rome had been entered and sacked in A.D. 410 by the Goths under Alaric, in 455 by the Vandals under Genseric, in 472 by the Germans under Ricimer (not to dwell on two later sackings between 540 and 553 by the Goths under Totila), specifically after the establishment by Theodoric in A.D. 493 of the kingdom of the Ostrogoths in Italy, it was manifest that the Romans were no longer the dominant race. The Goths were the dominant race and sneered and scoffed at all Roman customs, usages, ways, practices, and habits. It no longer was an advantage to be a Roman; it was a disadvantage even to seem to be a Roman. Most of all, it suddenly became socially unfashionable to be a Roman. The toga vanished, reclining on sofas at meals went out of use, and full-blooded Romans, if any such survived, took pains to sit at meals and to dress like Goths. It was unfashionable not only to look like a Roman or to act like a Roman, but even to feel or think as Romans had felt and thought. Romans were mostly ashamed of everything that had been Roman, including Roman literature.

To these adverse conditions were added the ranting diatribes of the Christian clergy against what they stigmatized as obscene, indecent, immoral, iniquitous, ungodly, and poisonous writings.

Some lovers of literature preserved for us Vergil, Horace, Ovid, and others, but most poets perished. We have no Latin historian complete, and where one is extant incomplete, nineteen survive only in tantalizing fragments or as mere names. All the orators have perished except Cicero. All the tragic poets except Seneca, and he was only nominally a writer of tragedies. All the satirists are gone except Horace, Juvenal, and Persius. No Latin mime has come down to us.

Practical needs preserved the works of Cicero almost entire, as all law was in Latin, all court pleading in Latin, court pleaders were numerous and every one of them wanted to model his pleadings on the style of the greatest orator and most successful barrister Rome had produced.

War was the most important of human concerns after the smash of the Empire, and all ambitious commanders aimed to model their methods on those of Rome's greatest general, so Cæsar's *Commentaries* on his wars had a steady sale and were recopied almost as often as Cicero's orations.

But in general the few booksellers and the few copyists had to write and offer for sale what was in demand. In the universal impoverishment and with parchment necessarily very expensive the demand was always too small for the trade. But the least paltry demand was for copies of the Gospels, of the Testaments, of the church fathers, and so copyists put in their time and booksellers offered for sale copies of the Bible, of Tertullian, Arnobius, Lactantius, Fulgentius, Augustine, Ambrose, and such like.

If Christianity had not existed, even if the Empire had collapsed as completely as it did, what little copying was done would have been of pagan orators, historians, philosophers, poets, or satirists and we should have had most of what was worth while in Latin literature. Actually the trifling demand was for Christian writings or for Latin writers of practical value.

There was no thought for the writings of archaic poets like Nævius, Pacuvius and Ennius, they vanished with Lucilius, Laberius, and other humorists and satirists. Few could afford the huge collections of rolls or codexes necessary for the works of such voluminous historians as Livy or such unwieldy encyclopædists as Varro or Nigidius Figulus. They vanished also, for their books were not recopied and the copies in existence perished one by one by fire, dampness, destruction, or mere age.

It cannot be too emphatically set forth that the benefit conferred on future generations by the preservation to us and our posterity of many works of Latin authors through their having been copied and recopied in mediæval monasteries is a trifle compared with the loss of our possible heritage from Roman times through the voluble jeremiads of the Christian clergy denouncing all interest in classic literature as un-Christian, impious, and wicked.

In the east, where there was no general invasion until the Mohammedans began overrunning that part of the Empire from A.D. 635 onward, where inroads had never brought any general devastation, the clergy were as furious against Greek literature as their western brethren were against Latin literature. And they were even more nasty-minded.

Homer survived all their assaults, for the tradition of admiration and love for the Iliad and Odyssey was too strong for even Christian bigotry to efface. But Sappho, who was called by the Greeks "the Poetess" as Homer was called "the Poet," they succeeded in eclipsing.

Lesbos, before Sappho's time, in her time and long after was prosperous. It had many wealthy families. It was fashionable at weddings to have a chorus of girls sing songs of praise of the bride from the bridegroom's point of view. Such singers were liberally paid and such singing grew to be a recognized and lucrative profession. Sappho was an impresaria with an organized troupe of such songstresses. She was highly original and was not content, like her predecessors and competitors, with the traditional tunes and words. She composed new airs for old songs, new words for popular airs, and new songs out and out. Her songs had an originality and perfection marking her as the greatest feminine literary genius this world has yet produced. For a thousand years she was a favorite composer and her songs were widely sung and her poems widely read. Their origin and nature were, however, much misunderstood. Most of all by the Christian Puritans. Love songs to women written by a woman! Horrors! So in many cities of the Greek world after Christianity triumphed the eleven books of Sappho's poems were hunted out of libraries and burnt in public squares under the supervision of pietistic bishops. They succeeded in robbing all future generations of her beautiful and original poetry.

What we have left of Greek poetry, oratory, historians, and philosophy was preserved largely because of the stubborn persistence of traditional methods and usages in education, almost as difficult to change, alter, or modify as religious observances. The Iliad and Odyssey had been used as educational textbooks from time immemorial. They survived in spite of centuries of vituperation from Christian pulpits. But every other Greek epic poem has perished utterly. Hesiod is often called an epic poet, but his poems are not properly so classed.

Of Greek tragedies we have those selections from Æschylus, Sophocles, and Euripides which were thought best for use in schools; besides these, the contents of one volume of a library edition of Euripides preserved to us by accident.

The comedies of Aristophanes were universally read in Byzantine schools. They survive, while all other Greek comedies have perished.

What little of Greek lyric poetry is extant was mostly preserved in anthologies for use in schools.

The hundred-odd orations of the ten Attic orators which have come down to us were preserved by their constant use in Byzantine schools.

So of Greek historians. Reading from Herodotus, Thucydides, and Xenophon formed a regular part of Byzantine edution; therefore their works have been saved, while those of more than a score of Greek historians really great have perished utterly.

Aristotle's teachings were continuously used in education and so most of his works are extant. Plato was preserved because he, or Socrates as reported by him, put forth some arguments aiming to prove the immortality of the soul which were very congenial to Christians. All the greater philosophers have perished.

When Ferdinand and Isabella of Spain finally vanquished the Moors in A.D. 1492 and overran and conquered and annexed Granada, one of their first concerns was to issue an emphatic edict that every one of the thousands of bathtubs in the former Kingdom of Granada should be smashed to atoms. Bathing was a Mohammedan habit and therefore abominable in the eyes of all pious Christians.

Very similar was the spirit of the Christian clergy of the

late Roman Empire from long before their triumph in A.D. 381 and certainly after it, toward all pagan customs and products, most of all idols, temples, and books on divination, but almost as virulent against all statues, all pagan buildings, and all pagan books.

CHAPTER XXVIII

SUMMARY

FOR ages before Rome was founded, and for centuries after the fall of Rome, conditions on the steppes, plains, and grasslands in the interior of the Great Continent were such that the incessant and inexorable struggle for existence, unmodified by any external or internal influences, eliminated all unfit for survival and made it impossible for any to survive except the fittest. From generation to generation only the fittest survived, and this maintained the fighting efficiency of the desert hordes at the highest level; even, perhaps, increased their fighting efficiency from age to age.

For centuries before the founding of Rome conditions in Italy brought it about that a different kind of remorseless and incessant competition for survival, the strife between each walled town and all its neighbors, created an even more stern, rigorous, and grim struggle for existence.

From the severest of these Italian conditions Rome emerged, becoming supreme on account of the possession by her citizens not only of matchless fighting powers, but also of preëminently felicitous, rooted, and steadfast instincts for coöperation, subordination, and mutual forbearance, and for fair dealing, not merely with each other, but with all mankind.

These congenital instincts of the Romans were the product of their vivid, profound, and earnest belief in the existence, might, overlordship, coöperation, and countenance of their ancestral gods.

Inside Rome the inexorable operation of the tendency to survival only of the fittest through the unescapable operation of the struggle for existence began to be mitigated as soon as it came to be felt that provision against a family's dying of starvation was a concern not solely of the man of the family, but also and even more positively of the community at large and of the government of the Commonwealth; which came to pass very early. As official solicitude for the adequate feeding of the populace increased, so the completeness of the operation of the struggle for existence in eliminating the unfit diminished; more unfit survived and the military efficiency of the Romans of Rome waned, though for centuries this impairment of their potentiality for victory was gradual, slow, imperceptible, and, in fact, extremely slight.

Outside Rome the potential fighting value of the populations was positively and rapidly impaired in proportion as any town or district engaged in warfare less frequently than every summer, and as ever smaller and smaller proportions of the total of its able-bodied full-grown men were drafted when the community was involved in warfare. As Rome's power grew and her sway extended, it came to pass that at first a few, then more and more, and then many able-bodied men never were drafted at all and lived out their lives without any participation in warfare.

To some extent from the end of the Hannibalic wars districts here and there slumbered for a generation without any drafting of recruits from them and with only little volunteering for service, and these districts were more numerous and extensive from age to age.

After the pacification of the Roman world by Augustus upon his establishment of the Principate, whole regions basked in complete immunity from any participation in warfare and in them generation after generation lived and died exempt from any military service.

This effect of *Pax Romana* very greatly impaired the potential military value of the populations of the sheltered regions and so positively diminished the total fighting power of the Empire as a whole.

Although this waning of universal capacity for victory throughout the territories controlled by the Roman Commonwealth began as early as 168 B.C., when Roman supremacy in the Mediterranean world was visibly established, yet, for more than two and a half centuries, until the death of Trajan in A.D. 117, Roman power increased and Roman sway extended.

This was because the wide local deteriorations of large portions of the Empire were more than countervailed by the positive and continual augmentation of its total fighting power through the effects of better and better leadership, better and better organization, ever keener military enthusiasm and ever greater cohesion, concord, and optimism among all Romans everywhere. This process of improvement continued up to the death of Tiberius in A.D. 37, and its momentum extended its effects not merely up to the death of Nero in A.D. 68, but for almost a century longer.

This increase in the total fighting power of the Commonwealth, which more than compensated for the diminished potential military value of a large percentage of the Empire's denizens, was caused by the universal faith of all pagan Romans in their high destiny as the chosen people of Jupiter, hallmarked as rulers of the world forever, by their belief in the overlordship, coöperation and countenance of their ancestral gods, and especially by the assurance of them given by Jupiter's avouchment for his acceptance of their deified chieftain, the prince of the Commonwealth, as his vicegerent on earth and as destined to deification after death.

It was the universal assent of the pagan denizens of the Empire to these ideas which created and maintained the Empire's prosperity by sustaining its civic and military morale. Universal faith in the godhead of the emperor, in his overlordship as vicegerent on earth of Jupiter, in the solicitude, guidance, and coöperation of the gods of Rome, in Rome's high destiny as mistress of the world forever, in the gloriousness of war and the honorable nature of the profession of soldiering, was first impaired by the spread of Christianity through the slums of Roman cities after A.D. 41 and increasingly from year to year thereafter, and by its cancerous effects on the military and civic morale of the population.

The mere vague rumor that there was in existence a sect whose members regarded war as wicked, soldiers as no better than brigands, the Commonwealth's gods as malignant demons, and the Emperor as a mere man among men, had the effect of a corrosive poison wherever it reached.

All the other internal causes of the decay of Roman power and of the ruin of Rome, taken together, were of trifling moment compared with the baneful effects of the spread of Christianity.

As the Roman Empire may properly be evaluated as the successful holding off, for more than a thousand years, by the military power of Greco-Roman civilization, of the pressure from the plainlands of inner Asia, so Greco-Roman culture at large may be fairly evaluated as the successful maintenance for more than a thousand years of the Mediterranean pagan conception of life as the dealing of human beings with the actualities of the visible universe against the Asiatic conception of the visible universe as being merely a delusion of the human senses and the inner spiritual life of man as being the only actual reality, one manifestation of which Asiatic state of mind ultimately overwhelmed Greco-Roman paganism.

As long as the citizens of the Commonwealth and the denizens of the Empire unanimously believed that this world is a reality and worth living in and for, the Commonwealth prospered and its Empire extended.

As soon as a noticeable minority of the denizens of the Empire came to believe that this world is merely a fleeting show and that only reward after death is worth living for, the vitality of the Commonwealth began to be impaired.

As soon as that detrimental minority increased sufficiently to acquire partial control of the Commonwealth, its Empire began to crumble.

Very shortly after that pernicious minority achieved complete control of the Commonwealth it and its Empire dissolved, evaporated, and vanished.

It is worth noting that the Roman Commonwealth endured, at most, from the expulsion of the Etruscan kings in 510 B.C. to the launching of the Vandal fleet in A.D. 440, nine and a half centuries. Practically it came to an end when the northern savages flooded across the Rhine in A.D. 406, a minimum duration of 914 years. During its existence four classes controlled it one after the other: the Patricians, Plebeians, Roman Colonists and Christians.

The control of the Patricians lasted at least 143 years from 510 B.C. to 367 B.C., for the first Plebeian consul took office in 366 B.C.; at most until 300 B.C., by which time all offices whatever were open to Plebeians—by the most liberal calculation 210 years.

The ennobled Plebeian families controlled the Commonwealth from 300 B.C. to the death of Vitellius in A.D. 69—369 years.

Then, with the accession in A.D. 69 of Vespasian, born at Reate in Sabinum, the control of the Commonwealth passed to Pagans of colonial stock of Roman or Italian ancestry. Their control endured until, in A.D. 323, Constantine beat down his rivals, became supreme, and recognized and favored Christianity, a period of 243 years.

The Christians began to get control in A.D. 323 when Constantine's edict in their favor was promulgated, and they attained full control in A.D. 381, when Gratian promulgated his edict for the suppression of paganism.

Contrast of the performance, achievements, and results of the control of each of the four classes may be summed up as follows:

For 210 years the Patricians steadily aggrandized the power and prosperity of the Commonwealth.

For 369 years the ennobled Plebeian families did as well, or better.

The Pagan colonials achieved a full century of the greatest prosperity ever attained by any people or government, and a century and a half more of peace and of prosperity, waning, indeed, but, except by their first century, never surpassed on earth before.

The Christians won and held control of an Empire buffeted by foes, held off by defenders never adequately numerous and ever fewer and fewer, through at most 117 years of disasters ever closer together and more calamitous. They gained full control in A.D. 381, and barely a quarter of a century later, in A.D. 406, the defenses of the Empire crumbled and its frontier legions were annihilated; and thirty-four years later, barely fifty-nine years after they had attained mastery, the Empire and Commonwealth had vanished forever.

CHAPTER XXIX

WHAT THE WORLD HAS LOST BY THE FALL OF ROME

IT IS not an overestimate to assert that the Roman Empire, in the Principate of Hadrian, contained 20,000 walled towns, every one of them provided with sewers, aqueducts, public baths, paved streets, and public squares, basilicas, porticoes, and temples; each with at least one stone circus or hippodrome for chariot races and one stone theatre for dramatic performances, each of those in the west with at least one stone amphitheatre for gladiatorial shows and beast fights, most of those in the east with at least one stone odeon for public recitations and readings, and most seacoast towns with adequate harbors. Outer harbors were ample anchorages adequately protected by breakwaters, if necessary. Inner harbors were mostly artificial, closely resembling the vast docks now existing at London, Hamburg, Bremen, Boulogne, Cherbourg, and other modern marts.

Cities mostly had magnificent amphitheatres, circuses, theatres, odeons by twos and threes, public baths likewise, basilicas and colonnaded stone porticoes by the dozens, and temples by scores, even some by hundreds.

The Empire contained twenty cities each of which had more than 100,000 denizens.

At the acme of its prosperity, the chief cities of the Empire were Antioch, Alexandria, Rome, Aquileia, Treves on the Moselle, Carthage, and Capua. Of these, besides Rome, Aquileia and Capua were in Italy.

As the Greeks and Romans built their public edifices, particularly their temples, for all time, there is no reason why, if the Empire had endured, the world might not now enjoy most of these towns and cities with their civic life unbroken since their foundation, and their public utilities and buildings intact and in use from their construction until today.

Very moderate exertions toward repair and not a great deal

of rebuilding after earthquakes would have kept in good condition and in uninterrupted use till today, the 350,000 miles of Roman roads and their tens of thousands of stone bridges.

Even after fifteen centuries of neglect many stretches of Roman roadways are still usable as roads, and some few Roman bridges are still in use. Had the Empire endured, they might have lasted ten thousand years or longer.

Had civilization not perished throughout the vast expanse of territory which the Greeks and Romans had civilized, most of the hundreds of inner harbors of the Empire's seaports might have been in continuous use till our days.

Of the hundreds of stone amphitheatres which adorned the towns and cities of the western Empire, some few, like the Colosseum at Rome and the great Amphitheatre at Thysdrus (El Djemm) in Africa (Tunisia) were partly ruined by earthquakes. But even these two, the largest ever built, suffered more from quarrying stone from them. Most were destroyed solely by being used as quarries.

A few remain nearly complete, as at Syracuse and Catania in Sicily, at Nîmes, Arles, and Frejus in France, at Pola in Istria, and at Verona, Capua, Pæstum and Pompeii in Italy. Had the Empire survived we might have a full thousand with all their decorations of marble slabs, mosaics, reliefs, and countless statues of marble and bronze.

Every Roman city or town had its circus and every Greek city or town its hippodrome, great stone buildings providing tiers of seats from which an audience of from 20,000 to 200,000 could view chariot races. The arrangement of a Roman Circus and a Greek Hippodrome differed, but not greatly, and the styles of edifice were very similar. The Circus Maximus in Rome, while still partly of wood, held 150,000 spectators in the times of Augustus and 225,000 after it had been rebuilt by Claudius. After Domitian extended it entirely in stone, it was claimed that it accommodated 385,000 seated spectators, which appears incredible. Yet Antioch asserted that its hippodrome equalled in size the Circus Maximus at Rome. And later the great Hippodrome of Constantinople was believed to surpass it both in dimensions and magnificence. Of the hundreds of Roman Circuses and Greek Hippodromes few traces remain. They were too tempting as handy quarries, at first for their incrustations of marble slabs, then for their monolithic pillars, later for any movable block of stone. Constructed as they were, all might have lasted until now, if respected and let alone, and most were good for thousands of years of usefulness.

The same is true of the hundreds of *stadia* for foot races and other athletic sports, with which all Greek cities were provided. Not so enormous as the circuses and hippodromes of the great cities, they were yet both imposing in size and magnificently decorated. Every one of them, if appreciated by its possessors, might still be in use as when first constructed, and our world would be the richer for having them.

All Greek cities, besides their privately owned *palæstræ* where boys were taught wrestling and other athletic sports, had *gymnasia,* public edifices where grown men kept themselves fit by wrestling, boxing, discus throwing, jumping, pitching quoits, running, and playing various ball games more or less like modern tennis, court tennis, fives, racquets, handball, squash, and such.

Gymnasiums took up a good deal of space, as each had an inner and an outer court, both of ample size, and usually had a small *stadium* attached. Like all Greek public buildings, the *gymnasia* were built to last forever.

Every town in the Roman Empire had its theatre; cities had two, three, or more, according to their size, population, and wealth. A Greek theatre was always hollowed out of the flank of a convenient hill so that the tiers of seats could be laid on the natural rock or earth, around more than half of the flat circular paved space called the orchestra (dancing floor), beyond which, facing the middle of the curve of seats, was the stone stage with its very simply decorated stone background.

Most Roman theatres were built from the ground up, and some were of stupendous girth, width of stage buildings, and height. The best preserved is at Orange in France.

At the acme of the Empire it possessed more than 20,000 stone theatres of the two types. Remains of a few score exist. The rest were quarried away by the brutish and degraded barbarian successors of the civilized Romans.

Most of the theatres accommodated from 10,000 to 50,000 spectators.

Odeons, which existed by thousands in the part of the Empire populated by Greeks, were theatres of moderate dimensions, for the public recitations and musical festivals which the Greeks loved. Many of the smaller had roofs.

The *Thermæ* of Rome were dazzling, gorgeous, and of stupendous dimensions; those of other large cities scarcely less so. Every city of the Empire had its *Thermæ,* not merely adequate for the accommodation of its bathers, but ample, roomy, and lavishly decorated. Every town had *Thermæ* suited to its needs. The maintenance of these public baths depended, of course, on the maintenance of the liberal water supply afforded to most cities and towns of the Empire by their magnificent aqueducts. Such aqueducts and baths, with the cleanly and ennobling habits of life that went with them, might very well have lasted on to our days, improving from age to age.

The beautiful open squares of the towns and cities of the Empire differed in plan in the east and west, for a Greek *agora* was not laid out like a Roman forum. But they were all alike in that the most important public buildings abutted on them, particularly basilicas, and they were flanked by colonnades of handsome stone pillars, called porticoes.

The healthy out-of-doors life of the ancient cities and towns, lived mostly in their public squares, in the spacious roofed squares called basilicas, and under the open colonnades was a fine and noble habit of life and might very well have lasted on for thousands of years.

Rome had more than ten public squares, more than twenty basilicas, and more than sixty colonnaded porticoes.

The ancients—Egyptians, Babylonians, Phœnicians, Greeks, and Romans alike—generally paid little attention to solidity in house building and lived in dwellings of wood or adobe (unburnt brick), only exceptionally in mansions of burnt brick, stone or concrete.

But the temples of their gods they built to last forever, and on them they lavished munificent expenditures, prodigious labor, infinite care and sedulous pains. Nothing was too good for them as to either material or finish.

Most Egyptian temples were wholly of stone, often in huge blocks, and so unerringly dressed that not even a razor blade can be inserted into the cracks of walls existing undamaged. Of stone fitted with such exactness were their foundations, walls, columns, roof beams, roof slabs, even sliding doors, weighing tons, so cunningly devised and so accurately balanced that they opened and closed at a mere touch and worked perfectly for centuries.

The Greeks were equally pains-taking. They never used any binding agent like mortar, but erected walls which stood because the blocks were so impeccably squared, smoothed and laid that they never needed the metal clamps with which they often, but not always, locked stone to stone. The Parthenon, in its time the most perfect Greek temple, was of such construction. The most profusely adorned of all Greek temples was the Temple of Artemis-Diana at Ephesus. And the Temple of the Sun at Heliopolis (the modern Baalbec) was rated the most magnificent of all temples built under Greek influence and according to Greek methods. Several of the outside foundation stones of its stylobate are single blocks larger than an American Pullman sleeping coach.

The Romans built chiefly of concrete faced with stone. The solidity of their construction outdid even the Greeks and Egyptians. The Temple of Venus and Rome built in Rome by Hadrian and Antoninus Pius was their masterpiece in design and decorations.

Many Egyptian temples had been demolished by Persian and other invaders. But at the accession of Theodosius in A.D. 379 hundreds existed as perfect as when completed centuries, even in some cases tens of centuries, before.

As to Greek temples in good repair at the same date, it is not extravagant to reckon that their numbers much exceeded 10,000 and may have exceeded 20,000.

Of Roman temples the numbers were not so great, but every Roman colony had at least one, most had more than one, and many had three, four, or five. Allied towns all over the western Empire were as well supplied. There must have been ten thousand and possibly there were more.

Of all the Greek temples, not one remains, and of the Roman temples only the Pantheon at Rome and the little Temple of Augustus at Nîmes, now known as the Maison Carrée.

As decorations to the towns and cities they adorned, few edifices ever erected on earth have surpassed the temples of the Greco-Roman world. As they were built to last forever, we might very well now have fifteen thousand or more as perfect as when they were completed.

All cultured persons of our days find that the world is better off for the existence of the lovely Taj Mahal at Agra in India. It is probable that, as a work of art, the Mausoleum at Halicarnassus greatly surpassed it. And the great Mausoleum of Augustus and the great Mausoleum of Hadrian at Rome (of which last the core exists as the imposing "Castle of St. Angelo") were not only stupendous by mere bulk and magnificent in every way, but as works of art of a very high quality. These and the twenty-six pyramids which were the glory of Egypt were all possessed of their pristine beauty and in perfect preservation at the death of Theodosius in A.D. 395. Had not Greco-Roman civilization been extinguished, intelligent appreciation of their value as part of the common wealth of the communities which had inherited them might well have preserved them intact till now.

The roads leading out of Rome and of every city and town of her Empire were flanked for furlongs, even for miles, by gravestones, monuments, tombs, every size and style of sepulchre, and here and there a mausoleum of some opulent family or distinguished magnate. As mortuary taste and artistic traditions in ancient times were far better than in ours, most of these erections were positively decorative to their neighborhood and valuable assets of the community possessing them. Few remain, for they have mostly been demolished as building materials or to be burnt in lime kilns. Our world might well possess them by myriads.

Most Roman towns were adorned by at least one stone triumphal arch, commemorating the prowess of some distinguished general. Some had one archway, some two equal archways, many a large middle archway flanked by two smaller openings. All were decorated with reliefs and statues, those built later profusely. Most were topped by a four-horsed chariot with the portrait statue of the individual honored. Many had also groups of statuary atop. Of the thousands with which the Empire was beautified about a hundred remain more or less ruined, a few nearly perfect. Of the many erected in honor of Augustus one exists at Aosta and one at Rimini. Of the twenty-one which adorned Rome in its prime, five are still standing. Few were shaken down by earthquakes. Most were torn down as material for later buildings. Had the Empire endured, the world might very well today possess thousands fit to last thousands of years yet.

It was a common saying at the acme of Rome's prosperity and magnificence, about the time of the Principate of Hadrian, that, not reckoning statues indoors in private residences, palaces, the Imperial Palace, and the countless public buildings, the city had, out-of-doors, in view of pedestrians or idlers, 400,000 life-size statues of bronze or marble, 40,000 groups of two or more life-size figures, 4,000 statues above life-size, 400 equestrian statues, 40 quadrigas, and 4 statues of colossal dimension. This inventory shows too much fondness for round numbers to be accurate, and the recurrence of the number four marks it as largely fanciful. It was probably much exaggerated. But it shows that Rome had, in the open air, an enormous multitude of statues of various kinds. Statuary in comparable numbers adorned every town and city of the Empire. The originality of the sculptors declined after the death of Nero (A.D. 68), and perfection of finish deteriorated from the death of Domitian (A.D. 96). After the Great Pestilence of A.D. 166 the art rapidly decayed. From the death of Caracalla (A.D. 217) no sculptors worthy to be called artists existed any longer and the art was practised by incompetent artisans.

The artistic tradition, which had become worthless and contemptible after the Great Pestilence, was totally annihilated by the destruction of the Empire. But just as the copyist's profession survived without a break from generation to generation until the invention of printing and even later, so the shop habits of the handicraft of statue making and of the craftsmen and workmen who made them survived with a tradition of practices and usage unbroken until our day and likely to endure for ages yet.

The monochrome statues of bronze or marble with which we are familiar are the result of the fact that when art revived in Italy many classic statues had already been discovered and recovered and more were unearthed and restored to view. The artists of the Renaissance saw that they were lovely, striking, original, and beautifully finished and were impelled to imitate them. But as in the lapse of centuries every trace of paint had vanished from the marble or bronze, the Renaissance artists did not suspect that every one had been painted all over, and imitated what they saw but did not reproduce works of art such as the classic artists had created. Our world's present sculptors' tradition is a renewal and emulation, not a continuance, of the sculptors' tradition of the ancient world.

But the craftsmen's tradition of the ancient sculptors' ateliers has never died out. Its product may be seen in countless Roman Catholic churches and in the shop windows of such firms as vend Roman Catholic church goods. Their statues and statuettes are painted or otherwise tinged with various washes or pigments. These figures display the living shop tradition handed down unbroken from generation to generation from such sculpture studios as that in which Phidias learned his art.

The most costly and magnificent of the cult-statues of Greco-Roman temples were of the kind called chrys-elephantine, the portions representing flesh being of ivory and those portions representing hair or garments being of pure gold. Of such unsurpassably costly and precious materials was the colossal statue of Zeus in his temple at Olympia in Elis, the crowning masterpiece of Greek plastic art. Such also was the colossal Athene Parthenos in the Parthenon at Athens. All Greco-Roman statues of bronze or marble were colored all over with lively and appropriate tints and hues like the already mentioned statuary now displayed in Roman Catholic churches and in the shops which have such wares for sale. But these modern polychrome sculptures are the product of artisans, not of artists, and do not possess the charms of originality, tastefulness, and finish which can be created only by genius or talent of the highest order, and which were present in their finest manifestation in classic polychrome sculpture as it existed in Rome's heyday.

In attempting to imagine what Rome looked like with its host of life-size statues in the open air on its roofs, balustrades, façades, and along its colonnades, streets, and squares, how Antioch, Alexandria, Aquileia, Treves, Carthage, or Capua appeared with their almost as countless out-of-door statues, what any city or town of the Empire at its acme looked like with its myriads, we must keep in mind that every statue was brilliantly colored all over.

For instance, making artificial eyes of glass or enamel was a recognized profession and selling them a regular trade in the Greco-Roman world. But they were not put into the eye sockets of living human beings, but into those of statues. Our monochrome eyeless busts and statues would have appeared comically absurd to Romans and Greeks, all of whose statues or busts were made natural with expressive eyes as exactly like human eyes as a highly developed art could make them; as like as our artificial glass eyes for living people.

The art of sculpture, as we have said above, declined after the times of Nero, still more after the times of Domitian, and positively after the Great Pestilence. But before the art began to decline artists of great originality and skill had crowded the towns and cities of the Empire with millions of statues of great artistic merit and of great beauty. The word millions is not extravagant. It is difficult for us to conceive of the number of statues in the Empire at its acme. When the Romans captured the Etruscan town of Volsinii in 265 B.C. they found in it 2,000 life-size bronze statues. They captured hundreds of such towns. And the making of statues was an honored art and a profitable trade for over four centuries after the storm of Volsinii, and the accumulation of statues went on from generation to generation. Had the Empire endured or Greco-Roman culture survived we should have hundreds of thousands instead of the few hundred still in existence.

Portraiture by statues or busts was carried to an amazing degree of perfection in the times of the late Roman Republic and early Empire. It was an art of highly creditable achievements even in the Republic from before the Hannibalic wars and on until the times of Aurelian up to A.D. 275.

We have hundreds of Roman portrait busts and statues. We might very well have an unbroken series of portrait statues of the Roman consuls from soon after the sack of Rome by the Gauls in 390 B.C. for six centuries. Likewise, of not only all the emperors to Aurelian, but of thousands of officials, generals, and other military officers. And all, originally, were colored accurately to nature and had natural eyes.

Triumphal columns, each standing alone and each supporting a colossal portrait statue of the person honored by it, were not numerous in the Roman world. Probably fewer than half a hundred were ever erected. The most magnificent was the column of Trajan, still standing, but robbed of its portrait statue, which was pulled down and replaced by a statue of a Christian saint.

The purpose of these columns is now generally misunderstood. The Forum of Trajan was of comparatively cramped extent and was flanked by very lofty buildings. The column was set up to put the portrait statue of the great Emperor on a level or nearly on a level with the upper galleries of the high buildings about the open space, so that the statue might be fittingly viewed, which was impossible from the pavement of the

Forum without setting it so low that it would be dwarfed by the tall edifices all about.

This was imitated by Marcus Aurelius and by other emperors.

Hence most of the triumphal columns, though there were such before Trajan's times, with the idea of honoring the man commemorated by setting his portrait statue aloft, not on a lowly pedestal.

Triumphal columns were notable adornments to whatever cities possessed them.

Being by the nature of their materials indestructible if cared for, the countless mosiac pictures which adorned walls of public buildings all over the Empire (not to dwell on the hundreds of acres of mosaic pavements) might very well still be in existence as perfect as when completed.

And the Roman fashion of making wall mosaics largely of bits of glass with the most brilliant hues in every shade of every color as well as in silver and gold, made Greco-Roman mosaic pictures particularly gorgeous and splendid.

It is impossible that any care could have preserved for us the uncountable fresco paintings, many of vast expanse, which adorned the walls of public buildings throughout the Roman Empire at its acme. But as not a few executed as early as 450 B.C. were still in good condition as late as A.D. 150, six centuries after they had been painted, it is possible that we might still have hundreds of them, perhaps even thousands. And their artistic perfection equalled anything our times have produced or possess from the past. The fairly good preservation of the many mediocre frescoes unearthed at Pompeii makes it the less improbable that the gems of this variety of art might still exist.

As for panel pictures in tempera or encaustic pigments, whereof thousands upon thousands were painted in Greek cities between 420 and 40 B.C., many hundreds of which were works of art of a very high order, it is possible that the best might still remain to us. Zeuxis died about 400 B.C. and Apelles before 300 B.C. Many of their panel pictures were still in good condition in A.D. 400, fully 700 years after they were painted. Our modern pictorial treasures, as the forty-odd paintings of Jan Vermeer of Delft, may very well be in good condition in A.D. 4000. Zeuxis and Apelles were painters comparable to Titian and Raphael. At the acme of the Empire's prosperity every city had two or more picture galleries, and few thriving towns were without one at least. Rome had many.

Likewise few towns lacked a museum of curios, jewelry, admired specimens of goldsmithing and silversmithing, painted vases, decorated pottery, pieces of household furniture by acclaimed artists or artisans, mementoes of distinguished persons, and so on. Rome had many of these, five of jewelry only.

At its acme, during the Principate of Hadrian, A.D. 117–138, and even until it began to crumble after 375, the Empire housed a stupendous accumulation of archives. As papyrus was extremely perishable and its predecessors, bark and linen, almost equally so, Italian towns had, even before Rome's rise began, developed the custom of engraving their treaties, laws, lists of officials, and town records in general on plates of bronze of convenient size and thickness. These were usually kept in a special public building and generally in its vaults and cellars, where they would be now to the amount of tens of thousands of tons of bronze, literally millions of tablets, if most of the record offices had not been burnt in the course of the barbarian ravagings and if the consequent impoverishment had not impelled every town to melt down its records to be coined into money.

Moreover, throughout the Roman world at its acme there existed an amazing accumulation of stone slabs inscribed with laws, and with records of every conceivable sort. These might have been heirlooms of the human race, enduring even for millions of years.

Paintings in fresco, tempera, or encaustic are by their materials perishable. Mosaics and statues, while far more durable, are, with all edifices and other structures devised by human ingenuity and erected or constructed by human effort, only relatively less perishable than paintings or statuary. The mere lapse of time must ultimately annihilate all.

But written words, whether constituting archives, records, or literary compositions, are potentially capable of lasting as long as the human race. For their preservation there is necessary only the appreciation of each generation of mankind, their interest and repeated copying.

Had the Greco-Roman civilization and culture endured or had it evaporated on account of slow, gradual, and imperceptible modifications, alterations, improvements, and changes through the inevitable effect of countless innovations, our world might still possess the entire body of Greco-Roman archives and literature.

The vast literature of Greece and Rome constituted a treasure greater in value than all the paintings, mosaics, statuary, columns, triumphal arches, mausoleums, temples, basilicas, baths, theatres, gymnasiums, *stadia,* hippodromes, circuses, amphitheaters, bridges, roads, aqueducts, sewers, towns, and cities of the ancient world, collectively.

The recognized chief departments of Greek literature were epic poetry, dramatic poetry, lyric poetry, elegiac poetry, and epigrammatic poetry, and in prose, oratory, history, philosophy, and romances.

Latin literature had all of these, though none so copiously as the Greek, and had also that idiosyncratically Roman department, satire.

Neither the Greeks nor the Romans thought much of their prose romances, which were hardly reckoned as literature at all.

At the acme of Rome's prosperity the thousands of libraries throughout the Empire (Rome itself had twenty-nine public libraries) contained countless copies of all the most acclaimed treasures of Greek and Latin literature and many, many copies of myriads of inferior or mediocre productions of authors whose very names are forgotten. Yet it is not extravagant to say that not one single book of all those in the libraries of the Roman Empire in the time of Hadrian would, if now recovered, fail to arouse keen interest and hearty congratulation among classical scholars all over the world.

Of the dozens of Greek epic poems, widely read throughout the Greek world from long before Alexander's time, and more widely read for six centuries after his time, we might very well have all and would be the richer for possessing the noble poems narrating the exploits of Hercules, Theseus, and other heroes, the voyage of the Argo, the two sieges of Thebes, and those tales of Troy not narrated in the Iliad and Odyssey, which two, while indubitably far superior to any others, were by no means the only Greek epics admired by ancient readers and critics.

The libraries of the Roman Empire preserved rolls containing more than 10,000 Greek comedies and more than 30,000 Greek tragedies. Besides part of the rollicking dramas of Aristophanes and some much-mutilated plays of Menander lately recovered from Egyptian rubbish dumps we have no Greek comedies. Horace brackets Eupolis and Cratinus with Aristophanes, and we might easily cherish a thousand Greek comedies, if we had them.

It would be difficult to exaggerate the extent to which all true lovers of good literature would be better off if we had all the plays of, say, three hundred Greek writers of tragedies, instead of part of those of merely three.

The treasures we have lost in losing all but a very trifling trove from Greek epigrammatic, elegiac, and lyric poetry are immeasurable both in numbers and quality.

Besides the orations of the ten Attic orators we have no complete oration of any of the hundreds of Greek orators of lofty repute. Even of the ten we have less than half of the speeches read by all educated persons of the Greco-Roman world.

We might easily have as complete as Plato all the great Greek philosophers of every period, school, and region. As already stated, Plato has been preserved because much of his output was congenial to Christian attitudes of mind. Of those philosophers whose views displeased the early Christians, all, save Aristotle and Plato, are totally lost.

Latin poetry never achieved either the sublimity or perfection of the best Greek poetry of each class. But rejoiced as all classicists are over the poems which have been preserved for our delight, no classicist can fail to mourn the loss of all the Latin comedies, except those of Terence and Plautus, and all the hundreds of noble tragedies which Romans produced. And while we have specimens of Roman epigrammatic, elegiac, and lyric poetry, we might have much more of all three sorts. Of Ennius, the greatest Roman poet, we have only tantalizing fragments.

No Roman philosopher achieved greatness, yet there were many Latin works on philosophy in the libraries of Hadrian's time, all of which we might have yet.

All the hundreds of orations by acclaimed Latin orators are lost to us except those of Cicero alone.

Most of all do lovers of learning, of books and of literature, mourn our great losses of most of the long series of Greek and Roman historians. All classicists dream of recovering Livy complete and anyone who has enjoyed the thirty-five books of his great work which are extant would put aside all other claims on his time to revel in the lost 115 books if they could be recovered.

We might very well have complete fully fifty Greek historians and as many Latin historians.

Besides the twoscore great historians who preserved for the information and pleasure of all future generations the majestic story of the Greco-Roman world from its first records to the ruin of the Empire even minor writers would be precious.

We might have, for instance, hundreds of memoirs like those of Sosilas and Silenus, Greek soldiers, both of whom were staff officers to Hannibal from before he laid siege to Saguntum until after the battle of Zama, and both of whom wrote up their recollections of their great chieftain.

Trajan's own account of his conquest of Dacia was, for three centuries, as popular as Cæsar's tale of the subjugation of Gaul. It is totally lost to us.

The mere enumeration of the treasures of Greek and Latin literature which we know we have lost would fill a large book;

and the lost treasures we do not even know of far outnumbered those of which we know.

So far, in adumbrating what the world has lost by the fall of Rome we have enumerated material treasures. But the organization, orderliness, industry, skill, thrift, and concomitant proclivities and instincts which produced all this material wealth; and the disposition, habits, and customs which went with the possession and use of its various components were worth more than any or all of the material treasures of the Empire. The habit of being civilized, of getting on smoothly and without violence, strife or dissensions with one's kinsfolk, associates, neighbors, and all mankind, was worth more than all that went with it.

The annihilation of these racial customs, habits, and instincts was a great loss to our world; as their maintenance and the slow, gradual, and imperceptible modification of them into better and better conditions from age to age would have been a great gain to mankind.

Herodotus, who died about 440 B.C., says that in his days the habit of going armed, universal not many centuries before, had entirely gone out of fashion, so that in few districts of the Greek world did one ever see a man going about his ordinary affairs girt with a sword or dagger.

This means, of course, that protection of the lives and property of individuals had ceased to be an individual concern, as every citizen of every Greek city felt adequately protected against foreign inroads by the military power of his Commonwealth and felt adequately protected against criminals by its police power.

With civic traditions like those of Greece both in origin and nature the carrying of arms became, even more than in Greece in the days of Herodotus, and from the same causes, wholly obsolete throughout the Roman Empire. Only soldiers under military oath went armed, and they only outside the walls of towns and cities. For centuries, all over the Roman world, the carrying of arms was even more unfashionable and unthinkable than it is in Great Britain today. And this was the result not of edicts or enactments, but of the spontaneous feeling of the population, so safe that an armed man would have appeared ridiculous and would have felt absurd.

Contrast this with present-day conditions in the United States, Mexico, Central and South America, Spain, Italy, Greece, Bulgaria, Rumania, even France. Except Switzerland and England, no region formerly part of the Roman Empire has yet regained the conditions of peacefulness and personal safety which it enjoyed under the rule of Rome. And what peacefulness exists today has been painfully and very gradually regained by slow improvements in the disposition of the descendants of the barbarian invaders who destroyed the Roman Empire. All over Europe, all gentlemen carried arms until the French Revolution, and the custom of duelling was still universal two centuries ago, vanished from England within a century, and still survives in an attenuated form in France.

Had the Roman Empire not perished, its traditions of peacefulness might have endured, bettering from generation to generation, and all mankind would be the better for it.

AFTERWORD

From the time I was a half-grown lad I have wanted to write a book on this theme and of such scope as this.

But from the time when the idea took definite shape, while I was at college, I had in mind a very different sort of book, for I envisaged a scholarly treatise, every statement in which should be substantiated by a quotation from an original source, the Greek or Latin given in full, with an accurate English translation. Long before middle age I realized that the limitations imposed on me by imperfect health made it unlikely that I could hope to finish such a book before I died of old age at the full term of human life. Moreover, it was plain to me that if I did complete such a work it would never be published except at my own expense. Therefore I never began it.

Sometime in 1923 I was asked by a well-known New York publishing house whether I would write for them a book for general readers on the true causes of the fall of Rome. I declined, alleging that general readers do not want the truth; they want an agreeable rehash of what they already happen to believe; also that any fair presentation of the true causes of the fall of Rome would appear to general readers intensely anti-Christian; so that, if I did write what they asked for, they would not publish it. There the matter dropped.

But when, later, the idea was suggested to the present publishers, they fancied it and asked for a popular treatment of the topic, with no show of erudition.

That is the sort of book I have written, very easily, for I have been saturated with the subject since childhood and more and more from year to year. But I grieve that I have not been able herein to demonstrate the truth of every one of my assertions, as, with better health and luck, I might have done in a much longer book.

An entirely fair presentation of the interaction between Christianity and paganism, from the Christian point of view, may be found in *Christianity and the Roman Government, a Study in Imperial Administration,* by E. G. Hardy, London, George Allen & Unwin; New York, The Macmillan Company (1925), Pp. xiii, 161.

In this also can be found two genuine accounts of the manner in which actual Roman officials dealt with Christians brought before them, in fact, not as in the fantastic inventions of the martyrologies, but with every solicitude to avoid harshness and to wean the wretches with whom they were confronted from their insane fanaticism.

My statement in Chapter XXVI (page 317) as to the proportions of Christians and pagans in the Empire when Constantine proclaimed Christianity may be compared with what Friedländer says in his *Sittengeschichte Roms* iii, 598. When Theodosius and Gratian suppressed paganism, Antioch, reckoned the most Christian city in the Empire, had fully four pagans to every one Christian; the Christians were not much over twenty per cent of the city's inhabitants. And, outside the walled cities and towns the population was almost wholly pagan even then.

What I have written of the genuine and earnest pagan belief in their gods may surprise many readers, but only because most earlier treatises on the subject are so biased that they put forward and emphasize every recorded utterance of any skeptic of the ancient world and ignore, garble, or misinterpret every evidence of pagan devoutness, piety, faith, or belief.

I claim that in this book for the first time there is printed a fair exposition of what Greco-Roman paganism meant to the millions of votaries, many of them highly cultured intellectuals, who for centuries devoutly and earnestly believed its tenets through their lives.

THE END